AF600657

# FIRST AMENDMENT FREEDOMS, PAPAL PRONOUNCEMENTS AND CONCORDAT PRACTICE

A comparative study in American
Law and Public Ecclesiastical Law

This dissertation was approved by the Reverend John J. McGrath, A.B., LL.B., J.C.D., Professor of Canon Law, as director and the Right Reverend Clement V. Bastnagel, S.T.L., J.U.D., and Doctor Stephen Kuttner, S.J.D., J.C.D., LL.D., as readers.

THE CATHOLIC UNIVERSITY OF AMERICA
CANON LAW STUDIES
No. 412

# First Amendment Freedoms, Papal Pronouncements and Concordat Practice

## A comparative study in American Law and Public Ecclesiastical Law

A DISSERTATION

SUBMITTED TO THE FACULTY OF THE SCHOOL OF CANON LAW OF THE CATHOLIC UNIVERSITY OF AMERICA IN PARTIAL FULFILLMENT OF THE REQUIREMENTS FOR THE DEGREE OF DOCTOR OF CANON LAW

BY

REVEREND WILLIAM NESSEL, O.S.F.S., A.B., M.A., J.C.L.
PRIEST OF THE OBLATES OF ST. FRANCIS DE SALES

THE CATHOLIC UNIVERSITY OF AMERICA PRESS
WASHINGTON, D. C.
1961

IMPRIMI POTEST:

JOHN J. CONMY, O.S.F.S.

*Provincial*

Wilmington, Delaware, February 1, 1961

NIHIL OBSTAT:

JOHN J. McGRATH, A.B., LL.B., J.C.D.

*Censor Deputatus*

Washington, D. C., March 1, 1961

IMPRIMATUR:

✠ PATRICK A. O'BOYLE

*Archbishop of Washington*

Washington, D. C., March 1, 1961

The *nihil obstat* and *imprimatur* are official declarations that a book or pamphlet is free of doctrinal or moral error. No implication is contained therein that those who have granted the *nihil obstat* and *imprimatur* agree with the content, opinions or statements expressed.



MURRAY AND HEISTER, INC.
WASHINGTON, D. C.

PRINTED BY
TIMES AND NEWS PUBLISHING CO.
GETTYSBURG, PA., U. S. A.

To
The Very Reverend J. Francis Tucker, O.S.F.S.
fifty years a priest

## FOREWORD

This dissertation consists of three parts: 1) Colonial Law, 2) American Constitutional Law, 3) A comparative study between the principles derived from Public Ecclesiastical Law and American Constitutional. In order to achieve the purpose of this dissertation the writer has used papal pronouncements and concordats as the main sources for the ecclesiastical law principles. However, the concordat considerations in this work are not intended to be an exhaustive study but only a survey. Several concordats analyzed in the third part of the dissertation could serve individually as the topic for a doctoral dissertation.

The purpose of this thesis is to state the juridic relations between Church and State in the United States, particularly as reflected in the right to preach, and to compare this condition with the juridic notions of Church and State contained in concordat practice during the twentieth century and in the writing of modern popes. The writer has abstracted such problems as the aid granted by the state to education from the field of inquiry. After careful consideration of the question, the writer is convinced that an inclusion of such topics would make the field of investigation too broad and would detract from the central object of the dissertation. Even education itself could serve as the basis of a separate study, inasmuch as the material available in concordat relations and American law is so extensive.

To determine the juridic status of religion and the right to preach in the United States, it is necessary to investigate the "no establishment clause," or the disestablishment clause as it is frequently called, and the free exercise of speech and religion clauses of the First Amendment. For this reason the two basic concepts traced through the Concordats, the Charters, the legislative enactments of the thirteen colonies of America, and the cases of the Supreme Court of the United States are the juridic status of Church and State and the free exercise of religion. The ultimate question which this thesis attempts to answer is: How does the juridic status of Church and State and the right to preach as contained in the public law of the United States compare with concordat practice and the principles enunciated by modern popes?

This work could not have been brought into being without the generous assistance of several persons. The writer is indebted to his former Provincial, the Very Reverend William D. Buckley, O.S.F.S., for the opportunity of graduate studies and for his constant encouragement. He also expresses his gratitude to the Faculty of the School of Canon Law of the Catholic University of America, to the Reverend Francis J. Powers, C.S.V., M.A., LL.M., S.J.D., his former professor of American Constitutional Law, to the staff of the Mullen Library at the Catholic University of America and of the Library of Congress in Washington, D. C., and finally to the members of his community at De Sales Hall in Hyattsville, Maryland, who assisted in the preparation of the manuscript.

TABLE OF CONTENTS

TABLE OF CONTENTS (Continued)

TABLE OF CONTENTS (Continued)

TABLE OF CONTENTS (Continued)

# PART I

## The Antecedents of the Federal Constitution: Establishment and Free Exercise of Religion in the Thirteen Colonies

The juridic concept of the relation between Church and State in the thirteen colonies cannot be adequately described in a few phrases, but the relationship as it existed does fall into one of four categories: 1) Initial Establishment of the Church of England, 2) Puritan Establishment, 3) Changing Establishments, and 4) Non-Establishment.[1]

In Virginia and the Carolinas the Church of England was established at the start of the colony, and this establishment was subsequently strengthened by colonial legislative enactments. This juridic condition of establishment persisted until the time of the Revolution.

The New England colonies, with the exception of Rhode Island, established the Congregational form of worship. Connecticut, Massachusetts, which then included Maine, and New Hampshire, which also encompassed Vermont, formed this juridic group.

New Jersey, Maryland, New York, and Georgia have a history of changing establishments. The original charter of Georgia did not establish a State religion. But this instrument was subsequently nullified and the Church of England was established both by royal decree and act of the colonial legislature. New York and New Jersey were originally Dutch settlements with a Dutch Reform Establishment. Military conquest of these territories by England at least *de facto* brought about an establishment of the Church of England. Religious freedom in Maryland was granted to Catholics and Protestants by Lord Baltimore (George Calvert, + 1632), who did not attempt to establish any Church. This free exercise of worship was also protected by legislative measures of the colonial

[1] Establishment, as used in this work, means that a particular religious group is juridically acknowledged to be the official religion of the State.

assembly. Eventually, the Church of England was given legal preference in the form of establishment.

Pennsylvania, in keeping with a liberal Quaker policy, was founded as a free colony. Delaware modeled its religious policy after the mother-colony, Pennsylvania. Rhode Island was begun as a haven of refuge for those who fled the persecution of the established colonies, especially the Puritan establishment.

Colonial progress towards disestablishment and religious freedom was very gradual. Separation of Church and State was not complete in some of the first state constitutions, and religious tests and other discriminations appeared in these constitutions and state legislative enactments during the nineteenth century. The juridic status of Church and State and the free exercise of religion in these thirteen colonies will form the basis for discussion in the remainder of this chapter.

## ARTICLE 1. CHURCH OF ENGLAND ESTABLISHMENTS

### *Section 1. Virginia*

#### A. Juridic Relations between Church and State in the Formative Period

Virginia definitely had an established religion—the Church of England. Sanford H. Cobb was equally as positive about the precise time of the establishment, but the writer cannot be as definite in his judgment. Cobb believed that the Church of England was established in the first Virginia charter granted by King James II in 1606. He cited a quotation from Anderson's ***History of the Colonial Church*** purportedly taken from the first charter of Virginia as the basis for his claim. The first charter of Virginia does not contain this passage.[2]

---

[2] Sanford H. Cobb, *The Rise of Religious Liberty in America* (New York: The Macmillan Co., 1902), p. 75 (hereafter cited Cobb). The text in Cobb's work reads as follows: ". . . the charter, after outlining the method of colonial administration, adds a prescription 'that the said presidents, councils, and ministers should provide that the Word and Science of God be preached, planted, and used not only in the said colonies, but also as much as might be among the savages among them, ac-

Cobb stated that the "second charter of 1609 repeated the terms of ecclesiastical establishment." If he means the terms cited above from Anderson's work and said to be a part of the original charter, he is in error. The charter of 1609 does not contain this passage, nor does the third charter of Virginia.[3]

However, another passage cited by Cobb in part, when read in context, demonstrates at least the preference for, and probably the establishment of, the Church of England in Virginia.[4] All three charters speak of the propagation of the "Christian Religion" as one of the purposes of the foundation of the colony. Christian religion definitely does not include the Roman Catholic religion, as is evident from the previous footnote, and it probably does not include any other Protestant religion than the Church of England. In the colonial documents and acts the term Protestant is generally used to express all Christian religions, except the Roman Catholic religion. It is a valid presumption to conclude that the expression Christian religion, as used in these Virginia charters, had the restricted meaning of the Church of England. The early charters certainly gave a preferred position to the Church of England, if "Christian religion" is equivalent to the Church of England, and probably intended to give it an "established" position, as in England.[5]

---

cording to the rights and doctrine of the Church of England.'" Cf. Francis N. Thorpe, *The Federal and State Constitutions, Colonial Charters, and Other Organic Laws of the States, Territories, and Colonies now or hereafter forming the United States of America* (7 vols., Washington: Government Printing Office, 1909), VII, 3783-3789—"The First Charter of Virginia, 1606" (hereafter cited Thorpe).

[3] Cobb, p. 75; Thorpe, VII, 3790-3802; 3802-3812.

[4] Cobb, p. 75; "The Second Charter of Virginia," Thorpe, VII, 3802. "And lastly, because the principal Effect which we can desire or expect of this Action, is the Conversion and Reduction of the People in those Parts unto the true worship of God and Christian Religion, in which respect we shall be loath that any person should be permitted to pass to affect the Superstitions of the Church of Rome, we do hereby Declare, that it is our Will and Pleasure that none be permitted to pass in any Voyage from Time to Time to be made into the said Country, but such as first shall have taken the Oath of Supremacy. . . ."

[5] For the use of the term "Christian religion" in the Virginia Charters of 1606, 1609, 1611-1612, cf. Thorpe, VII, 3784, 3802.

Sir Francis Wyatt (+ 1644) was sent to Virginia as governor in 1621. The first article of his instructions at least bordered on an act of establishment. It directed the new government to oversee the service of God and the observance of His laws. It further provided that the people were to be trained in the true religion "and to the Order and administration of Divine Services according to the Church of England . . . and to cause that the Ministers should be duly respected and maintained."[6]

The first assembly of Virginia legislated on religious matters. Act three required that "there be a uniformity in our Church as near as may be to the Canons in England, both in substance and in circumstance, and that all persons yield readie obedience under paine of censure."[7] This assembly also imposed a penalty for absence from religious services without an allowable excuse.[8] Therefore, a colonist who refused to attend the services of the established Church was constantly harassed by threat of heavy penalties.[9] Neither dignity nor position excused a person from this rule of compulsory Church attendance. The 1631-1632 session legislated that the council and burgesses were bound to attend services one hour after sunrise at the third beat of the drum or suffer the penalty for neglect.[10]

The General Assembly was determined to preserve the Establishment in Virginia. During the 1629-1630 session this assemblage

---

[6] Cobb, p. 80, quoting Anderson's *History of the Colonial Church,* I, 328.

[7] William Waller Hening (ed.), *The Statutes at Large Being a Collection of the Laws of Virginia from the First Session of the Legislature* (I-XIII, old series, New York, Philadelphia, Richmond, 1820-1823), I, 123 (the volumes consulted were published as follows: I, II in New York (1823); III, XIII in Philadelphia (1823); IV, VII in 1820, IX in 1821, and X, XI, XII in 1823, all in Richmond) (hereafter cited Hening, *Statutes*).

[8] Hening, *Statutes,* I, 123. The fine for one absence was one pound of tobacco; fifty pounds for one month. A similar act was passed in the 1631-1632 session. Cf. Hening, *Statutes,* I, 155, Act II.

[9] It is interesting to note that a minister who absented himself from his Church lost half his salary, and one who was absent beyond four months forfeited "his whole means and cure."—Hening, *Statutes,* I, 123-124, Act V. Cf. *ibid.,* I, 290 (1644-1645 session) for a law binding a minister to residence within his parish.

[10] Hening, *Statutes,* I, 162, Act XVIII.

declared that all ministers must conform to the laws of the Church of England.[11]

The government taxed the colonist to support the ministers and to build and repair churches. They also established stole fees.[12] These many acts clearly demonstrate that the assembly in the colony of Virginia exercised a prerogative which the parliament exercised over the mother church in England—the regulation of the internal and external life of the Church of England. Beyond all shadow of a doubt, Virginia had an establishment from the time of the arrival of Governor Wyatt.

The government of Virginia supported, maintained and protected the Established Church, and also controlled much of its internal life. The ministers of the Church of England received protection from a statute passed by the Assembly of 1623-1624. Anyone who made unfounded remarks about a minister and thereby hindered the effectiveness of his apostolate was subject to a heavy fine. Moreover, he also had to publicly beg the pardon of the minister he had so offended.[13]

All the ministers had to conform to the laws of the Church of England. Those who were faithful to these regulations were supported by public taxes.[14] The assembly enacted in 1632 a law stating that every minister "havinge cure of soules in the colony shall preach one sermon every Sunday in the year, havinge no lawful impediment. . . ."[15] In districts where ministers were few and parishes somewhat numerous, the law recommended that the ministers preach at various places on a rotary basis. The same session

[11] Hening, *Statutes,* I, 149, Act I—"It is ordered, that all ministers residing and being, or who hereafter shall reside or bee within this colony, shall conforme themselves in all thinges according to the cannons of the church of England. And if there shall be any that, after notice given, shall refuse to conforme himselfe, hee shall undergoe such censure, as by the said cannons in such cases is provided for such delinquents . . ."; *ibid.,* I, 155 (1631) for another uniformity act.

[12] Cf. Hening, *Statutes,* I, 144, 149, 161, 185, 207, 242. This covers sessions from 1629-1643.

[13] Hening, *Statutes,* I, 124.

[14] Hening, *Statutes,* I, 149; I, 155 (1631 session); I, 144, 149, 161, 185, 207, 242 (from the 1629-1643 sessions).

[15] Hening, *Statutes,* I, 157.

acts contain a law directing that "all preachinge, administeringe of communion, and marriages be done exclusively in church except in case of necessity."[16]

In addition to specifying the time and place for preaching, this assembly outlined the subject matter for "Sunday School" instruction: "The minister is to catechise and instruct the young and the ignorant of his parish in the ten commandments, articles of faith, Lord's prayer, catechism . . . ," and this was to be for a half an hour or more before the evening prayer each Sunday. Parents and masters were subject to a fine, if they refused to send their charges to church, and the latter for refusing to learn.[17] The Church wardens were charged with the duty of presenting masters and mistresses who were delinquent in these matters.[18]

The assembly made an effort to provide for all emergencies. This body empowered ministers to appoint ordained deacons to read the Communion prayers in their absence.[19] These several enactments provide ample evidence to support the assertion that preachers and preaching were under the close supervision of the assembly in the sixteen thirties.

## B. The Colonial Period

All former Assembly laws and acts were repealed by the assembly of 1642-1643.[20] The Church of England retained its legal position and the members of the Virginia Church had to conform to the rites and rules of the Mother Church. Act one of the session declared that "the liturgy of the Church of England, for the administration of the word and the sacrament, be duely performed according to the booke of common prayer allowed by his Ma'tie and confirmed by consent of Parliament."[21] Any minister who refused to conform to the orders, laws and constitutions of the Church of England could not "be admitted to teach or preach publicly or privately."[22]

[16] Hening, *Statutes,* I, 158; cf. also *ibid.,* p. 183.
[17] Hening, *Statutes,* I, 157, 181.
[18] Hening, *Statutes,* I, 156, 182.
[19] Hening, *Statutes,* I, 208.
[20] Hening, *Statutes,* I, 239.
[21] Hening, *Statutes,* I, 241.
[22] Hening, *Statutes,* I, 277 (March, 1642-1643 session).

The government did not relinquish its authority over the confirmation or dismissal of the ministers. The ministers were to be elected by the commander and commissioners, or the vestry in case of non-residence, and presented to the Governor. A minister could be suspended by the Governor and his Council for neglect or misbehaviour, but only the assembly could remove a minister.[23]

Roman Catholics were the object of harsh legislation in the assembly of 1642-1643. All Catholics were barred from public office, and if by "sinister or corrupt means" they obtained an office and refused to take the prescribed oaths, they were to be dismissed and fined one thousand pounds of tobacco upon conviction by the assembly.[24] Popish priests were forbidden to stay in Virginia and were expelled within five days after their arrival.[25] Cobb observed that "this section was to guard against the danger of 'infection' from Roman Catholic Maryland."[26]

The assembly again specified the time for preaching. A minister was obliged to preach on the last Wednesday of each month, a day set aside for fast, prayer, and humiliation.[27] The law also revived "the last act made the 11 January, 1641, concerning the ministers preaching . . . in the forenoon and catechising in the afternoon

---

[23] Hening, *Statutes,* I, 241-242, Act I (1642-1643).

[24] Hening, *Statutes,* I, 268-269.

[25] Hening, *Statutes, loc. cit.*: ". . . that it should not be lawful under the penaltie aforesaid for any popish preist [sic] that should hereafter arrive to remain above five days after warning given for his departure by the Governor or commander of the place where he be or they shall be, if the wind and weather hinder not his departure. . . ."

[26] Cobb, p. 85; Lord Baltimore came to Virginia temporarily in 1628, while making arrangements for the establishment of his own colony. The Governor and his Council would not allow him to remain, even for a brief period, unless he took the oath of supremacy. As a Roman Catholic, Baltimore could not acknowledge the ecclesiastical headship of the King of England. He offered to take a modified oath, but the Virginians would not accept this. Even Baltimore's personal friendship with the king was not sufficient reason to permit him to remain in Virginia. Cf. Cobb, p. 83, and Samuel E. Morison and Henry S. Commager, *The Growth of the American Republic* (4th ed. rev., 2 vols., New York: Oxford University Press, 1955), I, 47 (hereafter cited Morison and Commager).

[27] Hening, *Statutes,* I, 289-290 (1644-1645). If he had two parishes, or three, he was to choose a separate Wednesday for each of these.

of every Sunday. . . ." Any minister who failed to comply with the provisions of this law was fined five hundred pounds of tobacco.

No opposition was brooked from the ministers. "Those who refuse to read the common prayers as prescribed in the Common Prayer on the Sabboth are deprived of any tithes or duties from their parishioners." Such economic sanctions were powerful means for forcing the recalcitrants to conform.

The assembly did not slacken its efforts to have regular preaching. Ministers were directed to preach every Sunday, one Sunday a month in the chapel of ease, the other Sundays in the parish church.[28]

Furthermore the colonial legislature was adamant in its directive that a non-conformist and non-ordained minister be not permitted to preach. Only ministers who were ordained by some bishop of the Church of England could officiate in the colony of Virginia. These ordained ministers also had to conform to the orders, constitutions, and laws of the Church of England.[29] Anyone who pretended to be a minister and "contrary to this act presumes to teach or preach publiquely or privately, the governour and councill are hereby desired and empowered to suspend and silence the person soe offending. . . ." If he persists to preach or teach, they can "compell him to depart the country with the first conveniency as it hath beene formerly provided by the 77 Act made at James Citty the second of March 1642."[30]

But a layman could substitute for a minister, provided that he did not preach. The assembly directed every parish that did not have a minister every Sunday to choose "a person of good life and conversation to read divine service every intervening Sunday at the parish church, when the minister preacheth at any other place."[31] This same legislature passed a compulsory church attendance act, thereby assuring the preacher of an audience.[32]

---

[28] Hening, *Statutes*, II (March, 1661-1662; cf. also I, 181 (Sept., 1632); I, 290 (February, 1644-1645); I, 311 (March, 1645-1646).

[29] Hening, *Statutes*, II, 46.

[30] Hening, *Statutes*, II, 46.

[31] Hening, *Statutes*, II, 46-47.

[32] Hening, *Statutes*, II, 48 (March, 1661-1662). "Every person must attend preaching and divine service on Sundays and holydays. Those who absent themselves are subject to a fine of fifty pounds of tobacco."

To preserve uniformity in the Established Church this assembly required the canons of the Church of England be observed and that its liturgy be read.[33] The subject matter for teaching and preaching was also specified. No minister or reader could teach any other catechism than that of the Church of England, as contained in the Book of Common Prayer. The act further stated "that the minister expound no other than that, that our fundamentals at least may be well laid, and that noe reader upon presumption of his owne abilities do attempt the expounding that or any other catechisme ore the scripture."[34]

In its role as guardian of orthodoxy, the assembly did not content itself simply with the regulation of the life of the Establishment. It passed acts from time to time to prevent the growth of "heretical religious bodies" in Virginia. In additional to the anti-Catholic legislation mentioned above, the lawmakers directed their animosity against the Quakers, who were even more unwelcome in Virginia than Catholics. In the 1659-1660 session the assembly passed an Act Suppressing Quakers. A ship commander or master who brought Quakers to Virginia was fined 100 lbs. sterling. Any Quaker apprehended was to be imprisoned until he "do adjure this country or putt in security with all speed to depart from the colonie and not return again. . . ."[35] The residents of Virginia were forbidden to entertain Quakers who had been questioned by the Governor and his Council. Virginians were also warned not to permit Quaker meetings to be held in the vicinity of their homes under the penalty of 100 lbs. sterling.[36]

In 1661 Quakers and non-conformists were fined 20 lbs. sterling for each month that they were absent from Church services. If

---

[33] Hening, *Statutes,* II, 47; cf. also I, 49 (March, 1629-1630); I, 241 (March, 1642-1643); I, 277 (March, 1642-1643).

[34] Hening, *Statutes,* II, 47; cf. I, 157 (February, 1631-1632).

[35] Hening, *Statutes,* I, 533, Act IV; cf. also II, 180-183, Act I, II. The latter part of act two said that "if Quakers or other separatists after conviction give security that they shall not unlawfully meet in the future, they shall be discharged from the said penalties." If exiled Quakers returned, they were again punished and driven from the colony. Should they return again, they were treated as felons.

[36] Hening, *Statutes,* I, 533.

their absence was prolonged to one year, the dissenters had also to give proof of good behaviour.[37] The Quakers suffered during the entire period of the Restoration, when Sir William Berkeley (+ 1677) returned as governor. After his time the Quakers were not molested, as far as the records reveal, but they did not obtain relief at law in matters of conscience, such as military service and oaths, until the eighteenth century.[38]

However, the English Toleration Act of 1689 brought some relief to dissenters. The ones dissenting from the Church of England who qualified under the act of Parliament in every way did not fall under the penalty provided for those who absented themselves from the services of the Church of England.[39]

A very broad anti-heresy act was legislated in the session of April, 1699. If anyone reared as a Christian "shall be writing, printing, teaching or advisedly speaking, deny the being of God or the Holy Trinity or shall assert or maintain that there are more Gods than one" or deny that the scripture of the Old and New Testaments is of divine authority, upon lawful conviction in court shall be duly punished. First offenders were declared incapable of holding office. A second offense carried a disability to sue and a disqualification to be a guardian or executor or to take any gift or legacy, incapacity to hold office, and a three-year prison term.[40]

The effects of the English Toleration Act upon the legislators

---

[37] Hening, *Statutes,* II, 48, Act X. This act also forbade the holding of Quaker assemblies; cf. also Hening, *Statutes,* II, 180, Act I (1663).

[38] Cf. Hening, *Statutes,* III, 298; VIII, 242; IX, 434 (1775); and IX, 189 (1776); X, 201, 314, 362, 417; XI, 252, 503. The later legislation also provided relief for Mennonites.

[39] Hening, *Statutes,* III, 170, 171. This law obliged everyone over 21 to attend Church services one Sunday every two months. Fine upon conviction was five shillings or fifty pounds of tobacco for each offense. The Act was renewed in October, 1705. Cf. *ibid.,* III, 360. These acts were more lenient than earlier legislation, March, 1661-1662, which required attendance every Sunday and holiday under the same penalty. Cf. *ibid.,* II, 48.

[40] Hening, *Statutes,* II, 168-169; same act in III, 358-359 (October, 1705). There was a statute of limitation attached to the law. The information had to be given to the Justice within three months after the spoken word, and prosecution had to follow within twelve months after the information was legally given.

of Virginia benefited some of the Protestant sects. The Presbyterian minister Francis Makemie (+ 1708) was licensed to preach by the legislature in 1699. In the next year the Huguenots who came to Virginia were permitted to have their own minister.[41] The same privilege was given to the German Lutherans in 1730. However, as Cobb has stressed it, these exceptions were rare.[42]

Other sects migrated to Virginia, such as the English Baptists who arrived as early as 1714. But these Baptists did not fight vigorously for liberty until late in the colonial period. The Scotch-Irish, mainly Presbyterian, came in 1729, and they were followed by the German Lutherans. These two groups settled in the mountain regions, and their distance from the seat of government served to shield their non-conformity. Furthermore, the government was not desirous of making trouble with these settlers who formed a barrier against Indian attacks. The Methodists came later, but they were not dissenters. They identified themselves with the Establishment, and the government did not interfere with their irregularities.[43]

Later in the colonial period the French and Indian War preoccupied the government, and it paid little attention to church affairs. However, the war did occasion the passage of an act entitled "An Act for Disarming Papists, and Reputed Papists, Refusing to Take the Oaths to the Government."[44] Those who declined to take the oaths appointed by the act of parliament were forbidden to possess arms, weapons, gunpowder, and ammunition. Any such person who possessed the same could be seized by the order of the court and be imprisoned. No Papist could keep a

[41] Hening, *Statutes*, III, 478; IV, 306. Cobb, pp. 97-98.

[42] Cobb, pp. 98-99. He notes that the majority of the population was adverse to the established Church, yet there was little growth of dissenting bodies. "Most of the aversion was due to irreligion, rather than to any force of conscience or desire for non-conformity." In fact the government was preoccupied far more with combating indifference, e.g., by obliging people to attend services and to have their children baptized, than with the suppression of opposition groups. Cf. Cobb, p. 99. This indifference was due in no small part to the low caliber of the clergy in Virginia at the time. Cf. Cobb, pp. 94-95.

[43] Cf. Cobb, pp. 99-107.

[44] Hening, *Statutes*, VII, 35-39.

horse whose value was more than five pounds, on pain of forfeiture. This Act was more political than religious in motivation.

In 1758 the assembly enacted the famous Two Penny Act, which contributed to the downfall of the Establishment. Briefly, it required that all debts be payable in tobacco or in money at the rate of 18 shillings, 8 pence for a hundred pounds of tobacco. This reduced the price of tobacco for payment of debts to two pence a pound. The clerical contract was fixed by law in terms of tobacco, so the Act spelled ruin for clergy. Conditions grew so grave that clergymen sued their vestry. The Act was upheld in the Cann case and the Warrington case, even though the court awarded damages to Rev. Mr. Warrington. A Rev. James Maury won his suit in 1763 through the able pleading of a then relatively unknown advocate, Patrick Henry (1736-1799). The Act was declared invalid, but the jury assessed damages at one penny. This case added much ill-feeling among the populace toward the Establishment, and laid the groundwork for the destruction of the Establishment in Revolutionary times.[45]

### C. Statehood Period

During the Interregnum, July, 1775, Quakers and Mennonites were exempt from militia service.[46] The following year the Virginia State Convention met to draw up a constitution and adopted the famous Bill of Rights. Section 16 of this document guaranteed "free exercise of religion, according to the dictates of conscience."[47]

The legislature of the First Commonwealth in October of 1776 declared all acts of parliament punishing religious opinion to be void in Virginia.[48] Dissenters, regardless of denomination, were exempt from levies for Church support. For the present the clergy were to be supported by means of voluntary contributions, and the

---

[45] Cf. Cobb, 108-111.

[46] Hening, *Statutes,* IX, 34; cf. also *ibid.,* p. 189.

[47] Hening, *Statutes,* IX, 111-112, sec. 16 (July 12, 1776); cf. also Thorpe, VII, 3814.

[48] Hening, *Statutes,* IX, 164, Act I.

Act for the provision of the clergy was suspended.[49] There were additional signs of the suspension of Establishment legislation during the Second Commonwealth, e.g., the Baptists and Methodists were privileged to be served under the officers of their own religion.[50] The subject of the ministers' salaries was finally settled in 1779, when the legislature enacted a law repealing all former acts providing for the salary of the ministers.[51]

The vestries were stripped of their powers and duties with respect to the poor by an act in 1780 which created the Office of Overseer of the Poor.[52] Prior to 1780 only the clergy of the Church of England could witness a marriage without a special license. Then the legislature empowered dissenting ministers, Quakers, and Mennonites to celebrate marriage without a license or any publication of the banns.[53]

During the Ninth Commonwealth an act for the incorporation of the Protestant Episcopal Church was legislated. It required that the revenue of any church which exceeded eight hundred pounds must be reported to the General Assembly. The act was later repealed and a new act authorized the Church of England to regulate its own religious concerns, discipline, and worship.[54] The second act was repealed in October, 1786, and each religious society was permitted to secure its own property and was authorized to regulate its own discipline: "Be it further enacted and declared, That so much of all the laws now in force, as prevents any religious society from regulating its own discipline, shall be, and is hereby repealed."[55] This definitely ended all trace of legal establishment in the State of Virginia.

---

[49] Hening, *Statutes,* IX, 164, Art. 2, and 165-166, Art. 6. The suspension of the salaries of the clergy of the Church of England was renewed in May, 1777 (Hening, *Statutes,* IX, 312), and the Second Commonwealth renewed the suspension in October, 1777 (*ibid.,* p. 387). This suspension was repeated by successive legislatures. Cf. *ibid.,* pp. 469, 579.

[50] Hening, *Statutes,* IX, 348.

[51] Hening, *Statutes,* X, 197.

[52] Hening, *Statutes,* X, 288.

[53] Hening, *Statutes,* X, 362, 381.

[54] Hening, *Statutes,* IX, 532; *ibid.,* pp. 536-537 (Oct. 1784).

[55] Hening, *Statutes,* XII, 266-267.

The post-war Virginia assembly was rocked by a controversy over a proposed piece of legislation called "A Bill for establishing a provision for teachers of the Christian Religion." The proponents of the bill sought state support for the spread of Christianity and believed that no sect should be given preferential treatment. According to Cobb, "the bill provided for a general assessment by civil authority, and allowed each rate payer to indicate the Church which should receive the amount of his tax. In the latter respect the proposed bill resembled the enactments in New England for relief of those not of the 'established order.' "[56] The bill passed a second reading, but final action was delayed for the purpose of giving the populace additional time to register their opinion. The delay afforded the opposition time to muster sufficient strength to cause the abandonment of the bill. Madison was a powerful force in the ranks of the opposition. Had the bill passed, it would have established Christianity as the State religion and imposed a tax for the support of this "religion" upon all Christians and non-Christians.

Jefferson composed a new bill, which was enacted into law in October, 1785, and was entitled "An Act Establishing Religious Freedom."[57] Part two of this act reads:

> That no man shall be compelled to frequent or support any religious worship, place or ministry whatsoever, nor shall be enforced, constrained, molested, or burdened in his body or goods, nor shall otherwise suffer on account of his religious opinions or beliefs, but that all men shall be free to profess, and by argument to maintain, their opinion in matters of religion, and that the same shall in no wise diminish, enlarge or affect their civil capacities.

It is significant that this important piece of legislation is not part

[56] Cobb, p. 495. George Washington (1732-1799), Patrick Henry (1736-1799), Richard Henry Lee (1732-1794), Christopher Marshall (1709-1797) favored the bill, but Thomas Jefferson (1743-1826), James Madison (1751-1836) strongly opposed it.

[57] Hening, *Statutes,* XII, 84-86. Cf. also Marke De Wolfe Howe, *Cases on Church and State in the United States* (Cambridge, Mass.: Harvard University Press, 1952), pp. 5-8.

of the fundamental constitution, but merely a legislative enactment of the assembly.

The 1830 Constitution of Virginia merely re-enacted the Declaration of Rights of 1776.[58] Article XVI of the Bill of Rights of the Constitution of 1850 contained a free exercise clause identical with the Constitution of 1776, and the Constitution of 1864 simply adopted the Bill of Rights from the Constitution of 1830, as amended from its original passage in 1776.[59] Therefore, these fundamental documents added nothing new to the enactments of the seventeen eighties.

In retrospect, it may be stated that the Church of England was probably established in the early Virginian Charters. It definitely achieved this legal status during the governorship of Wyatt. What may be termed a "rigid establishment" existed until the Toleration Act of 1689. Following this act the Establishment exhibited sufficient flexibility to permit legal toleration, or at least a toleration *de facto,* of several Protestant sects. Universal legal toleration was abruptly ushered in by the Bill of Rights of 1775, and the succeeding years were witness to a period of gradual legal disestablishment. This transition was completed by 1786.[60]

The established Church was subject to strict government control, especially during the seventeenth century. The appointment, suspension, removal, and salary of the ministers were regulated by the colonial government. The time, place, and subject matter of preaching and religious teaching were determined in the various acts of the assembly. Unauthorized persons were subject to heavy fines upon conviction of attempting to preach or teach religious matters. The Virginia government not only controlled the internal

---

[58] Thorpe, VII, 3820, Art. I.

[59] Thorpe, VII, 3831, 3835.

[60] Baptists, Quakers, Roman Catholics, and Jews did not fare well during the colonial period. Cf. Hening, *Statutes,* I, 268-269 (1642-1643), the antipopish act; I, 532-533, Acts suppressing Quakers; II, 48 (1661-1662), Acts against Quakers and non-conformists; II, 48 and 180 ff., Acts forbidding Quaker meetings and worship; II, 182, Fine for permitting Quaker meetings near one's home, or for entertaining Quakers; III, 183, If Quakers or other separatists, after conviction, give security that they will not unlawfully meet in the future, they are to be discharged from all penalties.

life of the Church, but also supported, maintained and protected it.[61]

Non-toleration of dissenters and of dissenting preachers and ministers was the general policy prior to 1689. Quaker preachers and Catholic priests were exiled from the colony, and if they persisted to exercise their ministry in Virginia, they were treated as felons. By the turn of the eighteenth century Presbyterians and Huguenots were given some relief, and their ministers were permitted to exercise their ministry. Other Protestant sects enjoyed a toleration *de facto* later in the century.

The Constitution of Virginia, 1776, granted legal toleration to non-conformists and complete religious freedom and the right to worship to all religious groups in Virginia.

## *Section 2. The Carolinas*

### A. Juridic Position of Church and State from 1663 to 1729

In order to escape the intolerant measures of Governor Berkeley (+ 1677) some non-conformists left Virginia and settled in the northern section of Carolina. Others migrated into this country not for religious motives but to secure better land. Both the economic and religious motives probably played a part in the decision of some colonists to settle in Carolina.[62]

The first legal document instituting the Colony of Carolina was the Charter of 1663 granted by Charles II (1660-1685) to Lords Edward Clarendon (1609-1674), George Albemarble (1608-1670), William Craven, John Berkeley, and Anthony Ashley Cooper (1621-1683), Sir Anthony Carteret, Sir William Berkeley

---

[61] The protection of the ministers dated back to the assembly of 1623-1624. Anyone who disparaged a minister in such a way that the culprit's derogatory reports alienated the parishioners from their minister and caused his ministry to be less effectual, and had not sufficient proof to substantiate his disparaging remarks, was fined five hundred pounds of tobacco. The guilty party also had to ask pardon of the aggrieved minister publicly before the congregation. Cf. Hening, *Statutes,* I, 124.

[62] Cobb, p. 115. For an early account of the Colony of Carolina, cf. Morison and Commager, I, 69 ff.

(Governor of Virginia) and Sir John Collection, the third.[63] In virtue of this Charter these eight men became the proprietaries over the territory now comprising the two Carolinas.

There is some doubt whether this Charter of 1663 officially established the Church of England in the Carolina colony. Commentators generally concede that it did, or at least that the original proprietaries considered the charter as having established the Church of England.[64]

The fundamental charter also contains the principle of religious toleration. This concession was made for the benefit of those who could not conform to the worship of the Church of England. The proprietaries are also given the discretion to grant liberty by legal means to non-conformists. The ones enjoying this dispensation from conformity must be faithful subjects to king and colony, not cause any civil or ecclesiastical disturbance, nor scandalize or reproach the conformists and their liturgy, form and ceremonies.[65] The Lord proprietors gave their solemn pledge to implement these charter guarantees: "We will grant, in an ample manner as the undertakers shall desire, freedom and liberty of conscience in all religious and spiritual things, and to be kept inviolably with them, we having power in our charter so to do."[66] Furthermore, the

---

[63] Thorpe, V, 2743. Lord John Berkeley (+ 1678) and Sir George Carteret (+ 1680) became proprietors of New Jersey in 1673.

[64] The pertinent passage is: "And furthermore, the patronage and advowsons of all the churches and chappels, which as Christian religion shall increase within the country, isles, islets, and limits aforesaid, shall happen hereafter to be erected, together with license and power to build and found churches, chappels and oratories, in convenient and fit places, within the said bounds and limits, and to cause them to be dedicated and consecrated according to the ecclesiastical laws of our kingdom of England, together with all and singular alike, and as ample rights, jurisdictions, privileges, prerogatives, royalties, liberties, immunities and franchises of what kind soever, within the countries, isles, islets, and limits a foresaid." Cf. also Cobb, 117; Carl Zollmann, *American Church Law* (St. Paul: West Publishing Co., 1934), p. 3 (hereafter cited Zollmann); William George Torpey, *Judicial Doctrines of Religious Rights in America* (Chapel Hill: University of North Carolina Press, 1948), p. 10.

[65] Thorpe, V, 2752, § 18.

[66] "A Declaration and Proposal of the Lord Proprietor of Carolina, Aug. 25-Sept. 4, 1663," Thorpe, V, 2755, § 5.

Concessions and Agreements of the Lord Proprietors, 1665, guaranteed the free exercise of religion to those "whoe doe not actually disturbe the civill peace of the said Province or Countyes. . . ."[67] Those who do so peacefully conduct themselves will enjoy full freedom in matters of conscience, "any Law, statute or clause conteyned or to be conteyned, usage or custom of this realme of England to the contrary hereof in anywise notwithstanding."[68] The Carolina Charter of 1665 also contains a section guaranteeing liberty and protection of the law to persons unable to conform to the Church of England as established in the colony. Its wording is a combination of the text cited above from the original charter and from the Concessions and Agreements of 1665. In all these documents the person loses his right to the free exercise of religion when he uses it to disturb the civil peace and order.[69]

The next significant document is the Fundamental Constitution of Carolina, 1669, which John Locke (1632-1704) is generally credited as framing.[70] Article 96 established the Church of England in no uncertain terms and restricted all public support to the established Church.[71] The government was to be guided by a definite set of rules listed in the charter, when it dealt with dissenting religious groups, and the government was also empowered to keep dissenters out of the colony. They may be kept out so "that civil peace may be maintained admidst diversity of opinion."[72]

Nevertheless, broad toleration was the recommended policy.

---

[67] Thorpe, V, 2758, § 8.

[68] Thorpe, V, 2785, § 8.

[69] Thorpe, V, 2752, § 18, 2757, § 8, 2771. Local assemblies were empowered to appoint and support preachers. Liberty was given "to any person or persons to keepe and mainteyne preachers or ministers as they please." Cf. *ibid.*, § 9.

[70] Thorpe, V, 2772. Cobb, p. 119. This constitution was amended by the Earl of Shaftesbury and it was only partially put into operation. In 1693 it was abrogated by the proprietors.

[71] Thorpe, V, 2783. This article was not drawn up by Mr. Locke, but inserted by some of the chief proprietors, against his judgment, as Locke himself informed one of his friends, to whom he presented a copy of these constitutions. Cf. *ibid.*, note a; cf. also Cobb, p. 120; Morison and Commager, I, p. 70.

[72] Thorpe, V, 2783-2784, Art. 97.

Jews, heathens, and other dissenters were not to be persecuted, but rather they were to be treated kindly and thus moved to receive the truth. "Therefore, any seven or more persons agreeing in any religion, shall constitute a church or profession, to which they shall give some name, to distinguish it from others."[73] To be recognized at law each church had to submit a record of church membership and worship in a public manner.[74]

Anyone over seventeen years of age who did not have a recorded church membership was denied the benefit and protection of the law and was automatically incapable of any place of honor or profit.[75] A person ceased to be a church member either voluntarily or upon an authorized excommunication. In both cases this was signified through the striking of his name from the public record. This demand for a public record of church membership was somewhat unusual; it was not found among the other colonies.[76] Provided that the particular church complied with the various charter regulations, it was guaranteed the right of peaceable church assembly. Undoubtedly, the dissenters were willing to co-operate with these rules, for they were thus able to secure a freedom not available to them in neighboring Virginia.[77]

In an effort to preserve public order the charter prohibited all provocative language directed against any church. It likewise provided that "no person whatsoever shall disturb, molest or persecute another for his speculative opinions in religion, or his way of worship."[78] The councillor's court, which consisted of one of the proprietors and his six councillors, was alone competent to hear cases concerning the invasions of liberty of conscience or the disturbance of public peace under the pretext of religion.[79]

The politically predominant group at the time of the passage of the Toleration Act of 1696 was the body of the Church of England. For this reason it was not surprising that all Christians,

[73] Thorpe, V, 2784, Art. 97.
[74] Thorpe, V, 2784, Art. 98, 104.
[75] Thorpe, V, 2784, Art. 104.
[76] Thorpe, V, 2784.
[77] Thorpe, V, 2874-2875, Arts. 102, 108.
[78] Thorpe, V, 2785, Arts. 106, 109.
[79] Thorpe, V, 2777, Art. 35.

except Papists, were guaranteed full liberty of conscience and the free exercise of religion.[80] However, this enactment marked a retrogression in the liberty of religion as guaranteed by the government of Carolina. Previous fundamental law tolerated all religious beliefs, including Jewish, Catholic, and pagan, provided the said group publicly worshipped one God. The Act of Toleration of 1696 explicitly deprived Papists of the free exercise of worship and implicitly denied this right to the other two groups.

Unlike her sister colonies Carolina had an excellent record during the seventeenth century in matters of the free exercise of religion. At the turn of the century these colonies adopted a more tolerant attitude, but Carolina manifested the opposite tendency.

In 1704 the legislature passed an act establishing the Church of England.[81] But this was not the end of civil legislating in church affairs. A second act was passed requiring the members of the legislature to belong to the Church of England and to communicate once a year. The intrusion took an even bolder form when the assembly introduced lay interference into the internal life of the Church to an alarming degree. It empowered an ecclesiastical court composed of twenty laymen to settle dispute, to exercise church discipline, and to remove ministers for cause.[82] An additional act was passed in clarification of the provisions of the establishment act. The 1704 Act was not to be construed so as to deny dissenting ministers the right to marry, baptize, or bury their dissenting congregations.[83] The legislature passed other establishment acts, but they did not impinge upon the civil or religious liberties of

---

[80] Thomas Cooper (ed.), *The Statutes at Large of South Carolina,* Vols. I-V (Columbia, S. C., 1836-1839), I, 131 (hereafter cited Cooper, Statutes of S. C.). "All Christians . . . (Papists only excepted) shall enjoy the full, free and undisturbed exercise of their consciences, so far as it be in the exercise of worship according to the professed rules of religion, without any lett, hindrance, or molestation by any power either ecclesiastical or civil whatever."

[81] Walter Clark (ed.), *The Statutes of North Carolina* (25 vols., Goldsboro, N. C., 1904-1908), XXII, 161 (hereafter cited Clark, *State Records of N. C.*). Cooper, *Statutes of S. C.,* II, 232, 236. This act also disenfranchised all who dissented from the Church of England.

[82] Cooper, *Statutes of S. C.,* II, 240.

[83] Cooper, *Statutes of S. C.,* II, 259.

dissenters, nor did they contain the lay ecclesiastical court provisions.[84]

Quakers and other dissenters, who comprised the majority of the populace at the time of the passage of the 1704 establishment acts, reacted vigorously, but the acts were sustained by the majority of the proprietors. The dissenters carried their grievances to the parliament, where they were favorably received. The attorney general and the solicitor general declared these acts to be "unreasonable and against the Charter and English custom," and Queen Anne (1702-1714) in Council voided the acts on June 10, 1706.[85] The Carolina legislature had only one course of action open to them—repeal the statutes.

Protestant dissenters still had some anxious times. The assembly enacted a law entitled "An act for the better and more effectual preserving of the Queen's peace" (1711). This law favored the established religion and could be interpreted to effect the arrest of dissenting preachers on the ground that their preaching was a divisive influence in the colony.[86] The situation was somewhat relieved by the passage of "A Liberty of Conscience Act" in 1715, which guaranteed freedom of public worship to Protestants.[87] The liberty act of 1715 was substantially reenacted in 1749.[88]

In 1729 the colony of Carolina was divided into the royal provinces of North and South Carolina. The French Huguenots were the most important ruling element among the ruling class of South Carolina, and "unlike other foreigners in the English colonies they quickly adopted the English language and joined the established Church of England."[89] The Church of England was much stronger in South Carolina during the eighteenth century than in North

---

[84] Cooper, *Statutes of S. C.*, II, 282 ff. (1706), 338 (1710), 366 (1711); Clark, *State Records of N. C.*, XXIII, ch. 8, p. 6; ch. 32, pp. 187-191.

[85] Cobb, pp. 125-128; Clark, *State Records of N. C.*, XXII, 151.

[86] Clark, *State Records of N. C.*, XXV, ch. 1, p. 153.

[87] Clark, *State Records of N. C.*, XXIII, ch. 9, p. 11, § II; Quakers also benefited from liberal legislation passed in this session, for their solemn affirmation could be substituted for the required oath.

[88] Clark, *State Records of N. C.*, XXIII, ch. 18, p. 324.

[89] Morison and Commager, I, 70.

Carolina for this reason and because of the deeper religious character of South Carolina's settlers and the superiority of their clergy.[90] However, in both North and South Carolina the legislatures retained the basic Church and State relationship that existed prior to the formation of the separate colonies. Disestablishment was not realized until the Revolutionary years.

### B. North Carolina After the Division of 1729

The 1749 session of the North Carolina Assembly made it clear that the Church of England existing within its colonial boundaries would be regulated not by the acts of parliament, but by the assembly laws.[91] In 1760 the exemption from the militia duty was extended to include Presbyterian ministers. The ministers of the Church of England enjoyed this privilege as early as 1715.[92] This was an indication of a more liberal spirit beginning to pervade the legislature.

### C. Statehood Period

The period of the Revolution sounded the death knell to establishment and to other forms of discriminatory ecclesiastical legislation. A constitutional congress assembled at Halifax, N. C., on November 12, 1776, and completed its work on the Constitution of North Carolina. This document was not submitted to the populace for their ratification; it became effective by vote of the convention. The initial section of the constitution consisted of a Declaration of Rights. Article 19 of this declaration granted liberty of worship to all men, regardless of religious affiliation.[93]

---

[90] Cobb, p. 132.

[91] Clark, *State Records of N. C.*, XXIII, ch. 1, p. 327, § VI.—The Common Law of England does not bind in this Province "which relates to Matters of Ecclesiastical [nature], which are inconsistent with or repugnant to the Settlement of the Church of England in this Province, by the Acts of the Assembly thereof. . . ."

[92] Clark, *State Records of N. C.*, XXIII, ch. 24, p. 29, § V (1715); p. 519, § IV (1760); ch. 3, p. 761, § IV (1766); ch. 2, p. 941, § III (1774).

[93] Thorpe, V, 2788; Clark, *State Records of N. C.*, XXIII, 978.—That all men have a natural and unalienable right to worship Almighty God according to the dictates of their own consciences.

All forms of establishment were abolished, and no one could "be compelled to attend any place of worship contrary to his faith or judgment, nor be obliged to pay" for any place of worship, or for the maintenance of any minister or ministry; "but all persons shall be at liberty to exercise their own mode of worship."[94] But all the freedoms guaranteed in this article were conditioned by the clause, "Provided, That nothing herein contained shall be construed to exempt preachers of treasonable or seditious discourses, from legal trial and punishment." The uncertainty of the loyalty of the ministers of the Church of England may have caused the insertion of this clause. In other colonies their loyalty was questioned, and these ministers were the object of abuse, and even of physical violence, in some of the northern colonies.[95]

There were still some items of religious discrimination to be abrogated. The celebration of matrimony according to the rites and ceremonies of the minister had been restricted to the Church of England. It was now extended to Presbyterians and other dissenting ministers.[96] On December 23, 1776, all regular ministers of the Gospel of every denomination having care of souls were empowered to celebrate matrimony according to the rites and ceremonies of their respective Churches.[97]

Among the Convention Ordinances there was one which secured the peaceful possession of church property: ". . . all Churches, Chapels, and other Houses built for the purpose of public Worship, shall be and remain forever to the Use and Occupancy of that religious Society, Church, Sect, Denomination. . . ."[98] This right of peaceful possession safeguarded the place of worship and preaching against arbitrary state action or unauthorized lay intrusion. The State also implicitly abrogated the old English oath injurious

---

[94] Thorpe, V, 2793, § XXXIV; Clark, *State Records of N. C.*, XXIII, 983.

[95] Thorpe, V, 2793. Preachers, so long as they functioned as such, were not permitted to hold public office.—*Ibid.*, § XXXI.

[96] Clark, *State Records of N. C., XXIII*, pp. 672, 673, ch. 9, §§ I, II (1776). The constitution of 1776 retained a religious test. Cf. Thorpe, V, p. 2793, § XXXII.

[97] Clark, *State Records of N. C.*, XXIII, p. 997.

[98] Clark, *State Records of N. C.*, XXIII, 986 (1776).

to Catholics, Jews, and many Protestant sects in 1776, and made this abrogation explicit by an act passed in 1778.[99]

North Carloina preserved the constitution of 1776, with some amendments, as the fundamental law of the State, until the end of the civil war. The new constitution of 1868 contained in its declaration of rights an absolute expression of the right to worship according to one's conscience independently of government control.[100] This legal conviction is still preserved today in North Carolina.

### D. South Carolina: Free Exercise After 1776

The South Carolina constitution of 1776 was strangely silent regarding religious matters, except for the charge that the Roman Catholic religion in Canada was being employed by Great Britain as an instrument to harass the neighboring Protestant settlements.[101] This lack of attention to religious matters on the domestic scene was amply supplied for in the constitution formulated in 1778. The Protestant religion was declared the established religion of South Carolina, and toleration was extended to "all persons and religious societies who acknowledge that there is one God, and a future state of rewards and punishments, and that God is to be publicly worshipped. . . ."[102]

All Christians were accorded equal religious and civil privileges. Before a group could be incorporated or deemed a church of the established religion, church membership had to consist of at least fifteen male persons not under twenty-one years of age united for the purpose of religious worship and agreeing to the following: 1. One God and a future state of reward and punishment. 2. Public worship of God. 3. The Christian religion is the religion. 4. Divine inspiration of the Bible. 5. The duty to bear witness to the truth.[103]

---

[99] Clark, *State Records of N. C.*, XXIV, pp. 13-14, ch. IV, p. 219, ch. X.

[100] Thorpe, V, p. 2802, Art. I, § 26.—"All men have a natural and unalienable right to worship, and no human authority should, in any case whatever, control or interfere with this right of conscience."

[101] Thorpe, VI, 3241-3242.

[102] Thorpe, VI, 3255, art. 38.

[103] Thorpe, VI, 3256. This constitution retained a religious test for office. Cf. *ibid.*, 3249, art. 3; 3250, art. 8; 3252, art. 13. These tests were abrogated by the Constitution of 1790. Cf. *ibid.*, 3259, §§ 5-8.

The Constitution also established a rule for the selection of ministers. No one could officiate as a minister of the established church who was not "chosen by a majority of the society to which he shall minister. . . ."[104] As is evident, the new State of South Carolina was not ready to relinquish its control over the internal and external affairs of the various churches. Not only did it retain the old establishment, but it broadened the scope of state establishment, and hence state interference in matters of cult, preaching, and discipline.

To preserve both ecclesiastical and civil peace the constitution of 1778 forbade: 1) all disturbing or molesting of religious assemblies, 2) the use of unbecoming and provocative language against any church, and 3) the employment of irreverent and seditious speech against the state government in religious assemblies.[105]

The constitution of 1790 contained a free exercise clause which implicitly disestablished the Protestant religion. During the next few years churches of several denominations, including Jews and Catholics, were incorporated.[106] Beyond any doubt everyone was guaranteed the right to worship God according to the dictates of his conscience by the Constitution of 1868, provided this liberty did not justify "practices incompatible with the peace and moral safety of society."[107] The constitution of 1895 guaranteed civil and religious liberties in words identical with the first amendment to the federal constitution:

> The general assembly shall make no law respecting an establishment of religion or prohibiting the free exercise thereof, or abridging the freedom of speech or of the

[104] Thorpe, VI, 3256. The minister had also to subscribe to the foregoing five articles and the additional declarations discussed in this Article XXXVIII.

[105] Thorpe, VI, 3257.

[106] Thorpe, VI, 3264, art. VIII; Cooper, *Statutes of S. C.*, V, 141, Baptists (1790); V, 181, Roman Catholics in Charleston (1791); V, 184, Jewish Congregation (1791); V, 184, Presbyterians (1791); V, 230, United Independent Congregational Church (1793).

[107] Thorpe, 3282, Art I, § 9.

> press; or the right of the people peaceably to assemble and to petition the Government. . . .[108]

Church and State relations in the Carolinas during the colonial years was far from static. The Charter of 1663 contained the principle of toleration for dissenters from the Church of England. It also gave the proprietors discretion to grant this liberty to dissenters by legal means, which they proceeded to do in a formal declaration in 1663 and by their Concessions and Agreements in 1665. Local assemblies were empowered to appoint ministers and to maintain them, and other persons could have and support ministers of their own choosing.

The 1696 Toleration Act was a step backward in religious liberty in the colonies. Only Christians were tolerated, with the exception of Papists. Further encroachments were made upon the liberties of the dissenting Protestants and also the Church of England by the Establishment Act of 1704. This act and others of a similar nature were voided by the Queen in 1706, and the Protestants were granted substantial relief by the Liberty Act of 1715.

Division of the colony in 1729 did little to legally alter the situation of toleration, but the new colony of North Carolina was of a more tolerant spirit than her sister colony, South Carolina. This difference manifested itself quite clearly when they became states. North Carolina completely abrogated all forms of establishment in her 1776 Constitution and granted liberty to everyone in matters of religion. The only restraint placed upon preachers was that this new liberty did not exempt them from conviction for sedition or treason. South Carolina was slower in granting equality. The Constitution of 1778 established the Protestant religion and thus legislated a far broader form of establishment than had ever existed in Carolina. It also made necessary an adherence to several points of dogma before a church could be incorporated or an established Protestant minister could preach or teach.

By 1790 at least implicit disestablishment was contained in the fundamental law of the land and equal religious liberty in matters of the free exercise of worship were extended to all the people.

---

[108] Thorpe, VI, 3307, Art. I, § 4.

In a constitution adopted over a century later, the disestablishment clause and free exercise clause were the same as that used in the first amendment to the Federal Constitution.

### ARTICLE II. CHANGING ESTABLISHMENTS

New York, Maryland, New Jersey and Georgia fall under this general heading because their history is marked by a change in relations between the colonial government and the church. New York and New Jersey were initially colonies of the Netherlands. The establishment was Dutch Reform and the colonial church was subject to the jurisdiction of the mother church in Holland. The English conquest dislodged the Dutch Reform Church, and a number of unsuccessful attempts were made to force the colonists to adopt legally the Established Church of England.

Maryland's initial religious policy was equal religious tolerance toward all her Christian inhabitants. In the course of time the people were subjected to an Anglican establishment. Georgia was founded in 1732 upon liberal principles, but Papists were excluded from its guarantees of religious freedom. The charter of Georgia was annulled in 1752 by the crown, and the Church of England was established. This establishment never was very successful; moreover, it was short-lived, for the Revolution marked its downfall.

#### *Section 1. New York*

##### A. Juridic Position of Church and State in the Formative Period

The Dutch motives for establishing a colony in New Netherland were primarily political and economic, and not religious. The Dutch West India Company was chiefly concerned with building a commercial empire. However, it did make some provisions for religion. Holland, herself, was anxious to establish colonies which would give her a place of power among the mighty colonial powers of Europe.[109]

The administration of Church affairs was an involved matter

[109] Morison and Commager, I, 59-61; Cobb, p. 301; "The Charter of the Dutch West India Company," Thorpe, I, 59 ff.

in New Amsterdam. The ecclesiastical authorities in the Netherlands, the colonial civil authorities, and to some extent the civil authorities in the Netherlands played a part in Church affairs in the colony. The first minister to conduct services in the colony of New Netherland was Jonas Michaelius (1584-1638), who recognized the consistory of Amsterdam as the superior ecclesiastical authority of the colony. Attempts were made by the various local Synods in the Netherlands to centralize the authority over the Church in the New World, "but the Classis of Amsterdam remained undisturbed in the direction and supervision of the colonial church of New Amsterdam."[110] This strong influence of the Classis over religious conditions in the colony is revealed in the ecclesiastical correspondence during the period of Dutch control of New Netherland.[111]

The States General frequently intervened in the civil affairs of New Netherland, but it usually followed a policy of non-intervention in ecclesiastical affairs. The States General approved the exclusive establishment of the Reformed Church in the Charter of Privileges and Exemptions of 1640. However, it did not interfere in the Lutheran struggle or in other separatist movements seeking freedom of public worship.

The Province of New Netherland was governed by a Director General, who was assisted by an advisory Council. The Director was the supreme magistrate and he retained control over the colonial Church, even after inferior local courts were established in the colony. Religious crimes were reserved to the jurisdiction of the Provincial Court. In general, the erection and support of schools and churches had to be approved by the Director General and his Council.[112] The appointment of ministers was more involved. Ordinarily, they were "appointed by the Directors of the Amsterdam Chamber, commissioned by the Classis of Amsterdam,

---

[110] Frederick J. Zwierlein, *Religion in New Netherlands* (Rochester, N. Y., 1910), p. 42; cf. also pp. 40, 41, 63. This book contains an excellent selected bibliography.—*Ibid.*, 331-351 (hereafter cited Zwierlein).

[111] *Ecclesiastical Records of the State of New York* (7 vols., published by the State under the supervision of Hugh Hastings, Albany, 1901), I, II (hereafter cited *Ecclesiastical Records of N. Y.*).

[112] Zwierlein, p. 44.

but inducted by some colonial official in the name of the Director General."[113] If the Director General appointed a minister for the Reformed Church, his appointment required the approval of both the ecclesiastical and civil authorities in the Netherlands. English ministers who came to New Netherland had to obtain the approval of the Provincial government before they could exercise their ministry.

Michaelius was the first Dutch minister to arrive in the colony.[114] He was sent in 1628 by the company, which agreed to be responsible for his support. The company issued a Charter of Privileges and Exemptions in 1629. Article 27 placed the burden of support for the minister of religion upon the Patroon and the colonists. Zwierlein considered this action to be legal recognition of the establishment of the Dutch Reform religion.[115]

On July 19, 1640, a new Charter of Privileges and Exemptions was published. This charter established the Dutch Reform Church to the exclusion of public worship by other sects.[116]

Some degree of toleration was permitted in 1642. Reverend Francis Doughty, Richard Smith and other Presbyterians came from New England and settled on Long Island. The company granted permission, with the council's approval, for them to settle with their minister.[117]

There were other instances of toleration, such as the patents issued in 1642 and in 1645 to Englishmen at New Town, Flushing

---

[113] Zwierlein, p. 45.

[114] Zwierlein, p. 63.

[115] Zwierlein, p. 66; Cobb apparently was not aware of this document, for he writes, "So far as is reported, the first formal expression of the company's policy in regard to religious matters was made in 1638 in the 'Articles for Colonization.'" Cf. Cobb, p. 303. Article 7 of these latter articles permitted liberty of conscience. For this reason the States General did not approve them. Cf. Cobb, p. 304.

[116] Zwierlein, p. 70, and Cobb, p. 304. And no other religion shall be publicly admitted in New Netherland, except the Reformed, as it is at present preached and practiced by public authority in the United Netherlands; and for this purpose the Company shall provide and maintain good and suitable preachers, schoolmaster and Comforters of the Sick.

[117] E. B. O'Callaghan, *History of New Netherlands* (2 vols., New York, 1885), I, 257. Cobb, p. 307. Zwierlein, pp. 148 ff.

and the Great Plains of Long Island. According to the patents the Englishmen were allowed to use their own liturgy and exercise their own worship.[118]

## B. Colonial Period

Peter Stuyvesant (1592-1682) became governor in 1645 and he extended the influence of the Dutch as far south as Fort Christina (Wilmington, Delaware) on the Delaware.[119] During the early years of his governorship he pursued a policy of toleration of other religious sects, notwithstanding the establishment of the National Reformed Church.[120]

In 1654, however, there was a shift in policy. The previous year the Lutherans of New Amsterdam had petitioned the governor and his council for freedom of worship for all the Lutherans in the colony and for permission to send a minister to the colony. When the Dutch clergy heard about the petition, they vigorously opposed it, and the entire question was referred to the Company in Holland. The Company refused to grant the request of the Lutherans, and it also asked the governor not to accept requests of this nature in the future. But the Company cautioned him to refuse as gently as possible and to employ moderate means of persuasion in order to induce the Lutherans to join the Established Church.[121]

However, the Lutherans continued to hold services in defiance of the prohibition. John Megapolensis (1603-1670) and Samuel Drisius, two Dutch Reform clergymen, complained to the governor that unqualified persons were preaching in Middleburg. Stuyvesant reacted strongly. In a proclamation issued "to promote the glory of God, the increase of the Reformed religion and the peace and harmony of the country," he forbade preachers not called by ecclesiastical or civil authority to hold meetings not in harmony with the established religion as set forth by the Synod of Dort. This regulation did not affect any patent in existence at the time and

---

[118] Zwierlein, pp. 154-156.

[119] Cf. Morison and Commager, I, 62-63; Zwierlein, pp. 106-135.

[120] *Ecclesiastical Records of N. Y.*, I, 341.

[121] Cf. Cobb, pp. 313-314; Zwierlein, pp. 188 ff.

disclaimed "any lording over the conscience, or any prohibition of reading God's holy word, and the domestic praying and worship of each one in his family."[122]

The Directors of the West India Company were displeased with the harsh treatment of the dissenters. They informed Stuyvesant on June 14, 1656, that they would have been more pleased had the placard against the Lutherans not been published. The Directors intended a more lenient treatment, so they ordered Stuyvesant to "let them worship in their homes."[123]

By force of treaty the Swedes on the South (Delaware) River were permitted to have a Lutheran minister.[124] Encouraged by this permission, the Lutherans also sent a minister, John E. Goedwater, to the North (Hudson) River.[125] He did not possess a permit to preach, but said that he expected one from the West India Company. The mayor and aldermen forbade Goedwater to conduct any private or public services in the city.[126]

On October 10, 1657, the Lutherans petitioned the governor and his council to revoke these orders. The governor replied that Goedwater was to prepare to sail home immediately.[127]

---

[122] *Ecclesiastical Records of N. Y.*, I, 342. Every unlicensed preacher was fined one hundred Flemish and anyone who attended the meeting was fined twenty-five pounds.

[123] *Ecclesiastical Records of N. Y.*, I, 352; Cobb, p. 314. Stuyvesant was directed not to publish similar things without their knowledge.

[124] *Ecclesiastical Records of N. Y.*, I, 377.

[125] *Ecclesiastical Records of N. Y.*, I, 388-390; Zwierlein, p. 202.

[126] Cf. "Facts contained in a Report of the Mayer and Aldermen of New Amsterdam Upon the Petition of Ministers Against Allowing Lutheran Services, July 14, 1657," *Ecclesiastical Records of N. Y.*, I, 388-390.

[127] This directive was issued at a meeting of the Director General and his Council in Fort Amsterdam, New Netherland, October 16, 1657. Cf. *Ecclesiastical Records of N. Y.*, I, 407. During the meeting a letter from Goedwater to the Director and his Council, dated October 15, 1657 (*ibid.*, pp. 407-408), was handed to the Director General. Goedwater said that he was not guilty of any crime. He was awaiting further orders from Holland, and he petitioned for a stay of sentence. The Director and his Council charged him with contempt and ordered him to set sail immediately on one of the two ships about to leave the harbor. Cf. *Ecclesiastical Record of N. Y.*, I, 408-409; also 409-411, which contains a letter from the Reverends Megapolensis and Drisius to the Classis in Amsterdam (Oct. 25, 1657) recounting the incident in detail.

Goedwater fled to a Lutheran farm and wintered there. The Lutherans alleged that he was quite ill, and the Fiscal was ordered to force him to return to Holland upon his recovery.[128] Minister Goedwater remained and, contrary to the Director General's command, he began to hold meetings and to preach. The Director General again issued a prohibition, but he remained obstinate and ignored it. Finally, he was arrested and sent back to Holland on the Brown Fish (*De Bruynvisch*).[129]

This spirit of intolerance was not shared by all the populace. The inhabitants of Flushing, Long Island, refused to lay violent hands upon Quakers and others not of the Dutch Reform Church. The Director General was appraised of this situation in a written statement on December 29, 1657. Tobias Feaks, the Schout of Flushing, was arrested. On January 1, 1658, the magistrates of Flushing were also taken into custody by order of the Director and his Council. Tobias Feaks was sentenced on January 28, 1658. At his hearing he admitted that he had received an order from the Director General not to admit, lodge, or entertain in his village (Flushing, L. I.) any member of the Quaker sect. He was charged with contempt and sedition for his part in the letter of defiance submitted to the Director General. Feaks was dismissed from the office of Schout of Flushing and banished from New Netherland. He was given an alternate sentence of a fine of 200 florins and the right to remain in New Netherland, provided he promised to avoid such errors in the future.[130]

Inhabitants of New Netherland who did not pay the tax for the support of the Established Church were heavily fined, even if they were dissenters. One such incident is recorded in the *Ecclesiastical Records*.[131] The Lutheran and Quaker incidents and the heavy

[128] "Mesapolensis and Drisius to the Amsterdam Classis, Sept. 24, 1658," *Ecclesiastical Records of N. Y.*, I, 433.

[129] *Ecclesiastical Records of N. Y.*, I, 449. Megapolensis and Drisius wrote an account of this to the Classis of Amsterdam, Sept. 10, 1659.

[130] *Ecclesiastical Records of N. Y.*, I, 412-415. For a discussion of the treatment given Jews, cf. Cobb, pp. 317-318.

[131] I, 420 ". . . they behaved very insolently and stubbornly, making none but frivilous excuses, one, for instance, that he was a Catholic, the other that he did not understand Dutch. Therefore the Fiscal demanded, that the aforesaid persons should be condemned to pay a heavy fine."

fines of dissenters reflect the policy of intolerance adopted by the government during the decade preceding the British rule of New York.

The Dutch colony passed into the hands of the English during the Summer of 1664. A small fleet under the command of the Duke of York, brother of Charles II, took the colony without a skirmish. "New Netherland became New York without a blow or a tear."[132] New York remained under British domination until the Revolution, except for a brief return of Dutch power in 1673-1674. The Dutch restored it to England by treaty in 1674.[133]

The Duke of York, who later governed England as James II, obtained a parliamentary approved grant from his brother, King Charles II. This grant included all the land between the Connecticut and Delaware rivers, together with Long Island, Nantucket, and Martha's Vineyard, and Maine east of the Kennebec. The Duke was lord and master of this domain under the king. He made no provision for an assembly. James instructed his governor not to impose the English language nor his own Catholic religion upon the Dutch settlers.

The established position of the Dutch Reformed Church ended with Stuyvesant's surrender in 1664. The Articles of Capitulation specifically guaranteed liberty of conscience in divine worship and church discipline to the Dutch.[134]

The Duke of York's Laws were promulgated on Long Island in 1665. Article 10 granted liberty of conscience to all in very wide terms of toleration.[135] No individual sect was established, but the civil power retained control over religious affairs. The legal effect was to establish religion as such. The Duke's Laws did not specify

---

[132] Morison and Commager, I, 63.

[133] *Ibid.*, pp. 72-73.

[134] Cobb, p. 325. "Articles of Capitulation on the Reduction of New Netherland," *Ecclesiastical Records of N. Y.*, I, 557-558, Art. VIII.

[135] *The Colonial Laws of New York from the Year 1664 to the Revolution* (5 vols., Albany, 1894), I, 25.—"That no Congregations shall be disturbed in their private meetings in time of prayer, preaching, or other divine Service. Nor shall any person be fined, molested, or imprisoned for differing in Judgment in matters of Religion who profess Christianity." (Hereafter cited *Colonial Laws of N. Y.*)

any particular Church, but only that a church of some kind be established in every town. Cobb summed up the legal situation quite aptly—"an establishment without a name."[136]

James II (1685-1688) made the civil government the head of every church, Reformed, Anglican or otherwise, in the entire province. This situation was without parallel in the colonies, where legal establishment was given to one Church, and other churches or sects were merely tolerated or prohibited.

The Duke of York's Laws with respect to religion applied only to Long Island and Staten Island until 1674. One of these laws required a minister to produce testimonials of his ordination and present them to the governor, before the minister could officiate.[137] Another law commanded that "the minister of every Parish shall Preach constantly every Sunday and shall pray for the Kinge, Queene, Duke of Yorke, and the Royall family."[138]

Events of the last thirty years of the seventeenth century helped to form a complicated picture of religious conditions in New York. The first of these was the recapture of New York by the Dutch in August, 1673. The Province was renamed New Amsterdam and the Dutch Reformed Church was reestablished.[139] The English on Long Island petitioned for freedom of religion under the Dutch rule on August 14, 1673.[140] They desired to worship God according to their belief without any imposition, and not to be forced to bear arms against their own nation. The Dutch replied that "they are allowed Freedom of Conscience in Worship of God and Church Discipline."[141]

The English in New Jersey also petitioned for freedom of religion, and they were granted the same privileges as were permitted

---

[136] Cobb, p. 327.

[137] *Colonial Laws of N. Y.*, I, 25; *Ecclesiastical Records of N. Y.*, I, 570, § 4.

[138] *Colonial Laws of N. Y.*, I, 25; *Ecclesiastical Records of N. Y.*, I, 570, § 5.

[139] Cobb, pp. 322-323.

[140] *Ecclesiastical Records of N. Y.*, I, 629-630.

[141] *Ecclesiastical Records of N. Y.*, I, 530. The oath of allegiance to the new government did not bind them to fight against their own nation.

in Netherlands.[142] The Lutherans in Albany were given freedom on September 26, 1673, provided that they did not offend the Congregation of the Reformed religion, the State religion.[143] The degree of freedom permitted during the Dutch restoration was less than that granted to the populace by the Duke of York. However, it was more liberal than the degree of freedom allowed under the Dutch rule.

The Dutch restored New York to England again in 1674. James II bestowed upon the colonists an extremely broad liberty of conscience. In his instruction to the governor of New York he wrote, "You shall permitt all persons of what Religion soever quietly to inhabitt within the precincts of your government, without giving them any disturbance or disquiet whatever for, or by reason of, their differing Opinions in matters of Religion: Provided they give noe disturbance to ye public peace nor doe molest or disquiet others in the free exercise of their religion."[144] King James II, a Roman Catholic, neither attempted to establish his religion, nor did he suppress other religions in New York.

Catholicism enjoyed a more favorable position at Court with the Restoration of the Stuarts in 1660. King Charles II's brother was an acknowledged Catholic. Charles desired to be more tolerant towards Catholics and other non-Anglican groups. His motives were, at least in part, political. He had concluded a secret treaty with Louis XIV of France (1643-1715) in 1670, whereby he agreed to assist in an attack on Holland. In 1672 at the outbreak of the Dutch War, he issued a Declaration of Indulgence for Catholics and Non-Conformists. He suspended the penal laws of Elizabethan times and extended a degree of freedom of worship.

---

[142] *Ecclesiastical Records of N. Y.*, I, 631-632.

[143] *Ecclesiastical Records of N. Y.*, I, 636.

[144] "Secret Instruction of James II to Governor Dongan of New York, May 29, 1686," *Ecclesiastical Records of N. Y.*, II, 915; Cobb, pp. 328-329. Cobb quotes the same instruction, but says that it is James' instruction to Governor Andros. Andros was governor for a second time, and this was after Dongan's term. A directive was given to Andros which is cited later in this writer's work, and while it is substantially the same as Dongan's instruction, it is not the instruction quoted above. Cf. *Ecclesiastical Records of N. Y.*, II, 954.

Parliament, in a surge of anti-popery, opposed this action and forced the king to revoke his tolerant measures. The method of moral pressure employed is a familiar one. Charles needed money to conduct the Dutch War. Parliament passed a revenue bill with a rider revoking the Declaration of Indulgence and substituting a stringent Test Act. This act required every office holder to receive Holy Communion in the Anglican Church and to take an oath repudiating Transubstantiation. It also contained oaths of supremacy and allegiance.[145] The initial act applied only to England, Wales, Berwick, and Jersey. When James II became king in 1685 he voided the test act. It was renewed during the reign of William and Mary (1689-1702), and remained in force until 1829. The act originally did not apply to New York. It was introduced into the colony in 1691 under Governor Sloughter.[146]

A picture of religious conditions in New York is supplied by Governor Andros in a report in 1678. Article 26 is concerned with religion: "There are Religions of all sorts, one Church of England, Several Presbyterian and Independents, Quakers and Anabaptists of Severall sects, some Jews, but Presbyterians and Independents most numerous and Substantial."[147]

During the governorship of Andros the colonists were on the point of rebellion, because they lacked any form of representation.[148] Trouble about taxation finally forced the next governor, Thomas Dongan, to summon a representative assembly in 1683. This body passed the Charter of Liberties which guaranteed free and unmolested exercise of religion and, for the future, accorded equal privileges at law for all Christian Churches.[149] Cobb maintained that the Duke of York approved the broad terms of this

---

[145] *Church and State Through the Centuries,* trans. and ed. Sidney Z. Ehler and John Morrall (London: Burns and Oates, 1954), pp. 213-215 (hereafter cited *Church and State*).

[146] *Ecclesiastical Records of N. Y.,* II, 1012.

[147] E. B. O'Callaghan, *The Documentary History of the State of New York* (4 vols., Albany, 1849-1851), I, 62.

[148] Cf. Morison and Commager, I, 72; Henry W. Elson, *History of the United States* (New York, 1926), pp. 126-127.

[149] "The Charter of Libertys and Privileges Granted by His Royal Highness to the Inhabitants of New York and Its Dependencies, October 30, 1683," *Ecclesiastical Records of N. Y.,* II, 864-865.

charter, but recalled his approbation when he became king. Elson is not very clear, but he gives the reader the impression that they were never approved.[150]

Charles II died suddenly and the Duke of York, James II, acceded to the throne. In his secret instructions to Dongan on May 29, 1686, the Church of England was given a favored position, but toleration was still to be the policy.[151] However, the government did not hesitate to take action against a minister, when his preaching disturbed the public order, as a case on record demonstrates. Rev. Mr. James was arrested on the grounds that he preached a seditious sermon on October 17, 1686, in Easthampton, New York. In his sermon he condemned an action of the Town government. James maintained that the changing of the landmarks by the officials was wrong, and that it would still be wrong, even if done by order of the king. He then proceeded to curse all those responsible for this action. His speech was viewed as seditious and also contemptuous of His Majesty's Laws and authority. Dongan and his Council, following a report by the attorney general, issued a warrant for his arrest on November 18, 1686. The warrant charged that he had preached a seditious sermon tending to stir up strife and create a public disturbance. Rev. Mr. James voluntarily appeared and submitted a petition begging to be relieved of the penalty imposed upon him. He admitted that he had erred, but said it was the first time in nearly forty years of preaching that he had been called before the authorities for an accounting.[152]

Religious pluralism in New York seems to have thrived under James' policy of toleration. Governor Dongan stated in his report on the conditions of the Province in 1684 that New York had a minister of the Church of England, a French Calvinist and a Dutch Lutheran. There were also many Quaker preachers, both men and women, some Anabaptists, Jews, and Roman Catholics dwelling in New York. In this same report he mentioned that he had promised the Indians of the Five Nations a piece of land

---

[150] Cobb, p. 334; Elson, *History of the United States,* p. 127.

[151] *Ecclesiastical Records of N. Y.,* II, 915; cf. also Cobb, pp. 334-335.

[152] *Ecclesiastical Records of N. Y.,* II, 924-928.

in English territory near Saratoga. He pledged that he would send them three priests, English Jesuits, and build a Church for them. The motivation for all this was primarily political. Dongan hoped to destroy any French claim to the country and have the French priests return to Canada.[153]

Governor Dongan wrote to Monsieur de Denonville in Canada on July 26, 1686. He promised to do all in his power to see that the Fathers who preached to the Indians in his domain were not ill treated.[154]

Denonville replied rather sharply and critically on October 1, 1686. He wanted Dongan to take more effective measures against those who were disrupting the work of the missionaries, and also to stop the English merchants who were selling liquor to the Indians.[155] Dongan replied on December 1, 1686, and he seemed quite disturbed. He wanted to know who it was that pretended to have orders from him to disrupt missionary activity. Not only had he issued an order to the contrary, but he had even written to the King of England about the need to send some Fathers hither to preach the Gospel to the natives.[156]

Dongan's motives appear from all the correspondence investigated to have been predominantly political. Be that as it may, the facts demonstrate that a more than merely tolerant attitude toward Roman Catholic priests existed in government circles of New York during Dongan's rule.

Governor Dongan was ordered to resign in 1688, and Governor Andros was placed in charge of New York, New Jersey and New England. In his commission he was directed as follows: "You are to permit a liberty of conscience in matters of religion to all persons, so that they be contented with a quiet and peaceable enjoyment of it. . . ."[157]

---

[153] *Ecclesiastical Records of N. Y.*, II, 877, 921; E. B. O'Callaghan, *Documentary History of New York*, I, 95 ff., especially, pp. 116-117.

[154] *Ecclesiastical Records of N. Y.*, II, 921.

[155] *Ecclesiastical Records of N. Y.*, II, 923-924.

[156] *Ecclesiastical Records of N. Y.*, II, 928. Additional correspondence passed between the two. Cf. *ibid.*, pp. 938, 939, 942, 945, 946.

[157] *Ecclesiastical Records of N. Y.*, II, 954. Elson, *History of the United States*, p. 127.

King James had issued in 1687 a "Declaration of Indulgence" which suspended the Test Act and gave liberty of public worship to all non-Anglican subjects. He issued a second declaration in 1688, after he had appointed men to the parliament who were more disposed to his proposal. However, Anglican protests and non-Conformist distrust of the Catholic Church weakened the position of James. Succeeding events connected with the declarations damaged his prestige, and a bloodless revolution drove James II from England. William of Orange, his Dutch son-in-law and a Protestant, was brought to power.[158]

Governor Sloughter arrived in New York in 1689 with instructions from William and Mary to grant the Church of England a favored position. He was further ordered "to permit a liberty of conscience to all Persons (except Papists), so that they be contented with a quiet and Peaceable enjoyment of it, not giving offense or scandall to the government."[159] He was also given power over the ministers of the Church of England. His secret instructions read: "If any person preferred already to a benefice (in the Church of England) shall appear to you to give scandal either by his Doctrine or Manners, you are to use the best means for the removal of him, and to supply in such manner as we have directed."[160]

The "toleration" section of the Instructions of William and Mary to Sloughter became colonial law in 1691. The Governor and his Council assented to a bill giving liberty of conscience," provided always that nothing mentioned herein or contained, shall be extended to give liberty for any persons of the Romish religion, to exercise their manner of worship contrary to the laws and statutes of their Majesties Kingdom of England."[161] The act also

---

[158] *Church and State*, p. 216; cf. *ibid.*, pp. 216-219, for a reproduction of the second Declaration, 1688.

[159] *Ecclesiastical Records of N. Y.*, II, 991.

[160] *Ecclesiastical Records of N. Y.*, II, 991. Governor Fletcher, his successor, was given the same directive. Cf. *ibid.*, p. 1033. The Test Act of 1673 did not apply to New York, but was introduced there by Sloughter in 1691. *Ibid.*, p. 1012.

[161] "Journal of the Council of New York, 1691, May 12, Henry Sloughter, Governor," *Ecclesiastical Records of N. Y.*, II, 1015-1016. The law as passed: "No Person or Persons which profess Faith in God by Jesus Christ,

discriminated against non-Christians. To those who were granted the right of toleration, i.e., the free exercise and public worship, there was given the warning that this toleration must not be used as a cloak for public disorder and civil strife.

The government's anti-Roman attitude culminated in an Act Against Jesuits and Popish Priests, August, 1700.[162] The act can best be appreciated when viewed within the framework of events preceding and immediately following its passage. The Jesuits had been laboring among the Indians of the Five Nations for years. French Jesuits worked among them even in the days of Dutch control of New York. Later, some English Jesuits came to preach to the Indians through the influence of Governor Dongan. As explained above, Dongan primarily did this to nullify the French claim over these Indians and their lands. After James II fell from power, anti-Roman directives were imposed upon New York and a concerted effort was made to win the Indians to Protestantism. The French Jesuits influenced a number of the Indians to move into the Canadian area to preserve their faith.

The Earl of Bellomont (Beaumont) held a conference at Albany with the Indians of the Five Nations from August 26-31, 1700. The purpose of this gathering was to turn the Indians against the Jesuits, against the Roman Catholic Church, and against Canada, and to win them over to England and Protestantism.[163] The act of 1700 was part of the plot. The schemers now had the legal weapon they needed to pursue their objectives.

---

his only Son, shall at any time be any way molested, disquieted, or called in question for any Difference of Opinion, or matter of Religious Concernment, who do not under that pretence disturb the Civil Peace of the Province, etc., and that all and every such Person and Persons may from time to time, and at all times hereafter, freely have and fully enjoy his or their Opinion, Persuasions and Judgments in matters of Conscience and Religion throughout all this Province; and freely meet at convenient places within this Province there to Worship according to their respective Persuasions, without being hindered, or molested, they behaving themselves peaceably, quietly, modestly, Religiously, and not using this liberty to Licentiousness, nor to the civil Injury or outward Disturbance of others. Always Provided. . . ." Cf. *ibid.*, p. 1016.

[162] *Ecclesiastical Records of N. Y.*, II, 1368-1370; *Colonial Laws of New York*, I, 429.

[163] *Ecclesiastical Records of N. Y.*, II, 1376-1383.

The anti-Popist Act of August 9, 1700, was very explicit. It forbade all Roman Catholic priests either to remain or to enter New York Province. Any priest apprehended there after November 1 was to be considered an "incendiary and a disturber of public peace and Safety and an Enemy to the true Christian Religion."[164]

Although the crown ordered the Church of England to be established, Governor Sloughter made no formal effort to have it established by the colonial legislature.[165] Sloughter was succeeded in 1692 by Governor Fletcher, who vigorously pursued a program of formal establishment. The legislature of 1692 refused to act on the matter. Fletcher pressured the next assembly, and they yielded somewhat to his demands. A committee was appointed and they reported out "a bill for a religious establishment of an entirely nondescript character, the like of which is not to be found elsewhere."[166] The bill became law on September 22, 1693.[167] The act was more remarkable for its omissions than for its requirements. It created an established Church in four Counties, but not in Albany or Kingston, or rather it established six Protestant ministers, but of no specified denomination. The law contained no reference to the Church of England or the Book of Common Prayer, nor any acknowledgment of the supremacy of the crown. Strange as it may seem, the Reformed Church had as solid a legal claim to establishment as the Church of England.[168]

Cobb claimed that establishment belonged to neither the Dutch

---

[164] *Colonial Laws of N. Y.*, I, 429. First conviction brought perpetual imprisonment. If the priest escaped and was recaptured, he was to suffer capital punishment. Anyone harboring a priest was subject to heavy fines. The law remained on the books until 1784.

[165] Cobb, p. 377; Elson, *History of the United States*, pp. 128-129. He recounts the usurping of the government prior to the arrival of Sloughter. He claims it was part of the anti-Catholic sentiment which swept over England and the colonies during the reign of James II.

[166] Cobb, p. 338.

[167] *Colonial Laws of N. Y.*, I, 328-331.—An Act for Settling a Ministry and Raising a Maintenance for them in the city of New York, County of Richmond, Westchester and Queens County.

[168] Cobb cited an incident in which a Colonel Lewis Morris of the Church of England admitted that the dissenters had as strong a claim as the Church of England.—Cobb, p. 339.

Reform Church nor the Church of England. In fact, he maintained "the only named Church that was ever 'established' on the soil of New York was the Reformed Church, which fell with Dutch power," and he is right.[169]

However, *de facto* the Church of England was regarded during the eighteenth century as the established Church. Cobb himself cited actions of Governor Cornbury which demonstrate that Cornbury considered the State Establishment to be an Anglican one. Cornbury seized a Presbyterian Church in Jamaica early in the eighteenth century and prohibited a Presbyterian preacher from preaching there. He did this on the grounds that the church was built with public taxes and appertained to the Established Church. Then he turned over possession of the place to the Anglicans.[170]

The act of 1693 was consistently interpreted by the governors of New York as establishing the Anglican Church, or as Cobb preferred to phrase it, "By dint of constant perversity of statement, (the established Church) had become entirely the Church of England."[171]

This establishment was never extended beyond the original limits of the act of 1693, the four Counties, despite the efforts of the clergy of England to have the government expand its coverage. Furthermore, the *de facto* extant establishment of the English Church reflected the will of the governors and their councils, but not the attitude of the majority of the people. This *de facto* extant establishment remained in New York's four Counties until the Revolution.

The Dutch Reform Church continued to do well under the eighteenth century laws. The Dutch Church of Albany petitioned for a charter, which was granted on August 10, 1720. By force of this charter the Dutch Reform Congregation was given the free exercise of worship, provided that it did not disrupt the public

---

[169] Cobb, pp. 339-341.

[170] Cobb, p. 346. "Of course, Cornbury's false premise was that the establishment was Anglican, coupled with another equally false, that any property for religious purposes, paid for at any time by tax, must belong to the Church of England. Governor Hunter, Cornbury's successor, was of the same frame of mind." *Ibid.*, pp. 347-348.

[171] Cobb, p. 361.

order or disturb the National Church of England or any other Reformed Protestant Churches.[172]

The governor of New York continued to exercise his authority over preachers. An interesting case is recorded in the records about 1707. Reverend Francis Makemie (1685-1708), a Presbyterian minister, preached in the house of a Mr. Jackson in New York. For this bold action he was arrested and charged with preaching apart from the governor's permission. So successfully did he plead his case that the jury readily acquitted him. But the government was determined to have the last word, and so the court ordered him to pay the court costs of some two hundred dollars.[173]

Three years later a dispute arose between two ministers of separate congregations regarding the right to preach in a given town. By a decision aimed at pacifying both parties Governor Hunter directed that the Justices of Kings County allow both to preach in their respective churches and ordered "that no molestation be given to either of them."[174]

During the eighteenth century governmental licensing of preachers was retained. The records reveal instances where this option to license or to refuse to license was exercised. Nicholas Eyers, a Baptist minister, obtained permission to preach on January 23 1721/22.[175] However, the Moravian preachers were not afforded the kindness of this dispensation. Count Nikolaus Ludwig von Zinzendorf (1700-1760), founder of the Moravians, protested on December 31, 1744, against the ill treatment of his missionaries in New York.[176] The Moravians had been ordered to stop preach-

---

[172] "Charter of the Reformed Protestant Church of Albany, August 10, 1720," *Ecclesiastical Records of N. Y.*, III, 2156, Part IV, § 2.

[173] *Ecclesiastical Records of N. Y.*, II, 879.

[174] *Ecclesiastical Records of N. Y.*, III, 1866 (Sept. 15, 1710).

[175] *Ecclesiastical Records of N. Y.*, II, 2187-2188. ". . . I have thought fit to grant unto the said Nicholas Eyers that he enjoy the Priviledge, benefits and advantages which dissenting Ministers may enjoy in virtue of a Statute made an enactment at Westminster Ent. an Act for Exempting their Majesties Protestant Subjects dissenting from the Church of England from the Penaltys of Certain Laws in the first year of King William and Mary Provided always that he shall comply with the Rules and orders or directions mentioned and Expressed in the same Statute with Regard to Anabaptists or such Dissenting Protestants."

[176] "Count Zinzendorf to the Board of Trade in New York," *Ecclesiastical Records of N. Y.*, IV, 2865.

ing and to leave the Province on November 27, 1744. But they remained obstinate and continued to be the object of persecution.[177]

The persecutors were soon to become the persecuted. The spirit of the Revolution of 1776 reflected itself in the treatment of the Episcopal clergy. Generally considered, the sympathy of this clergy was with the English, so they did not attempt to speak out in their sermons in favor of the revolution. According to one account, the Episcopal clergy were often threatened, ill treated, beaten, and even temporarily imprisoned.[178]

## C. Statehood Period

The Constitution of 1777 brought relief to those who had long been the object of intolerance, but not every discrimination against these sects was removed. All laws of the crown and the colony remained in force, except those establishing and maintaining any particular denomination of Christians.[179] As a result the Ministry Act of 1693 and all its amendments were repealed, and freedom of religion was established.[180] However, the notorious anti-priest act of 1700 remained as law in New York State.

Public opinion was opposed to this and other discriminatory laws. When Father Farmer boldly came to New York in 1784 and held Catholic services, this was quite evident, for no one molested him. The New York legislature, partly because the act embarrassed them before the French Catholics, repealed the Law of 1700 against Popish Priests and Jesuits in 1784.[181]

---

[177] *Ecclesiastical Records of N. Y.*, IV, 2861-2862.—The Moravians were ordered "to desist from further teaching and preaching and to depart from this province. . . ." The Honorable William Livingston staunchly defended the Moravians on January 4, 1753. Livingston later served as a delegate to the 1787 Constitutional Convention. Cf. *ibid.*, V, 3332-3333.

[178] *Ecclesiastical Records of N. Y.*, VI, 4293—from the correspondence of the Rev. Charles Ingles of Trinity Church, New York.

[179] "New York Constitution of 1777," Thorpe, V, 2635-2636, Art. 35.

[180] Thorpe, V, 2635-2636; *Ecclesiastical Records of N. Y.*, VI, 4300.

[181] *Ecclesiastical Records of N. Y.*, III, 1450-1451. A naturalization law enacted in 1777 virtually excluded Catholics from citizenship. Catholics were required to take the religiously discriminatory naturalization oath until 1806, when the law was finally abrogated. *Ibid.*, p. 1451.

The free exercise of worship had a confusing history in New York during colonial times. Under the initial Dutch charter, only the Dutch Reform Church had a right to public worship. An exception was made to this rule for a Presbyterian minister in 1642. When Stuyvesant became Director General in 1645, he continued this spirit of toleration. This attitude changed sharply in 1654 during the Lutheran controversy. He then forbade all forms of Lutheran worship, except the worship conducted by a man in the privacy of his home. No outsider could participate. The Company rescinded this directive and allowed a free exercise of worship to Lutherans in their homes. The Lutherans still were forbidden to have a minister. During this period the Quakers also suffered persecution, and their ministers were prohibited from conducting services. Relief came with the rule of the Duke of York. He ordered that no one be disturbed during prayer, preaching or divine services. The Duke's Laws required that a minister give proof of his ordination to the governor before he could exercise his ministry. One of these laws obliged the minister to preach every Sunday.

The reoccupation of New York by the Dutch was significant at least in one aspect. The Dutch were far more tolerant to the Lutherans and allowed them the free exercise of public worship. Once again under British rule, New York witnessed the end of Dutch establishment and a policy of toleration for all inhabitants under the kingship of Charles II and James II.

The reign of William and Mary brought a new form of toleration to New York. It failed to embrace Roman Catholics, Jews and other non-Christians. Roman Catholic priests were subject to life imprisonment and death, if they dared to exercise their priestly ministry. Protestants were given the right of public worship, but their preachers had to be licensed by the colonial government. But Moravian preachers were not granted this privilege; instead they were ordered out of the Province. Even the ministers of the Church of England were subject to civil control under various ministry acts.

The Constitution of 1777 brought an end to all forms of establishment and guaranteed the free exercise of worship. Not until

1784 were the legal impediments which had been imposed upon Roman Catholic priests by the act of 1770 removed, and the free exercise of public worship made possible for Catholics for the first time in almost a century.

The Dutch Reformed Church was the established religion during the years of Dutch rule. But no English establishment existed during the reign of Charles II and James II over New York. Even though William and Mary ordered Sloughter to seek establishment, there was no establishment made by the colonial legislature in the time of his governorship. His successor, Fletcher, pressured the assembly into passing a ministry act, but it is extremely difficult to prove from the wording of this law that the act established the Church of England. The better opinion is that the Church of England was not *de iure* established in New York. However, the practice of the governors and their councils during the eighteenth century demonstrates the "supposed" existence of an Anglican establishment. Therefore, it is valid to conclude that there was at least a *de facto* extant Anglican establishment. This establishment, whether extant *de iure* or *de facto,* was abolished by the New York Constitution of 1777.

## *Section 2. New Jersey*

### A. The Juridic Position of Church and State in the Formative Period

The ownership of New Jersey passed through several hands between 1644 and 1680, and the transfers resulted in "a heterogeneous settlement, a minimum of social cohesion, and a bad confusion in land titles which bedevilled New Jersey politics until the Revolution."[182]

The Duke of York ceded the lands between the Hudson and the Delaware rivers as the Province of Nova Caesarea or New Jersey to Lord John Berkeley (+ 1678) and Sir George Carteret (+ 1680), the proprietors of Carolina.[183] In 1674 Berkeley sold

---

[182] Morison and Commager, I, 73.

[183] "The Duke of York's Release to John Lord Berkeley and Sir George Carteret, 24th, June, 1644," Thorpe, V, 2533.

half of his share in New Jersey to two Quakers. Carteret kept the northeastern part and the two Quakers had title to the southwestern share of the Province. The widow of Carteret sold East New Jersey in 1680 to a group of proprietors, and the two Quakers shared their title of West New Jersey with William Penn (1644-1718). These property and title shifts had an effect upon the juridic status of religion in the various sections of New Jersey.

In 1644 Berkeley and Carteret issued "The Concessions and Agreements of New Caesarea or New Jersey" in order to attract settlers to New Jersey. Liberty of conscience, liberal land titles, and an assembly were among the concessions.[184] This liberty in religious matters was granted to those "behaving themselves peaceably and quietly, and not using this liberty of conscience to licentiousness, nor civil injury or outward disturbance of others."[185] Unless a person actually disturbed the civil peace of the province, he could in no way be "molested, punished, disquieted or called into question for any difference in opinion or practice in matters of religious concernment."[186]

In 1672 the proprietors issued a document declaring the true intent of these concessions. The Governor and Council were given power to constitute and appoint such ministers and preachers nominated by the several corporations and to establish their maintenance. The General Assembly was specifically excluded from any role in the selection of ministers and preachers. In addition to ministers appointed by the Governor in Council, liberty was given "to any person or persons to keep and maintain what preachers or ministers they please."[187]

B. West New Jersey

The Charter of West New Jersey, 1676, declared that no human authority "hath power or authority to rule over men's

[184] Thorpe, V, 2537; *Ecclesiastical Records of N. Y.*, I, 569.

[185] *The Grants, Concessions and Original Constitutions of the Province of New Jersey, The Acts between 1644-1702*, ed. Aaron Leaming and Jacob Spicer (Philadelphia, 1758), p. 14 (hereafter cited *Grants and Concessions*); Thorpe, V, 2537.

[186] *Grants and Concessions*, p. 14.

[187] *Grants and Concessions*, p. 55; Thorpe, V, 2545.

consciences in religious matters."[188] Therefore, no one in the Province "shall be any way upon any pretence whatsoever, called in question, or in the least punished or hurt, either in person, estate or privilege, for the sake of his opinion, faith or worship towards God in matters of religion."[189] On the contrary, every person "may . . . freely and fully have, and enjoy his and their judgments, and the exercise of their consciences in matters of religious worship throughout all the said Province." These charter guarantees were reiterated by an act of the West Jersey Assembly in November, 1681.[190]

## C. East New Jersey

The constitution drawn up for this province in 1683 guaranteed the freedom of worship under the following conditions: "All persons living in the Province who confess and acknowledge one Almighty and Eternal God, and hold themselves obliged in conscience to live peaceably and quietly in a civil society, shall in no way be molested or prejudged for their religious persuasions and exercise in matters of faith and worship, nor shall they be compelled to frequent or maintain any religious worship, place or ministry. . . ."[191]

This respect for conscience was reflected in the proprietors' treatment of a discriminatory act submitted to them in 1682. The Lord proprietors refused to approve a section of the law passed by the assembly (March 5, 1682, session), which would have punished Quakers who could not bear arms for reasons of conscience.[192] The constitution did not establish any religious sect as the State church. Fifteen years later the assembly retreated

---

[188] *Grants and Concessions,* p. 393; Thorpe, V, 2549, ch. XVI.

[189] *Grants and Concessions,* p. 393.

[190] *Grants and Concessions,* p. 425. Thorpe, V, 2567. This document pledged liberty of conscience, outlawed all religious tests for public office, and did not establish a church.

[191] Thorpe, V, 2579-2580, Art. XVI. "The Fundamental Constitution of the Province of East New Jersey in America," *Grants and Concessions,* pp. 153-166.

[192] *Grants and Concessions,* p. 281. This was a generous act, because the colony needed protection against unfriendly Indians.

from this position of almost complete freedom of worship. It was caught up in the spirit of the times. William and Mary had been instrumental in proclaiming a "toleration act" (1689) which explicitly excluded Roman Catholics. The crown exerted pressure upon the New York Assembly to pass a similar act. Undoubtedly influenced by the crown's activity East New Jersey adopted the same course of toleration in 1698.[193]

Between the adoption of the constitution in 1683 and the passage of this toleration act, there had been great political turmoil in Jersey. When James II ascended the throne he demanded the charter of the Jerseys on writs of *quo warranto*. Ownership of the soil was left with the people and East and West New Jersey were united with New York and New England. Andros was appointed to govern the entire area. Upon the fall of James and the expulsion of Governor Andros, a state of anarchy followed. This sad condition continued for some ten years.[194]

Political unrest and disillusionment motivated the proprietors to offer a surrender of their charter to the crown and petition for union with New York. In 1699 they referred these matters to the Lord of Trades and stipulated certain conditions to be met before they would surrender the charter and merge with New York. Article 10 stated that no Protestant be subject to a religious test for holding any public office or employment in the government.[195] But the reply was not what the proprietors had hoped for: "This article must be regulated by the Acts of Parliament, and the usage of New York itself."[196]

---

[193] "An Act declaring what are the Rights and Privileges of His Majesty's Subjects, inhabiting within this Province of East New Jersey," *Grants and Concessions of N. J.*, pp. 368-372. Those believing in Jesus Christ as the Son of God were given full freedom in matters of religion, provided they did not disturb the civil peace of the Province. "This shall not extend to any of the Romish Religion, to exercise their Manner of Worship, contrary to the Laws and Statutes, of his Majesty's Realm of England." This act, of course, denied all non-Christians toleration.

[194] Elson, *History of the United States*, p. 132.

[195] *Grants and Concessions*, pp. 588-591.—The Proprietors' Memorial to the Lord of Trades (1699).

[196] *Grants and Concessions*, p. 596.

### D. Reunion of the Two Colonies

Two years later both Jerseys united in a petition to be placed under the immediate jurisdiction of the crown.[197] Queen Anne accepted this surrender on April 17, 1702, and appointed her cousin, Lord Edward H. Cornbury (1661-1723), as first governor.[198] In her instructions to Cornbury the Queen used the stereotyped form regarding religious liberty; "You are to permit a Liberty of Conscience to all Persons (except Papists) so that they may be contented with a quiet and peaceable Enjoyment of the same, not giving Offense or Scandal to the Government."[199] Although legal disparagement of Papists already existed in East New Jersey, it was introduced for the first time in West New Jersey by Lord Cornbury.[200]

Furthermore, Lord Cornbury was empowered by the Instructions of Queen Anne to regulate Church benefices and the exercise of the ministry of the Church of England. No minister could be given an ecclesiastical benefice, unless he produced a certificate of orthodoxy from the Bishop of London. This was a requirement in other colonies and reflected the policy of the crown in colonial Church affairs.

Moreover, the Queen instructed Cornbury "to inquire whether there be any Minister within your Government, who preaches and administers the Sacraments in any Orthodox Church or Chapple, without being in due Orders, and to give account thereof to the said Lord Bishop of London."[201]

---

[197] "Surrender From the Proprietors of East and West New Jersey, of Their Pretended Right of Government to Her Majesty, 1702," Thorpe, V, 2585.

[198] "The Queen's Acceptance of the Surrender of the Government," Thorpe, V, 2584.

[199] *Grants and Concessions,* p. 633, n. 51.

[200] Cobb, p. 405.—He stated that New Jersey hitherto "had no discrimination against Romanists." His treatment of New Jersey does not include the session act of 1698 cited above, so he undoubtedly was not aware of its existence. However, his evaluation of the discrimination against Papists was quite sound· "We may consider it, therefore, that this specifying of Protestants was rather for conformity of phrase to the English statute, than for any hostility to Roman Catholics" in Jersey.

[201] *Grants and Concessions,* p. 639. He was also directed to encourage the conversion of negroes and Indians to the Christian religion. Cf. *ibid.,* p. 642.

The assembly of New Jersey imposed the obligation of taking an oath of supremacy which originated during the reign of Charles II, contrary to his personal desires. The oath was suspended during the reign of James II and revived by William and Mary. It was still in effect in Queen Anne's time. This oath was frankly anti-Roman, and the assembly confirmed this by its declaration that anyone who refuses to take the oaths and declarations in this act shall be "esteemed and adjudged a Popish Recusant Convict, and as such to forfeit and be proceeded against."[202] But Protestant dissenters who could not for conscience' sake take the oaths and declarations were excused, for the act was not intended to apply to them.[203] This act could be a contributing argument for an Anglican establishment in New Jersey, but it could not by itself establish the Church of England in New Jersey.

Succeeding assemblies did not legislate intolerance, for the records are silent on matters regulating the exercise of religion. Every governor of the colony, even after its separation from New York, received the routine instructions given to Cornbury about extending liberty of conscience to all Christians, except Papists, and regulating benefices.[204]

Number fifty-three of the Instruction, which runs for pages, directed him as follows: "You shall take especial care, that God Almighty be devoutly and duly served throughout your government, the Book of Common Prayer as by Law established, read each Sunday, and Holy-day, and the Blessed Sacrament admin-

---

[202] *Acts of the General Assembly of the Provinces of New Jersey, 1702-1776*, ed. Samuel A. Allison (Burlington, N. J., 1776), p. 62, § 1, "An Act for the Security of His Majesty's Government of New Jersey, May 5, 1722" (hereafter cited acts of the *Acts of the General Assembly*). Cf. pp. 63-64 for the oath.

[203] *Acts of the General Assembly*, p. 66. Quaker dissenters were permitted to affirm. Cf. 1713-1714 assembly, *ibid.*, p. 32, ch. 54; 1727-1728 assembly, *ibid.*, pp. 75-78, ch. 124. For a discussion of Quaker difficulties in New Jersey, cf. Cobb, pp. 409-415.

[204] "Instructions for our Right Trusty and well beloved Edward Lord Cornbury, our Captain General and Governor in Chief and over our Province of Nova-Caesarea or New Jersey, in America, November 16, 1702," *Grants and Concessions*, p. 633, § 51.

istered according to the Rights of the Church of England."[205] This directive either presupposed that the Church of England was already established in New Jersey, or that the force of the Instructions could so establish it. Cobb disclosed the anomalies of this Instruction. Not a single Church of England existed in New Jersey, and of the churches that were in New Jersey, most of them were either Dutch Reform or Presbyterian.

The Queen's Instruction admits of two interpretations: either the Instruction intended to force the Anglican religion upon these Congregations, or to confer power upon the Governor over such Episcopal Churches as might later be established. This would mean that the royal authority carried the Church of England into the Province under the term "as established by law." However, Cobb contended that the Church of England was never formally established in New Jersey. The Anglican Church and the Common Prayer were established by law in England. But it is not difficult to prove that English Ecclesiastical Law did not extend to all parts of the domain, because, as Cobb correctly stated, "in no other colony had this general dominion been thought sufficient for the establishment of the Church."[206]

According to the records unilateral action in the form of an Instruction never created a colonial establishment. The colonial assembly established the Church of England in Virginia and the Charter in Carolina. Royal authority never exercised such power in New England or Pennsylvania. In New York it is evident from Fletcher's insistence that the assembly pass an establishment act that royal authority alone did not establish a church in New York. The situation in Maryland was more involved. First William assumed direct control over the Province, and then the action of William and Mary and their Council with respect to the establishment of the Church of England had the force and effect of a charter. Even this royal activity was supplemented by an act of the colonial assembly. In New Jersey, however, no such provisions were made. Establishment was taken for granted with no decree or law to sustain it. The New Jersey legislature never

---

[205] *Grants and Concessions*, p. 638.

[206] Cobb, p. 407.

formally enacted a law establishing a church. Therefore, the Church of England was never formally established in the colony of New Jersey. Cornbury's Instructions are not sufficient grounds for maintaining the contrary.[207]

Succeeding events further sustain Cobb's contention that the Anglican Church was not formally established in New Jersey by the crown or by the legislature. During the governorship of Cornbury the assembly was predominantly Quaker, and such an assemblage would not have seriously considered establishing the Church of England. Much to the displeasure of those in sympathy with the Church of England, Governor Morris, who succeeded Cornbury, refused to be a party to any scheme to disable the Quakers and establish the Church of England. In 1713 the Quakers were allowed to qualify as jurors and for public duties by affirmation. This was subsequently confirmed by Queen Anne.[208]

The English government continued to view the Church of England as established in New Jersey. Cobb admitted this. Every royal governor, even after 1738 when New York and New Jersey were again separate colonies, received the stereotyped instruction regarding liberty of conscience and the conferring of ecclesiastical power upon the governor. But in New Jersey this amounted to nothing. Long before the Revolution the Church party had given up any real hope of obtaining legal establishment from the assembly. Yet, they still clung to the fiction of establishment, or at least tacit establishment.

There is sufficient evidence to support the contention that colonial New York had a *de facto* extant establishment of the Church of England, but the same cannot be demonstrated for colonial New Jersey. Morison and Commager seem to agree with this contention. They list New Jersey among the colonies in which there was "a separation of Church and state" at the outbreak of the War for Independence.[209]

---

[207] Cf. Cobb, pp. 407-408.

[208] *Acts of the General Assembly,* p. 32, ch. 54. This act was renewed in 1717, 1725, 1727.

[209] Morison and Commager, I, 241; Zollman, p. 3. He is of the opinion that the Church of England was established in New Jersey.

## E. Statehood Period

Legal disestablishment and the free exercise of religion were ushered in with the Revolution. The New Jersey Constitution of 1776 was very explicit in its disestablishment clause, but it seemed only to grant a guarantee of civil liberties to Protestants. ". . . no Protestant inhabitant of this colony shall be denied the enjoyment of any civil right, merely on account of his religious principles."[210] Unfortunately there was no guarantee for the civil rights of Roman Catholics, Jews, and other non-Protestants. This anomaly was removed by the Constitution of 1844.[211] However, the Constitution of 1776 did safeguard everyone's right to worship according to the dictates of his conscience. It likewise forbade any compulsory attendance or support of any religious worship.[212]

New Jersey was apparently troubled by religious impostors toward the end of the eighteenth century. On March 18, 1796, the legislature enacted a statute against such activity.[213]

In an "Act for Suppressing Vice and Immorality (March 16, 1798)" the state legislature imposed a fine of two dollars upon a person convicted of wilfully disquieting, interrupting, or disturbing any assembly of the people gathered together for religious worship "either by making a noise, or by rude and indecent behaviour, or profane discourse, whether within the place of worship or out of it, so near the same to disturb the order and solemnity of the meeting."[215] Like the colonial government before

---

[210] Thorpe, V, 2597, Art. XIX. This article further provided that faith in any Protestant sect was a prerequisite for public office.

[211] Thorpe, V, 2599, Art. 4.

[212] Thorpe, V, 2597, Art. XVIII. These protections were repeated in the Constitution of 1844. *Ibid.*, p. 2599, Art. I, § 3.

[213] *Laws of the State of New Jersey, 1703-1799* (rev. by William Patterson, New Brunswick, 1800), p. 211, § 20: ". . . all impostors in religion, such as personate our Saviour Jesus Christ, or suffer their followers to worship or pay them divine honors, or terrify, delude, or abuse the people by false denunciations of judgment, shall, upon conviction, be punished for every such offense by a fine, not exceeding one hundred dollars, or an imprisonment at hard labor, not exceeding six months, or both, at the discretion of the court."

[215] *Laws of New Jersey*, 1702-1799, p. 332, § XIII.

it, the state punished such activities on the grounds that they were a menace to society and a disruption of the public order, which the state by its very nature has a duty to preserve.

In summary it may be said that liberty of conscience and the free exercise of worship were guaranteed by the Concessions and Agreements of 1644, provided that this freedom was not used for a disruption of the public order or of ecclesiastical peace and harmony. In 1672 the Declaration of the True Intent of these Concessions empowered the governor and his council to appoint and support ministers nominated by the several corporations. The assembly was given no voice in these matters. The document also permitted anyone to have and support any minister of his liking. From this permission it is apparent that the appointment by the governor was not a license to preach, since it merely qualified certain nominated preachers for public support.

The West New Jersey Charter of 1676 granted full and complete liberty of worship. East New Jersey's Constitution of 1683 required a belief in one God, in addition to the usual requirement to live in peace and harmony and not to disturb the public order. In 1698 East New Jersey's assembly adopted the Toleration Act of William and Mary, including the discriminatory phrase against Papists. This was not abrogated until the formulation of the Constitution of 1776.

The Jerseys became a royal colony in 1702 at their own request, and the first governor, Lord Cornbury, was instructed to be intolerant of Roman Catholics. He introduced the first legal discrimination into West New Jersey. Cornbury was also given the power to regulate ecclesiastical benefices of the Church of England and to check on the orthodoxy of Anglican ministers. Other governors were given this same list of instructions.

The assembly enacted into law the oaths dating back to the days of Charles II. Dissenting Protestants were not obliged to take these oaths, but Roman Catholics were. The assembly acts were silent after this on matters of religious intolerance. The Constitution of 1776 revoked all the discriminatory laws affecting freedom of worship, including all traces of establishment.

The acts of the state legislature touched upon religious matters. Religious fakes and impostors were subject to heavy fines and imprisonment, and religious assemblies were protected from molestation and disturbances. These enactments were on the record as late as the middle of the nineteenth century.

No establishment existed between the time the Concessions and Agreements of 1644 were promulgated and 1702, the year in which the Jerseys became a royal colony. Queen Anne's Instruction to Cornbury either presupposed or intended the Establishment of the Church of England. On its face, the Instruction could not establish the Church of England in New Jersey, unless it is to be regarded as an exception to British colonial practice. The assembly of New Jersey did not pass an act for the establishment of the Anglican Church. The English government acted as if there were a formal establishment, so that establishment was taken for granted without any formal decree or law as its basis. If, contrary to the writer's opinion, there was an establishment in New Jersey prior to 1776, the New Jersey Constitution disbanded it.

## *Section 3. Maryland*

### A. The Juridic Condition of Church and State Relations in the Formative Period

Cobb succinctly described the anomaly of the relations between Church and State in Maryland: "A foundation of Roman Catholics in the avowed interests of religious freedom, it was wrested from their grasp and made hostile to both their faith and the rights of conscience."[216]

Maryland was founded by Lord George Calvert Baltimore (1580-1632), a Catholic convert and close friend of James I and Charles I. Baltimore unsuccessfully attempted to establish a colony in Newfoundland. He then settled for a short time in Virginia, but was expelled from this colony because he was a Roman Catholic. Lord Baltimore petitioned Charles I for a patent in the Chesapeake area, but died before the charter was issued. It was

[216] Cobb, p. 362.

confirmed to his son and heir, Cecil Calvert (1605-1675).[217] The original grant extended from the Potomac river to New England. Pennsylvania was later carved out of this donation.[218]

The initial paragraph of the charter stated that one of the motives for the foundation of the colony was "for extending the Christian Religion."[219] The charter did not explicitly establish any religion. One phrase in the charter might be used in support of an argument for implicit establishment. All churches, chapels and other places of worship were "to be dedicated and consecrated according to the Ecclesiastical Laws of our Kingdom of England."[220] Cobb considered this phrase to mean the right to establish any religion: "Under the terms of the charter it was competent for him (Baltimore) to establish Romanism, Episcopacy, Independency, or Presbyterianism. The power is plainly in the instrument, but its character is undefined."[221] Werline took the opposite point of view: "Indeed, nothing in the Charter gave Cecil Calvert, a Roman Catholic, the authority to establish in the province the religion of his choice."[222] The writer agrees with Cobb and Hanley. It is possible to conclude from the technical interpretation of the written document that Baltimore was given the power to establish the religion of his choice. But documents must be viewed within the historical framework in which they are composed. Establishment was not the intention of Baltimore. It was opposed to his political philosophy and his economic projects. Both Werline and Cobb held that the Calverts did not intend to establish

[217] Morison and Commager, I, 47; Albert W. Werline, *Problems of Church and State in Maryland During the Seventeenth and Eighteenth Centuries* (South Lancaster, Mass.: College Press, 1948), pp. 1-2 (hereafter cited Werline); Thomas O'Brien Hanley, *Their Liberties and Rights* (Westminster, Md.: The Newman Press, 1959), pp. 59-79 (hereafter cited Hanley).

[218] "The Charter of Maryland, 1632," Thorpe, III, 1669-1677 (Latin text); III, 1677 ff. (English text).

[219] Thorpe, III, 1677.

[220] Thorpe, III, 1679.

[221] Cobb, p. 364. Hanley admits that the charter could be so construed, but believes that the better interpretation is that the charter's vagueness was a product of the liberal religious philosophy of Church and State already espoused by Baltimore. Cf. Hanley, pp. 68-69.

[222] Werline, pp. 1-2. He cited some authors to support his claim.

the Church of England and that it is difficult to discover any evidence that they intended to establish the Catholic Church.[223]

If any doubt arose concerning the meaning of the charter, Lord Baltimore and his heirs were to be given the benefit of the doubt, "provided that no interpretation thereof be made, whereby God's holy and true Christian religion, or Allegiance due to Us, our Heirs and Successors, may in any wise suffer by Change, Prejudice, or Diminution. . . ."[224] Baltimore was made the official interpreter of the charter, so the solution to the problem of the true meaning of the charter's vague religious references must be sought in the interpretation *de facto* given to them by Baltimore and his heirs.

This vagueness was a source of consternation to both Protestants and Catholics. The Protestants objected that the loosely worded religious clauses gave too much power to a Roman Catholic proprietor. Baltimore's co-religionists complained that a Roman Catholic could not in conscience accept a charter in which freedom of worship was granted to several religious sects.[225] All

[223] Hanley agrees with this interpretation: "Such a meaning would be contrary to the commercial aspect of the Maryland project, which had to appeal to the Protestants as well as the Catholics if it would succeed." Cf. Hanley, p. 68. In another place, he says: "The important point is that this heterogeneously-founded charter left the door open to further development of the tradition we have been tracing. This is precisely what the Virginia Council foresaw when they wrote to the privy council complaining of the charter phrasing. The king made no denial of the charge, thus giving further support for this interpretation of the charter."

[224] Thorpe, III, 1686. Hanley interprets this provision as follows: "This proviso demonstrates a respectful reserve toward the church and conscience that ruled out state absolutism." Cf. Hanley, p. 68.

[225] Cf. Hanley, pp. 72-74, for a discussion of the objections raised by the Protestants in Virginia and the Roman Catholics in England and elsewhere. Both Cobb and Werline reject the Protestant objections to the charter. Cobb says that at the time it was politically impossible for Charles to state in a document of this nature that he was granting the charter to Baltimore, in order that Baltimore might found a place of refuge for his persecuted Catholic brothers. Cf. Cobb, pp. 367-368. Werline completely discounts the view that Baltimore intended to found a refuge for persecuted Catholics, because "Roman Catholics in England were not subject to persecution at that time." Cf. Werline, p. 1. Hanley is not in complete agreement with Werline. He believes one of the motivating forces for the establishment of the colony

these objections to the charter were refuted in *Objections Answered,* a pamphlet containing Baltimore's replies to Catholics and Protestants alike. Cobb believed that the Jesuit who most assisted Baltimore was Father Richard Blount (1565-1638), the provincial of the English Jesuits. Hanley credited Father Andrew White (1579-1656), who was to be one of the first missionaries to go to Maryland, as the Jesuit who was the greatest help in the preparation of *Objections Answered.*[226]

Lord Baltimore and his immediate heir made no effort to establish any Church in Maryland, so the most solid interpretation must be that the charter did not intend to establish any Church, or, if it did, it left the choice of the nature of the establishment to the discretion of the Baltimores.

Lord Cecil Baltimore instructed Governor Leonard Calvert (1606-1647) to present his Code of Laws to the assembly. Baltimore only intended this to be a "rubber stamp" ratification by the legislature. On January 25, 1638, the governor convened the assembly and presented the Code for their approval. A lively debate, which generated into a heated controversy, followed. The Code was rejected on January 29 by an overwhelming majority of 37-2. It was resubmitted and again rejected by the assembly.[227]

Cobb believed that the assembly rejected the Code and then simply made it their own. Hanley presented an entirely different version. The assembly vigorously opposed the imposition of the Code upon them by the governor. They then appointed a committee which drew up the various bills. The committee made use of the Code of Laws of Lord Baltimore, but the final product was in many respects a new piece of legislation.[228]

---

was "to make it as a haven for his coreligionists." Cf. Hanley, p. 65. Catholics were not subject to persecution, but even men in high favor with the king suffered from the legal disabilities still existing against Catholics. Cf. Hanley, pp. 59-66.

[226] Cobb, pp. 367-368; Hanley, pp. 73-76.

[227] Hanley, pp. 88-92. He recounts in some detail the political maneuvering of Governor Calvert and the debates between the governor and the leader of the opposition, Thomas Cornwallis. Cobb, pp. 369-371; Morison and Commager, I, 47-48.

[228] Cobb, pp. 369-371; Hanley, pp. 94-108. Hanley presents sufficient evidence to substantiate his position.

Hanley discussed the original text of one of the laws passed by the assembly—"An Act for Church Liberties." The act stated that Holy Church within the Province was to have and enjoy its rights, liberties, and franchises wholly and without blemish. The original version reads: "Holy Churches within this province shall have all its rights and Liberties." Hanley viewed the use of the term "Churches" as a mechanical error, because the singular was evidently intended.[229] He rejected the position of those who maintained that the assemblymen intended the use of the plural.[230] In the term Church, Hanley perceived a "recognition of the higher spiritual society with its autonomous functions as a moral person."[231]

The law, "An Act for Church Liberties," was significant for what it left unsaid. It did not violate the charter mandate that nothing injure God's true and holy religion. Nor did the act establish the Church of England. If the assembly had establishment in mind, it would have established the Roman Catholic religion, for it was a Catholic assembly. It is reasonable to conclude that each Church was left free to conduct its affairs.

The Act for Church Liberties secured liberty for each Church. A second liberty act prepared by the committee safeguarded the individual's right of conscience. It provided that the "inhabitants of this province shall have all their rights and liberties according to the Great Charter."[232]

Baltimore's code contained a blasphemy law, which enacted heavy penalties to be imposed by the justices. The assembly removed the magistrates from this delicate area. Undoubtedly, they realized the problems such a law would create in the pluralistic society of their colony. The assembly did not legislate any religious felonies as such. Civil disorders arising out of religious matters were to be treated under the title of "preserving the peace."[233]

---

229 Hanley, p. 103.

230 Hanley, pp. 103-104.

231 Hanley, p. 105.

232 Cf. Hanley, p. 105.

233 Hanley, pp. 105-106. He points out the error of Baltimore, which the assembly avoided: "The temptation was to name religious situations which might give rise to disorder. But the committeemen saw that once they were

In this same year three Catholic judges were called upon to decide a rather delicate issue. William Lewis, a Catholic overseer, was charged with using pressure upon some Protestant servants to embrace the Catholic Faith. On the basis of the testimony presented, the court found Lewis guilty of disturbing the peace and quiet of the colony and fined him five hundred pounds of tobacco.[234]

## B. The Colonial Period

In 1649 the Maryland Assembly passed a law of religious toleration.[235] This act was more restrictive than the liberty granted by the Catholic assembly of 1638-1639. It militated against the liberty of non-Christians and contained a blasphemy clause.[236] The act itself stated that one of the reasons for the passage of the law was the forestalling of discontent which might lead to public disorders or sedition.[237]

---

named the magistrate must begin defining religious matters. This Gelasian reserve kept the distinction of church and state clear." Cf. Hanley, p. 106.

[234] Hanley, pp. 83-86. He gives a detailed account of the situation, including the threatened intervention of Virginia.

[235] *Archives of Maryland* (61 vols., Baltimore: Maryland Historical Society, 1883-1944), I, 244-247; Morison and Commager, I, 47; Cobb, p. 376; Werline, pp. 6-8.

[236] "Be it therefore ordered and enacted (except as in the present act is before declared and set forth) that no person or persons whatever in this Province, . . . professing to believe in Jesus Christ, shall from henceforth be any ways troubled, molested, or discountenanced for, or in respect to, his or her religion, nor in the free exercise thereof within this province, or the islands thereunto belonging, nor in any other way compelled to believe or exercise any other religion against his or her consent, so that they be not unfaithful to the lord proprietor, or molest or conspire against the civil government." Cf. *Archives of Md.,* I, 244.

[237] In his evaluation of the early years of Maryland's history of religious legislation, Hanley comments:

> The prominence of the Maryland Ordinance of 1639 logically demands a reconsideration of the role of the proprietors and the Act of Toleration of 1649. Calvert did not at all times speak for the Maryland Catholics. Indeed, by and large he was not representative of their mind on a large range of matters. Neither is the Puritan-tinged Toleration Act of 1649 representative of the Catholics, who had lost their dominant position in the assembly by that time. Cf. Hanley, p. 123.

The section of the Toleration Act of 1649 dealing with blasphemy said that

The early sixteen fifties were years of discontent and revolt. The Puritan opposition met with success, and the assembly of 1654 passed an act repealing the Toleration Act of 1649. The new law declared that no one who professed the Roman Catholic religion could be protected in the province. Liberty of dissent was granted to those who could not embrace the predominant religion, which at that time was Puritanism, but this liberty was not extended to "popery, prelacy, or licentiousness of opinion." Cromwell (1599-1658) forced the new government to restore the Act of Toleration, and Lord Baltimore regained his rights.[238]

After the restoration of the colony to the Baltimores in 1658 and until 1689, the Baltimores were able to direct matters in the province largely as they desired. There was very much agitation among the Quakers because of the requirement of oaths. A relief act was finally adopted in 1681.[239]

A number of attempts were made during these years to have some form of establishment, particularly the Church of England, adopted in the colony. The proprietor steadfastly refused to countenance this or any other form of establishment.[240] The proprietory government was overthrown in the summer of 1689, and the sentiment of the revolutionaries was highly anti-Catholic.[241] This revolution played right into the hands of the Anglican minority, for it accelerated the union of Church and State in Maryland.

In 1692 William and Mary revoked the charter and sent Governor Copley to Maryland. He convoked an assembly which passed

---

the denial of the Trinity, or blasphemy, was a capital crime, and imposed a fine of five pounds upon all who spoke reproachfully of the Blessed Virgin Mary, the Apostles, or the Evangelists.

[238] Werline, pp. 9-12. He regarded this revolt as a religious one. Morison and Commager seemed to view it more as an economic revolt: The revolt of 1654 was a "class war of Protestant small farmers against the Catholic magnates and lords of manors. The majority won, and the Act of Toleration was repealed."—Morison and Commager, I, 48; cf. also Cobb, p. 379.

[239] *Archives of Maryland,* VII, 174. A number of attempts to pass such an act had been made between 1661 and 1681. Cf. *ibid.,* I, 411, 436; II, 356, 424, 427, 444-445, 447-448; 450, 455, 456, 492. Cf. also Werline, pp. 12-13.

[240] Cf. Werline, pp. 14-17.

[241] Cf. the Articles of Surrender in the *Archives of Maryland,* VIII, 107.

"An Act for the service of God and the Establishment of the Protestant Religion within this Province."[242] However, the act was disallowed on technical grounds.[243] Similar acts were passed in 1694 and 1695. The 1695 act was set aside by the King in Council on the grounds that it contained a clause declaring all the laws of England to be in force in Maryland.[244] The assembly enacted another one in 1696, and it too was declared null and void on November 30, 1699, by the King in Council.[245]

Undaunted by this rebuff, the assembly passed "An Act for the Service of Almighty God, and the establishment of religion in this province, according to the Church of England."[246] In 1702 the assembly repealed its own act and replaced it with "An Act for the Establishment of religious worship in this province, according to the Church of England, and for the maintenance of ministers."[247] This act remained in force through the entire colonial period with a few amendments. It provided for the adoption of the Book of Common Prayer and the establishment of the Church of England in Maryland.[248]

The Quakers were given their rights of toleration in an act of the legislature in 1704. In the same year the assembly passed legislation to prevent too great a number of Irish papists from being imported into the colony of Maryland.[249] This legislation forbade a "popish priest or bishop" to exercise his functions, under

---

242 William Kilty (rev. and col.), *The Laws of Maryland* (Annapolis, 1779-1780), I, ch. 2 (hereafter cited Kilty, *Laws of Md.*). The establishment law was passed on June 9, 1692.

243 Cf. Cobb, p. 388; Werline, p. 20.

244 Werline, p. 20.

245 Kilty, *Laws of Md.*, I, Ch. 18, July 9, 1696; Werline, pp. 20-21; Cobb, p. 388.

246 Kilty, *Laws of Md.*, I, Ch. I, 1700, April Session.

247 Kilty, *Laws of Md.*, II, Ch. I, Session of March, 1702.

248 Werline discusses in detail the support of Anglican minister by public tax and the opposition and disdain for the act on the part of Quakers and Catholics. Cf. Werline, pp. 21 ff.

249 Kilty, *Laws of Md.*, II, Session of 1704; Ch. IX; also Sept. session of 1704, Ch. 59. The act was repealed in 1718. Cf. the fourth chapter of that session.

the penalty of fifty pounds or six months in prison. For a second offense the cleric was deported to England.[250]

Protestant dissenters were given formal toleration on April 19, 1706, in "An Act declaring several Acts of Parliament, made in the Kingdom of England, to be in force within this province."[251] This act exempted Protestants who dissented from the Church of England from the penalties imposed upon dissenters by the previous legislation. The same assembly mitigated the anti-popish priest act of 1704 to the extent that it permitted priests to function in private homes.[252] The anti-popery act retained its full force in all other respects.[253]

Quaker meetings and preachers continued to enjoy the protection of the law. On October 25, 1725, the assembly passed an act fining those who disturbed the Quakers during the exercise of their worship, and it forbade the sale of liquor within one mile of the meeting house in Talbot County, and two miles in Anne Arundel County, during the Quaker meeting time. Papists continued to be the object of discriminatory legislation. The school act of November 2, 1728, placed an extra "duty of twenty shillings per poll on all Irish servants, being papists, to prevent the growth of popery by importation of too many."[254]

## C. The Statehood Period

All Protestants were permitted to have the exercise of public worship during the colonial period of the eighteenth century, but

[250] Cf. Cobb, pp. 397-398.

[251] Kilty, *Laws of Md.*, April Session of 1706, Ch. VIII; *Acts of the Assembly Passed in the Province of Maryland from 1692-1715* (London, 1723), p. 56 (hereafter cited *Acts of the Assembly of Md., 1692-1715*).

[252] *Acts of the Assembly of Md., 1692-1715*, p. 57.

[253] For additional anti-popery acts, cf. Kilty, *Laws of Md.*, Session of April, 1715, Ch. 36; *Acts of the Assembly of Md., 1692-1715*, pp. 108-111. This act was repealed on May 10, 1718, and another passed in 1720, which was in turn repealed on Nov. 24, 1724. Cf. Kilty, *Laws of Md.*, Session of April, 1718, Ch. 4; Session of Oct., 1720, Ch. 26; Session of Oct., 1720, Ch. 10. In general the acts tried to prevent the entrance of Irish papists.

[254] Kilty, *Laws of Md.*, Session of Oct., 1728, Ch. 8; cf. also Session of 1732, Ch. 23; Session of July, 1740, Ch. 9; Session of May, 1754, Ch. 14; Session of Sept., 1757, Ch. 22.

Roman Catholics continued to be restricted to worship in private homes. Disestablishment of the Church of England in Maryland was not achieved until the Revolution. The Bill of Rights of the Maryland Constitution of 1776 granted the free exercise of worship and an equal protection of the laws to those who were professing the Christian religion. No one was to be disturbed or molested on account of his religious persuasion or practice, "unless, under colour of religion, any man shall disturb the good order, peace or safety of the State" or infringe upon or injure the rights of others.[255] This same instrument declared that no one was "to be compelled to frequent or maintain, or contribute, unless on contract, to maintain any particular place of worship, or any particular ministry."[256]

A policy of general toleration existed during the proprietorship of the Baltimores. Under William and Mary the charter was revoked and the assembly established the Church of England, but not before a series of unsuccessful attempts around the turn of the century. Protestants were tolerated and permitted the right of public worship early in the eighteenth century. However, Roman Catholic clerics were prohibited from exercising their ministry publicly or privately. This was mitigated in 1706 to the extent that they could function in private homes. Such was the general state of affairs at the time of the Revolution, when the Church of England was disestablished and all Christians were given the right of free worship and equal protection of the laws. Jews were still discriminated against by the laws of Maryland. Not until 1851 were they granted full equality before the law.[257]

---

[255] Thorpe, III, Art. XXXIII.

[256] Thorpe, III, 1689. However, the legislature was given the discretion to levy "a general and equal tax, for the support of the Christian religion." The taxpayer was given the option of indicating the particular Church or charity to which he wished his tax to go. As mentioned elsewhere, several of the outstanding patriots, such as Washington and Patrick Henry, favored a tax support of religion, and other States, besides Maryland, had some program of tax support of religion after the Declaration of Independence. Cf. Werline, pp. 157 ff., for a more detailed discussion of this matter.

[257] "Constitution of Maryland, 1851," Art. XXXIV—Thorpe, III, 1715.

### *Section 4. Georgia*

General Oglethorpe (1696-1785) founded Savannah in 1733 under the charter granted by George II (1727-1760) for whom he named the colony.[258] The charter pledged freedom of religion to all except Roman Catholics.[259] Furthermore, it did not establish the Church of England.

In 1752 the charter was voided, and Georgia became a royal colony.[260] Six years later the colonial legislature formally established the Church of England. By 1769 only two established churches existed in the Colony of Georgia.[261]

The Georgia Constitution of 1777 granted a free exercise of worship and implicitly abrogated the Church of England establishment.[262] This was repeated in the Georgia Constitution of 1789 in substantially the same words.[263] The Georgia Constitution of 1798 was most explicit in these matters and also prohibited all religious tests:

> No person within this State shall, under any pretence, be deprived of the inestimable privilege of worshipping

[258] Morison and Commager, I, 98; Elson, *History of the United States*, p. 82; Thorpe, II, 765—Charter of 1732. E. Merton Coulter, *Georgia, A Short History* (Chapel Hill: The University of North Carolina Press, 1947), p. 16.

[259] Thorpe, II, 773—". . . there shall be a liberty of conscience allowed in the worship of God, to all persons inhabiting, or which shall inhabit or be resident within, our said province, and that all such persons, except papists, shall have a free exercise of their religion, so that they be contented with the quiet and peaceable enjoyment of the same, not giving offense or scandal to the government."

[260] Elson, *History of the United States*, p. 84. The king did not assume control until 1754, when Captain John Reynolds was installed as royal governor. Cf. Coulter, *Georgia, A Short History*, p. 83.

[261] Cobb, p. 421. No one was forced to be a member of the established Church, but no person was exempted from the tax for the support of the establishment. Cf. Coulter, *Georgia, A Short History*, pp. 106-107.

[262] Thorpe, II, 784, Art. LVI. "All persons whatever shall have the free exercise of religion; provided it be not repugnant to the peace and safety of the State; and shall not, unless by consent, support any teacher or teachers except those of their own profession."

[263] Thorpe, II, 789, Art. IV, § 5. "All persons shall have the free exercise of religion, without being obliged to contribute to the support of any religion but their own."

> God in a manner agreeable to his own conscience, nor be compelled to attend any place of worship contrary to his own faith and judgment; nor shall he ever be obliged to pay tithes, taxes or any other rate, for the building or repairing of any place of worship, or for the maintenance of any minister or ministry, contrary to what he believes to be right, or hath voluntarily engaged to do. No one religious society shall ever be established in this State, in preference to another; nor shall any person be denied the enjoyment of any civil liberty merely on account of his religious principles.[264]

Religious toleration existed in Georgia from the very beginning of the colony, except for Papists. They too were given freedom of religion in 1777. The establishment of the Church of England was quite late in arriving compared with the other English establishments, and it only enjoyed a relatively brief period of existence. It should not be surprising to find so little religious conflict and discrimination in the Colony of Georgia, for its very purpose was initially a refuge for the poor and religiously persecuted of the Old World.

## ARTICE III. PURITAN ESTABLISHMENTS

The New England colonies present a paradox. Although one of the purposes for founding these new communities was the preservation of the liberties of the free-born Englishmen, "they proposed to subordinate everything to the establishment and maintenance of what they deemed to be the true religion."[265] So deeply was this idea buried in the minds of these new settlers that every new settlement and congregational church was formed by means of a covenant. As a result the relations of Church and State in New England expressed themselves in the idea of a covenant.

### *Section 1. Massachusetts*

#### A. Juridic Position of Church and State in the Formative Period

The discussion of the Massachusetts colony in this section is centered about the Colony of Massachusetts Bay. Plymouth Colony,

[264] Thorpe, II, 800-801.

[265] Morison and Commager, I, 55.

itself, began with the arrival of the Puritans at Cape Code on November 11, 1620.[266] By the instrument known as "The Charter of New England, 1620" this colony formulated its fundamental law.[267] However, in 1635 the charter was returned to the king.[268]

A second group obtained a royal charter from Charles I in 1629 under the title of Massachusetts Bay Colony. Both the Company and its Charter were transferred to Massachusetts, and the colony became practically independent of England.[269] The charter expressed the desire that "our said People, Inhabitants here, may be soe religiously, peaceablie, and civilly governed, as their good life and orderlie Conversacion, maie wynn and incite the Natives of the Country, to the Knowledge and Obedience of the onlie true God and Savior of Mankinde, and the Christian Fayth, which is our Royall Intencion, and the Adventurers free Profession, is the principall Ende of this Plantacion."[270]

The Company Instructions to Endicott, April, 1629, clearly stated that the aim of the company was to spread the Gospel.[271] Further evidence of the company's religious concern was its support of the ministers and payment of one half of the expense involved in building churches. The colonists were given freedom to choose a form of religion—Independency, Presbytery, or Episcopacy—with or without dependence upon the Church of England.[272]

The people of Salem, Massachusetts, organized a Church and adopted a confession of faith and a covenant. One article of the confession of faith dealt with the power and the duty of the magistrate in matters of religion. They established union of Church and State and refused to concede freedom of conscience to the

---

[266] Cf. Morison and Commager, I, 52.

[267] Thorpe, III, 1827.

[268] Thorpe, III, 1860. For a detailed discussion of this colony and its religious practices consult: Cobb, pp. 133-148, and Thomas Hutchinson, *The History of the Colony of Massachusetts Bay* (3 vols., ed. Lawrence S. Mayo, Cambridge, Mass.: Harvard University Press, 1936), I, 55 ff. (hereafter cited *History of Mass. Bay*).

[269] Morison and Commager, I, 54; *History of Mass. Bay,* I, 10-14; Thorpe, III, 1846.

[270] Thorpe, III, 1857.

[271] Cobb, p. 155.

[272] Cobb, pp. 155-156.

individual.[273] Immediately, the colony started to apply the principle of denying all dissent and of subjecting religious matters to the magistrate. John and Samuel Browne, who were substantial promoters of the colony, were banished to England in 1630 because they refused to conform to the new style of Puritanism. The Browne brothers were Puritans who clung to the English Church and its liturgy, and they held services on their own authority using the Book of Common Prayer.[274] Cobb described the situation in the Bay Colony as that of Puritans who "were separatists from the Church of England as positively as the men of Scrooby, and differed only from the Pilgrims in that, having now the power, they merged Church and State together and suffered no dissent from their opinions in matters of religious worship."[275]

The General Court of 1631 ordered that "none should be admitted to the freedom of the body politick but such as were church members."[276] To qualify as a voter, a colonist needed a certificate from a minister stating that he was a member of a congregational church in good standing and one who regularly attended services. The Puritans, as Cobb observed, acted the same as the English government, except that parliament enacted the Episcopal establishment, whereas the General Court of Massachusetts established Congregationalism. The Bay Colony was not founded as a haven for the oppressed, but as a Puritan religious Commonwealth.[277]

The Puritans likewise did not countenance private relevations, as the famous case of Mrs. Hutchinson demonstrates. She was ordered by the Court to be banished from the province for "traducing ministers and their ministry by her notions."[278]

The most outstanding figure of the times to be banished was the

---

[273] *History of Mass. Bay,* I, 12; Cobb, pp. 157-158.

[274] *History of Mass. Bay,* I, 12-13; Cobb, pp. 159-160.

[275] Cobb, p. 161; cf. also *History of Mass. Bay,* I, 352-366, Ch. IV, "The Ecclesiastical Constitution of the Colony and the Special Religious Customs."

[276] *History of Mass. Bay,* I, 24-25; Cobb, p. 171. For the repeal of this law consult *The Colonial Laws of Massachusetts* (reprinted from the edition of 1672 with supplements through 1686, prepared under the supervision of William H. Whitman, Boston, 1887), p. 56 (1665) (hereafter cited *Colonial Laws of Mass.*); cf. Cobb, p. 227.

[277] Cobb, p. 172.

[278] *History of Mass. Bay,* I, 62-64; Cobb, pp. 188-190.

minister, Roger Williams (1603?-1683). He was a man of strong independent views, which he did not hesitate to propound in public.[279] Williams uttered dangerous opinions against the authority of the magistrates and wrote letters of defamation against the established Church and the magistrates. The court commanded him to leave the colony or be banished forceably within six weeks.[280] The doctrines of Williams were subversive to the civil order, not because he sought the overthrow of the civil government, but because he opposed the Church-State structure which the Puritans sought to preserve. His expulsion was logically based upon the alleged disturbance of the public order, for the attack upon the establishment was bound to disrupt civil peace.

Any group of men who desired to open a church needed the approval of the magistrates and the majority of the elders of other churches in the area. In the absence of such an approbation, these men were denied the freedom of the commonwealth.[281] There were other instances of civil interference in church affairs. The Church of Malden chose a minister without consulting the neighboring churches. Such action was viewed as a spiritual misdemeanor and a high offense against Church and State. The court fined all those who were a party to the affair, and the people of Malden were required to rescind their act and make a public apology. They complied with this order and acknowledged the competency of the civil authorities in religious matters. Their fines were remitted.[282]

In 1653 the civil authority intervened in the case of Mr. Powel. The Church at North Boston had chosen him to be their minister, but the civil authorities prevented him from assuming the office on the ground that he lacked a learned education.[283]

---

[279] *Hist. of Mass. Bay,* I, 34-36.

[280] Cobb, p. 186.

[281] An act passed by the General Court in 1635. Cf. *Acts and Resolves,* I, 147, n. 2 and Cobb, p. 173. The magistrates had inquisitorial power. Cobb (pp. 173-174) cites a number of cases wherein it was employed.

[282] "Ecclesiastical History of Massachusetts," *Collections of the Massachusetts Historical Society,* X (Boston, 1809), pp. 24-25.

[283] *Ibid.,* pp. 25-26.

## B. The Colonial Period

The condition of the Massachusetts Bay Church-State arrangement is even more adequately reflected in the Body of Liberties of 1641.[284] The civil authority enjoyed jurisdiction over the Established Church, but the Church authority did not supersede state jurisdiction in civil affairs.[285]

The Capital Laws of the 1641 body of laws contained the death penalty for certain religious crimes.[286] Deliberate blasphemy or witchcraft were punishable with death. Hutchinson recounts the famous trial of the widow, Ann Hibbins. She was condemned to death on charges of witchcraft in 1665. The jury found her guilty, but the magistrates refused to accept the verdict. The case was referred to the General Court, where the popular clamor prevailed against her.[287]

The 1641 body of laws granted certain liberties to the churches and these were repeated in the 1660 collection of laws. They con-

---

[284] The early history of published laws of the Colony of Massachusetts falls into four periods:

1. The Body of Liberties, 1641.
2. The First Collection of Laws, 1649.
3. The Revision of 1660.
4. The Further Revision of 1672 with supplements up to 1686.

[285] *Colonial Laws of Mass.*, p. 47, n. 58: "The Civill Authoritie hath power and libertie to see the peace, ordinances and Rules of Christ observed in every Church according to his word, so be it done in a Civill and not an Ecclesiastical way.

"N. 59: Civil Authoritie hath power and libertie to deale with any Church member in a way of Civill Justice, notwithstanding any Church relation, office or interest.

"N. 60. No church censure shal degrad or depose any man from Civill dignitie, office, or Authoritie he shall have in the Commonwealth."

[286] *Colonial Laws of Mass.*, p. 55, n. 94. Many of the Ecclesiastical Laws of the period under consideration can also be found in *The Laws and Liberties of Massachusetts,* reprinted from the copy of the 1648 edition in the Henry E. Huntington Library, with an introduction by Max Farrand (Cambridge: Harvard Univ. Press, 1929).

[287] *History of Mass. Bay,* I, 160. Any man legally convicted of worshipping "any other god, but the lord god" was also put to death.—*Colonial Laws of Mass.,* p. 55, n. 94, § 1. These capital laws were repeated again in the 1660 collection of laws.—*Ibid.*, p. 128.

cerned the internal life of the Church, such as censures, days of fasts and elections.[288] Provision was also made for the support of ministers of the established Church.[289]

Quakers, Roman Catholics, and other dissenters were also the object of legislation in the Bay Colony. The lawmakers enacted "A Heresy and Error Act" in 1644 and another in 1646. In the initial sections of these companion laws the legislators concerned themselves with the denial of points of dogma, while in the latter sections they legislated against Quakers and Quaker sympathizers. Heresy in the Bay colony was regarded as a serious civil offense, and punishment upon conviction ranged from a small fine to whipping, banishment, and even death.[290] Unfortunately these enactments were no idle threats, for the Quaker repressions erupted into a small scale persecution in 1656 and culminated in several hangings in 1660.[291]

During this period the Society of Jesus was singled out for persecution. As in the third century the mere fact that a person was a Christian made him guilty of a crime punishable by banishment and death in the Roman Empire, so by a law passed in 1647 called the anti-Jesuit act a Jesuit was automatically subject to banishment. If he should return, he could be put to death upon conviction. Even the observance of Christmas was made a criminal act under the anti-popery law of 1659.[292] Charles II demanded

---

[288] *Colonial Laws of Mass.*, p. 57, nn. 95, 96; pp. 147-148.

[289] An example of such a law is the one passed in 1654. Every town was ordered to provide a house and a salary for the minister. Each person was assessed and the fee was levied and collected like the other town rates. Cf. *Colonial Laws of Mass.*, pp. 148-149, n. 17 and p. 134, n. 2.

[290] *Colonial Laws of Mass.*, pp. 154-156, nn. 1-9. Some examples: An obstinate offender who denied the immortality of the soul, or the resurrection of the body, or Christ's redemption, was banished (n. 1); a denial of the divine inspiration of Scripture was punished by a 50 lb. fine and 40 strokes, maximum (n. 2). Obstinate offenders were subject to banishment or even death. Quakers were subject to banishment, or death, if they returned or remained obstinate in their practice (n. 9).

[291] *History of Mass. Bay*, I, 167-175. Cf. also *Transactions and Collections of the American Antiquarian Society* (Cambridge, 1857), III, 178-197.

[292] *The Colonial Laws of Mass.*, p. 153.

that this act be repealed in 1665.[293] The Baptists also had their share of persecution in the Bay Colony.[294]

Legal toleration did not appear in the Bay Colony until late in the seventeenth century. The Charter of Massachusetts Bay was revoked by the king in council in 1685, and Andros was designated as governor. His presence marked the beginning of agitation between the Congregationalists and the government.[295] James II issued a proclamation of toleration which was designed in part to remove Catholic disabilities. Its effect in this regard was never realized in Massachusetts, because the Charter of Massachusetts Bay, 1691, as granted by William and Mary, provided liberty of conscience for all Christians, except Papists.[296] Liberty of action for the Protestant Churches was now part of the fundamental law of the land. Union of Church and State manifested itself hereafter in anti-popery action and in the public support of the Congregational Church.

The legislature enacted a law in October, 1692, requiring each town to secure and support a minister. The town was to choose its minister by majority vote, and all were obliged to contribute to his support.[297] Section three of this act stated that all the churches in the province were to enjoy the free exercise of public worship. Because this assembly act incorporated into colonial law the toleration guaranteed by the Charter of 1691, the freedom given by the assembly act must be understood within the terms of the toleration grant. The assembly definitely abrogated by domestic legislation the exclusive legal position of the free public

---

[293] Cf. Cobb, p. 209. He notes that the act was not repealed until 1681. This was not the end of such laws in Massachusetts, for as Cobb remarks, "Men, now (1902) not much beyond middle life, can remember a childhood to which the festivity of Christmas was forbidden."

[294] *History of Mass. Bay*, I, 195 ff. Hutchison recounts some incidents.

[295] *History of Mass. Bay*, I, 303.

[296] Thorpe, III, 1881; *History of Mass. Bay*, I, 345-351.

[297] *Acts and Resolves of the Province of Massachusetts Bay, I-IV, 1692-1780* (Boston, 1869-1886), I, 62. "An Act for the Settlement and Support of Ministers and School Masters" (Ch. 26 of the Province Laws of 1692-1693); cf. also *ibid.*, pp. 102-103, Ch. 46 (hereafter cited *Acts and Resolves*).

exercise of worship held for some sixty years by the Puritan establishment.[298]

In a session begun in Boston on October 23, 1706, the assembly supplemented the aforesaid legislation with an "Act for Maintaining and Propagating Religion." Under the terms of section one of this act the Court of General Session of Peace was directed to appoint a jury to investigate whether all towns and districts had a minister and were supporting him properly according to contract. If a minister was neglected by a district and this was brought to the court's attention by someone other than a member of the jury, section two of the act empowered the court to enforce the law of support for ministers. When the orders of the court were ignored or circumvented, the court was instructed to file a report with the General Assembly, which in turn would remedy the situation as directed by law.[299] The members of the Church of England claimed that they were being unreasonably taxed for the support of divine worship according to the laws of the province. On May 26, 1742, the assembly passed an act whereby the taxes of persons attending the Church of England were to be paid to their own ministers.[300]

The charter provision of 1691 depriving Papists of toleration was implemented by an act of the assembly in Boston on May 29, 1700.[301] Under this infamous act all Roman clerics were banished from the province, and anyone who dared to remain was to be imprisoned for life. Should he escape and be recaptured, he was to be put to death. Anyone who knowingly aided such a cleric was to be fined "two hundred pounds, one moiety to the government,

---

[298] *Acts and Resolves,* I, p. 62, Ch. 26.

[299] *Acts and Resolves,* I, p. 597, Ch. 9. Under similar acts of 1715 and 1722 the assembly was directed to send ministers to towns lacking them. Such ministers were to be recommended by three or more ordained ministers. Cf. *ibid.*, pp. 26, 27, Ch. 17, p. 224, Ch. 4.

[300] *Acts and Resolves,* III, p. 25, Ch. 8. An act of broader scope was passed on October 17, 1754, entitled "An Act Favorable to Protestant Churches," for more effectively obtaining grants and donations for the support and maintenance of the ministers and defraying other costs relative to Public Worship (2nd session of 1754-1755), *ibid.*, pp. 778-779, Ch. 12.

[301] *Acts and Resolves,* I, pp. 423-424, Ch. 1. "An Act against Jesuits and Popish Priests."

one moiety to the informer, and they shall be set in pillory on three several days and then put on parole."[302] Furthermore, the procedure for apprehending the "culprits" was extremely simple. Any peace officer could arrest a person on the mere suspicion of being a Jesuit, seminary priest, or Roman cleric, and bring him to trial. A citizen arrest was equally uncomplicated, for the citizen could arrest these members of the clergy without a warrant and have them brought to trial. If the suspects were convicted, the informer was rewarded.[303] These clergymen finally received relief under the Massachusetts Constitution of 1780, which extended free exercise of worship to Papists and all other dissenters.[304]

C. The Statehood Period

In this same constitution all Christian sects were granted equal protection under the law.[305] What was the fate for the Congregational Establishment, which in the early years under the Charter of William and Mary practically had been reduced to the public support of its churches? It certainly did not enjoy exclusive establishment, because the constitution of 1780 ordered that "no subordination of any one sect or denomination to another shall ever be established by law." The eleventh amendment repeated this phrase.[306] Did this phrase mean a total disestablishment of all religion in Massachusetts? A careful reading of both Article III and Amendment XI favors the interpretation that it did not, but rather that a broad establishment of religion still existed, and that the Congregationalists continued to share in this establishment. Article III invested the legislature with the power to authorize and require towns and other political units to select, support and maintain "public Protestant teachers of piety, religion, and morality, in all cases where such provision shall not be made

[302] *Acts and Resolves,* I, pp. 423-424, Ch. 1, § 3.

[303] *Acts and Resolves,* p. 424, Ch. 1, § 5. The law made one exception. Roman clergy who were temporarily obliged to take refuge in the province by an act of God or some unusual circumstances were given a period of grace, before they were obliged to depart from the province.

[304] Thorpe, III, 1889, Art. II, p. 1890, Art. III.

[305] Thorpe, III, 1890, Art. III, *in fine.*

[306] Thorpe, III, 1890, Art. III, *in fine,* and p. 1914.

voluntarily."[307] Amendment eleven, which was ratified by the people on November 11, 1833, abolished tithes, discharged the towns and other political units of the responsibility and power for Church affairs, and made the existence, support and maintenance of all Churches voluntary.[308]

This evidence leads the writer to the conclusion that the Constitution of 1780 established the "Protestant Religion," at least in a wide sense, and this was not disestablished until 1833. Cobb cited some cases which support this contention. The most significant was the case of the church in Dedham. The majority of the members were orthodox, while the majority of the town were Unitarian. The minister resigned in 1818 and the town chose a Unitarian to succeed him. The church refused to accept him and carried their plea to the supreme court of Massachusetts. The court upheld the town vote, for, the court reasoned, "the constitution gives to towns, not to Churches, the right to elect the minister in last resort."[309] The church rights and property were handed over to the Unitarians, and the Orthodox Puritans had to provide a new church for themselves on a voluntary basis. Cobb stated that this happened in many places and "the old Puritan Church found itself turned out of house and home by the very powers it had contrived to give it lasting security. This was the death-blow to the long-moribund theocracy."[310]

Non-Protestant teachers and preachers were permitted to exercise their ministry under the Constitution of 1780, but they were still discriminated against. The constitution authorized only the public election and support of Protestant teachers or preachers and their churches. All such discriminations were abrogated by the eleventh amendment in 1833. Religious support was placed on a voluntary basis, and the local authorities no longer regulated any aspect of the internal life of the church or the choice of ministers or preachers.[311]

---

[307] Thorpe, III, 1890, Art. III.

[308] Thorpe, III, 1914, Amendment XI.

[309] Cobb, p. 515. Cf. Howe, *Cases on Church and State in the United States*, pp. 40-47. He reports the entire case.

[310] Cobb, p. 515.

[311] Thorpe, III, 1914, Amendment XI.

D. Protection Given to Puritan Preachers

It is fitting to give some attention to the specific freedoms and protections which the Puritan establishment granted to its preachers and membership. These protections for the Puritan religion were considered a matter of duty for the civil government, because the government considered itself the guardian of orthodoxy.[312] The civil authority had the power and liberty to deal with any church member, regardless of his position.[313] The government punished any church member guilty of heresy and did not tolerate the doctrines of dissenters. If anyone worshipped any God but the true God, or blasphemed the Trinity, or practiced witchcraft, he was subject to banishment or death.[314]

Although the civil government legislated in the area of religion, it did allow the Puritans a certain freedom of action in the internal affairs of the Church. In an act entitled "A Declaration of Liberties the Lord Jesus hath given to the Churches," the Puritans were granted the right to elect officers, "provided they be able, pious and orthodox."[315] In addition every church was free to admit, censure, or excommunicate members and to celebrate days of fast and prayer.[316]

Under a law passed in 1646 anyone who behaved with contempt towards a preacher, either by interrupting him in his preaching or by charging him falsely of erroneous teaching, upon conviction was publicly reproved by the magistrate. For a second offense the culprit was fined five pounds, or stood for two hours upon the block on a lecture day with a paper fixed on his breast on which was written in capital letters, AN OPEN AND OBSTINATE CONTEMMER OF GOD'S HOLY ORDINANCES.[317] Further

---

[312] *Colonial Laws of Mass.*, p. 47, n. 58, of the Body Liberties of 1641:—"The Civill Authoritie hath power and libertie to see that peace, ordinances, and Rules of Christ be observed in every Church according to his word. . . ."

[313] *Colonial Laws of Mass.*, p. 47, nn. 59, 60.

[314] *Colonial Laws of Mass.*, p. 55, n. 94; p. 128.

[315] *Colonial Laws of Mass.*, p. 57, n. 95; p. 128.

[316] *Colonial Laws of Mass.*, p. 57, n. 95, §§ 4, 6; p. 128.

[317] *Colonial Laws of Mass.*, p. 148, n. 14. The preface to this law stated that contempt for the word of God "is the desolating sin of civil states and Churches."

measures were taken to safeguard the office of preaching by the General Court, which in 1658 promulgated an act whereby no one could publicly preach or be ordained to the office of a teaching Elder when any two Organic Churches, Council of State, or General Court disapproved either on the grounds of doctrine or practice.[318]

The government also brought pressure upon the populace to attend the Congregational services. If any person was absent from a public meeting on the Lord's day, or other set days when Church attendance was obligatory, without a just cause, he was fined five shillings. He could be brought before the Magistrate from time to time for repeated offenses.[319]

From the laws just cited and the discussion in the previous sections, it is evident that an extreme form of Church-State structure existed in Massachusetts Bay from the early sixteen-thirties until the time of James II. The formula was not distinction and cooperation, but fusion and domination. Legally, the two societies appeared as one, with the State the guardian of orthodoxy and the supreme legislator in all matters, as well as the final court of appeals. The State was the Grand Inquisitor and took its job of snuffing out heresy and non-conformity very seriously. Although an absolute tyrant to non-Puritans, the State was most paternal toward the established membership, and surrounded the Puritan preachers with legal protection and support.

The Toleration Acts of James II and the Charter of 1691 from William and Mary greatly weakened the position of the Puritan Establishment, and the ministry act of 1692 left only a shell. The Massachusetts Constitution of 1780 did not destroy these remains, but rather made the Puritan Establishment a part of a much broader establishment—the Protestant religion. The remnants of the old Puritan Establishment were swept away in 1833 by the eleventh amendment.

The toleration policy of James II extended legal freedom of action to all preachers and liberty of conscience to all worshippers. The 1691 Charter of William and Mary and also the supplementary

---

[318] *Colonial Laws of Mass.*, pp. 147-148, n. 13.
[319] *Colonial Laws of Mass.*, p. 148, n. 155 (1646).

legislation restricted all non-Protestants from the enjoyment of these freedoms. These liberties were finally restored to everyone by the Constitution of 1780. One discrimination still remained; only Protestant preachers and teachers were legally entitled to state tax support. Equality in religious affairs was realized through the eleventh amendment—no religion received state support, and no religion was preferred over another.

### *Section 2. Connecticut*

#### A. Juridic Position of Church and State in the Formative Years

Thomas Hooker (1586?-1647) migrated with his congregation from Newton (Cambridge), Massachusetts, to Connecticut Valley in 1636. He founded the town of Hartford under a provisional government. This was authorized in virtue of a commission from the General Court of Massachusetts on March 3, 1635. Hartford and two other towns, Windsor and Witherfield, adopted a constitution on January 14, 1638/39.[320] This document, with some minor changes, remained the fundamental law of Connecticut until 1818. The founders of Connecticut believed that it was the duty of the government to maintain the liberty and purity of the Gospel, so they incorporated this ideal in the constitution of 1638-1639.[321]

The early settlers of this colony were of Puritan extraction, and the logical interpretation of this constitutional statement and the complementary one by the General Court was establishment of Puritan Congregationalism. As Cobb commented, "without formal definition or prescription of the form of Church polity, they simply assumed the form to which they had become attached in Massa-

---

[320] Elson, *History of the United States,* pp. 100-101; "Fundamental Order of Connecticut," Thorpe, I, 519; Cobb, pp. 238-242.

[321] Thorpe, I, 519. The first General Court made the same declaration in a more formal statement: "Forasmuch as the peace and the prosperity of the Churches and the members thereof, as well as Civil rights and Liberties, are carefully to be maintained: It is ordered by this court and decreed, that the civil authority here hath power and liberty to see that peace, ordinances, and rules of Christ be observed in every Church according to His word." Cf. *Connecticut Colonial Records,* I, 21, 524, 525, as quoted by Cobb, p. 243.

chusetts, and which they brought with them, would be the model for the Churches in their colony."[322]

## B. The Colonial Period

During the early part of this period church foundations and church attendance were closely regulated by law. Unless a group of persons obtained the consent of the General Assembly and the approbation of the neighboring churches, they were forbidden to embody themselves into a church.[323] Freedom of religious worship was restricted to the extent that the inhabitants of a town or of a plantation district were forbidden to attend a church distinct from, or in opposition to, the one publicly observed and dispensed by the approved minister of the place.[324] However, the act was not intended to hinder "any private Meetings of Godly Persons to attend any duties that Christianity and Religion calls for as Fasts and Conferences with the allowance of the Settled Minister or Ministers of the respective place."[325]

Everyone was bound to attend the preaching of the Word on the Lord's day and other set days. According to the law those who withdrew themselves "from hearing the Publick Ministry of the Word, after due means of Conviction" were fined five shillings."[326] A person who contemptuously insulted a minister of the Word during the course of his preaching, or falsely accused him of erroneous teaching, was subject upon conviction to fine and public ridicule. This act guaranteed the established preacher that he would have an audience, and took measures to see that it would be a docile one.

The Quakers were the first to be the object of intolerance under a law entitled "An Act for Suppressing Heretics, 1656."[327] It

[322] Cobb, pp. 243-244.

[323] *Acts and Laws of His Majesties Colony of Connecticut in New-England* (New London, 1715-1730), p. 29, "An Act Relating to Ecclesiastical Affairs" (hereafter cited *Acts and Laws of Connecticut*, 1715-1730 (comp.)).

[324] *Acts and Laws of Connecticut*, 1715-1730 (comp.), p. 29. Each breach of carried with it a fine of five pounds.

[325] *Acts and Laws of Connecticut*, 1715-1730 (comp.), pp. 29-30.

[326] *Acts and Laws of Connecticut*, 1715-1730 (comp.), p. 30. An individual could be excused for just and necessary causes.

[327] *Acts and Laws of Connecticut*, 1715-1730 (comp.), p. 49.

was the standard anti-Quaker act. Quakers were subject to exile and imprisonment, and anyone fraternizing with or aiding a Quaker was subject to a fine. Masters of vessels were obliged to transport them out of the colony again under pain of fine.[328]

The colony of Connecticut was granted a royal charter in 1662.[329] It placed no restraints upon religious preferences, nor did it make the acceptance of the Church of England mandatory. The question of Church establishment and religious affairs in general was left to the competency of the colonial government.

With the accession to power of William and Mary, the colony was not forced to abdicate its charter liberties. In 1708 the legislature passed a toleration act granting liberty of conscience to those who fell within the scope of the Toleration Act of William and Mary (1689). However, the law was not to be interpreted so as to prejudice the rights and privileges of the established Puritan Church.[330] Section two of this act declared that anyone who disturbed or disquieted the Established or Tolerated Congregations or misused their preachers was upon conviction to be fined according to law. The only difference at law between the Protestant preacher and the Puritan of the Established Church was that the former did not receive state support and the latter was subject to closer state control, e.g., in matters of appointment and removal the Puritan preacher was subject to the General Court. Non-Protestants at that time enjoyed no right of public assembly for worship.

The legislature decreed in 1723 that persons who "neglect the public worship of God in some Lawful Congregation and form themselves into Separate Congregations in private Houses" were to be fined twenty shillings upon conviction. They further ordered that "whatever Person, not being a lawful or allowed Minister of

---

[328] This act was repealed in May, 1706. Cf. *ibid.*, p. 129; Cobb, p. 261. The final portion of Quaker discrimination was removed by an act in 1729 which exempted Quakers from supporting the established Church.

[329] Thorpe, I, 529.

[330] *Acts and Laws of Connecticut,* 1715-1730 (comp.), p. 134. "An Act for the Ease of such as Soberly Differ from the Way of Worship and Ministry Established by the Laws of this Government"; cf. also Cobb, pp. 267, 268. This act was repealed in 1743.

the Gospel, shall presume to Profane the Holy Sacraments, by Administering or making shew of Administering them to any person or persons whatsoever," upon conviction was to be fined ten pounds for each offense, or thirty stripes.[331] Cobb observed that this is the only specimen of Connecticut law on religion which resorts to the whip for a penalty, and that he found no record of its being inflicted.[332] The preface of this law stated that it was directed against people who attended separate private meetings and did "not attend the Public Worship of God on the Lord's Day under color of gathering in private homes for preaching and for other parts of divine worship."[333] This undoubtedly referred to persons who banded together, but did not qualify under the law of 1708, and were probably disorderly in conduct. Cobb noted that "there is no record to show the denominations of these disorderly people."[334]

In 1728 the assembly gave its approval to an agreement reached by the Elders of the Puritan Churches at a meeting in Saybrook. Commonly known as the "Establishment Act of 1728," the law declared "that all Churches within this government: that are or shall be thus United in Doctrine, Worship, and Discipline be, and for the future shall be Owned, and Acknowledged by Law."[335] In an effort to clarify this action the assembly noted that the act was not intended as an encroachment upon the toleration given to certain dissenters, namely, to Protestant worshippers.[336]

---

[331] *Acts and Laws of Connecticut,* 1715-1730 (comp.), p. 290.

[332] Cobb, p. 269.

[333] *Acts and Laws of Connecticut,* 1715-1730 (comp.), p. 290.

[334] Cobb, p. 269.

[335] *Acts and Laws of His Majesty's English Colony of Connecticut in New England in America* (New London, 1750), p. 169 (hereafter cited *Acts and Laws of Connecticut,* 1750 (comp.)).

[336] *Acts and Laws of Connecticut,* 1750 (comp.), p. 169. "Provided always, that nothing herein shall be Intended or Construed to Hinder or Prevent any Society, or Church that is, or shall be allowed by the Laws of this Government, who Soberly Differ, or Dissent from the United Churches hereby Established, from Exercising Worship, and Discipline in their own Way, according to their Conscience."

This law was far more liberal than an earlier "Act Relating to Ecclesiastical Affairs," which stated "that no persons whatever within this

The next year a five shillings fine was ordered to be imposed upon anyone who disturbed a meeting or abused the moderator. This law also protected meetings for religious purposes and preachers of the Gospel.[337]

The Dissenters Law of 1743 repealed the Law of Toleration of 1708 and was far less liberal. The old law made it comparatively easy for a dissenting congregation to function. They simply petitioned their own county court for recognition of rights to organize and worship. Dissenters were obliged by the 1743 law to travel to Hartford and appear in person to take "the oaths and subscribe to the declarations provided by the Act of Parliament in cases of like nature."[338] This made the right to organize a church a *favor* of the assembly.

The 1770 session of the assembly removed the penalty imposed upon dissenting Protestants. They were excused from attending the public meetings of the Established Religion on the Lord's day "on account of their Meeting together by themselves on the said Day, for Public Worship of God, in a Way agreeable to their Consciences, anything in said Act to the contrary notwithstanding."[339]

As late as 1808 residents of Connecticut were still bound to attend public worship in some congregation allowed by law. This Sabbath observance law harks back to the Sabbath law of 1692.[340]

---

colony shall in any way Imbody themselves into a Church Estate without the consent of the General Assembly of this Colony, and the Approbation of Neighboring Churches." The 1728 did not demand that dissenting Churches already established again seek approbation under the new law. Cf. *Acts and Laws of Connecticut,* 1715-1730 (comp.), pp. 29, 30.

[337] *Acts and Laws of Connecticut,* 1715-1730 (comp.), p. 366.—"An Act to Prevent Tumults and Disorders in Town-Meetings, Society-Meetings and Proprietors-Meetings." This act received some slight revision in 1750, and was still substantially in effect in 1808. Cf. *The Public Statutes of the State of Connecticut* (Hartford, 1808), Book I, p. 492.

[338] *Acts and Laws of Connecticut,* 1715-1730 (comp.), p. 134—1708 Act; *Acts and Laws of Connecticut,* 1750 (comp.), p. 169—1743 Act.

[339] *Acts and Laws of Connecticut,* 1750 (comp.), p. 351.

[340] *Statutes of Connecticut* (1808), p. 578, § 1. This section 1 reads the same as the law adopted in the 1702 session.

## C. The Statehood Period

During the Revolution no State Constitution was formulated by the people of Connecticut, and no changes were made in the basic Church-State structure. In 1778 the Separatists, though Congregationalists, were exempt from paying taxes to support the established Church. This tax exemption was broadened by "An Act for Securing Rights of Conscience" enacted in 1784. No one professing the Christian religion who dissented from the worship and ministry established by law was subject to the penalty for not attending the established worship, provided that he attended his own public worship. Christians who attended and supported the form of worship according to their consciences were not taxed to support the established religion. Those who had no Christian Church affiliation were subject to the tax for the support of the established Church. All Protestant dissenters were permitted to use the same power and privilege for maintaining their respective societies as belonged to societies established. Under this law the Jews and other non-Christians were still subject to the said penalty and tax. All non-Protestants, including Roman Catholics, were still deprived of equal protection of the law in areas of Church organization and support.[341]

This act was implemented by the legislature in 1791.[342] The supplementary legislation concerned a certificate which a dissenter had to present as proof of his dissent from the established Church and in token of his support of the religion of his choice, in order to be exempt from the State tithe for the Establishment. The law further required that this certificate be signed by two of the civil authorities living in the town where the dissenter lived, or by one, in case but one officer lived in the said town. If these officers

[341] *Connecticut State Records,* I, 11, as cited by Cobb, p. 501. Protestant Churches were now supported by public taxes. Their Church members paid the tax to the town officials and designated the Church that was to receive the benefit of the tax.

[342] *Unbound Acts of the Connecticut Acts and Laws,* in the Anglo-American Section of the Library of Congress, May Session of 1791 (Second Thursday), pp. 403-404.—An Act, in addition to, and in explanation of, an Act entitled "An Act for Securing the Rights of Conscience in matters of religion, to Christians of every denomination in the State."

judged his claim to be legitimate, they were to issue him a certificate.[343]

The legislature of Connecticut not only concerned itself about the local observance of religion, it also passed a law in 1792 to obtain support for missionaries to preach the Gospel in the northern and western sections of the United States. They directed that a collection be made annually for a three-year period to assist these preachers. An annual report of receipts and expenditures was to be made to the assembly.[344]

Disestablishment and the free exercise of worship and of speech became a part of the fundamental law of Connecticut in 1818. All persons were given the right to worship according to their own choosing, provided that this liberty did not lead to license or to a disturbance of the peace and safety of the State.[345]

---

[343] The law indicated the form to be used: "We, having examined the claims of N. N., who says he is a dissenter from the ecclesiastical Society of N., and hath joined himself to a Church or Congregation of the name of N, and that he contribute his share or proportion towards supporting the public worship and ministry thereof, do upon examination find the above facts are true.

Date. Justices of the Peace."

[344] A bound photostatic copy of the Connecticut *Acts and Laws* in the Anglo-American section of the Library of Congress, October Session of 1792, p. 453: "That there be contributions in the several Religious Societies and Congregations in this State on the first Sabbath in the month of May annually for the term of three Years, and the Minister or Clerk of such Societies or Congregations shall receive and pay over such contributions to Reverend Ezra Stiles, Nathan Williams and Jonathan Edwards, who shall appropriate the same to the support of such Missioners as the general associations of this State shall from time to time employ in preaching the Gospel, in those settlements in the Northern and Western parts of the United States, where the Ordinances of the Gospel are not established. . . ." (The remainder of the law deals with the annual assembly report.)

[345] Thorpe, I, 537, Art. I, § 3.—"The exercise and enjoyment of religious profession and worship, without discrimination, shall forever be free to all persons in this State, provided, the right hereby declared and established shall not be so construed as to excuse acts of licentiousness or to justify practices inconsistent with the peace and safety of the State."
Sec. 4. "No preference shall be given by law to any Christian sect or mode of worship.".
Sec. 5. "Every citizen may freely speak, write, and publish his sentiments on all subjects, being responsible for the abuse of that liberty."

All Protestants, Catholics and Jews, and persons of any other religious sect, were now free to worship in a public or a private manner. Their preachers could expound their doctrines, provided they caused no serious breach of peace and public order. These liberties were obtained in the State of Connecticut more than a quarter of a century after they were guaranteed on the Federal level in the first amendment to the Constitution of the United States.

Compulsory church attendance laws existed from the early days of the colony into the nineteenth century. Private meetings of Christians were permitted, provided they did not interfere with attendance at the public worship of the Established religion on the Sabbath and other set days. Quaker meetings were prohibited in 1656 by the Law to Suppress Heretics. This law was repealed in 1706, and in 1708 Quakers and all other Protestants were allowed to incorporate and to hold public worship, provided they petitioned the County Court for this privilege. Catholics and non-Christians were not given this favor of the law. The Sabbath Act of 1723 requiring church attendance and the Establishment Act of 1728 did not alter the Toleration Act of 1708. The Toleration Act of 1743 was less liberal than the one in 1708. It obliged the Protestant sects to travel to Hartford and obtain the permission formerly granted by the local court. In 1770 Protestants were excused from the penalty of not attending the worship of the established religion, provided they worshipped publicly in conformity with conscience. All residents of Connecticut were still bound to attend public worship in one of the allowed Protestant religions. The Constitution of 1818 granted full freedom of worship to everyone and implicitly abrogated all mandatory attendance laws and discriminatory religious laws.

The preachers of the Established Church were given legal protection against all contemptuous, insulting and derogatory attacks. Protestant preachers were given this same protection in 1708. The Establishment Act of 1728 did not affect this position. In 1729 both the Congregations and their preachers were guaranteed government protection by an anti-disturbance act. Roman Catholics, Jews, and all non-Protestants were denied the right of religious assembly, and their preachers were forbidden to propagate their doctrines until the nineteenth century. The Constitution of 1818 secured these rights and privileges for everyone in the State of Connecticut.

The Establishment continued for more than a quarter of a century after the adoption of the Federal Constitution. In 1816 the penalty for non-attendance at church was totally abolished. The following year the anti-establishment element gained the position of power in the Connecticut government. The new legislature guaranteed every person of any Christian denomination the right to change his Church affiliation at will. Puritan Congregationalism was finally disestablished by the Constitution of 1818. This replaced the old colonial charter as the fundamental law of the State.[346]

### *Section 3. New Hampshire*

#### A. The Formative Period in Church and State Relations

There was a grant of New Hampshire as early as 1629, and three additional grants in 1635, but the first document of any significance for the present considerations of Church and State was the Agreement of the Settlers at Exeter in New Hampshire, 1639.[347] John Wheelwright (1592?-1679) was banished from Massachusetts, and by the end of 1638 a sufficiently large group had united with his followers for the establishment of three settlements,

[346] Thorpe, I, 537, Art. I, § 4: "No preference shall be given by law to any Christian sect or mode of worship."

The colony of New Haven, America, was founded in 1638 by Theophilus Easton (1590-1658) and John Davenport (1597-1670). They drew up a Fundamental Agreement on June 4, 1639 (Thorpe, I, 523 ff.). The union of Church and State in this colony is best termed a theocracy. This colonial experiment was brief in duration. New Haven united with Connecticut by order of the king under the Charter of 1662. Cf. Elson, *History of the United States,* pp. 100-101, and Morison and Commager, I, 81. No specific consideration is given to religious conditions in this colony of New Haven in this present work. For a treatment of these religious matters in New Haven Colony, cf. Cobb, pp. 280-290.

[347] Thorpe, IV, 2445; the 1629 and 1635 grants are reproduced in Thorpe, IV, 2433-2445.

Exeter, Hampton and Dover. In 1639 they decided to associate themselves under the afore-mentioned agreement for the purposes of government.[348]

The Agreement of 1639 was exceptionally brief compared with the usual colonial agreements. It took cognizance of religion in the following paragraph: ". . . do in the name of Christ and in the sight of God combine ourselves together to erect and set up among us such government as shall be to our best discerning agreeable to the will of God. . . ."[349] They bound themselves in the name of Christ "and for fear to submit ouselves to such Godly and Christian Lawes as are established in the Realm of England . . . and all other such Lawes which shall upon good grounds be made and enacted among us according to God, that we may live quietly and peaceably together in all godliness and honesty."[350] The term "Christian Laws" indicated that this colony was a Christian foundation, but the document itself was silent concerning any ideas of concrete establishment.

## B. The Colonial Period

New Hampshire was united to Massachusetts in 1641 and remained a part of that colony until the king separated them in 1679. He rejoined them in 1686, but in 1691 New Hampshire was again separated from Massachusetts and became a royal colony. The president and council were appointed by the crown, and the assembly was elected by the people. Until 1747 the governor remained under the supervision of the governor of Massachusetts.[351]

The Commission of John Cutt, 1680, marked the formal beginning of constitutional government in New Hampshire.[352] Cutt's Commission granted liberty to all Protestants and gave a preferred

---

[348] Elson, *History of the United States,* p. 104; Cobb, p. 290.

[349] Thorpe, IV, 2445.

[350] Thorpe, IV, 2445.

[351] Elson, *History of the United States,* p. 105. Thorpe, IV, 2521—The Voluntary Union of the two colonies in 1641; *ibid.,* p. 2522, the solution of the union in 1679; the reunion of 1686—*ibid.,* p. 2524.

[352] Thorpe, IV, 2446 ff.

position to the Church of England.[353] However, Roman Catholics, Jews and all other non-Christians were deprived of the right of religious toleration.

The assembly of 1680 passed a number of criminal and capital laws. Anyone who was convicted of blaspheming the Trinity or of denying God, his creation, or his government of the world, was subject to the penalty of death.[354] In addition witchcraft was also punishable with death.[355] Furthermore, the assembly made the contempt for the word of God or for the ministers of the Gospel a criminal offense, punishable upon first offense with twenty shillings or four hours in the stocks; second offense, forty shillings or whipping.[356] Like her neighbor Massachusetts, the New Hampshire assembly passed "An Act punishing the Profaning of the Lord's Day by unnecessary work, travel, etc." In a case decided on the basis of this law Robert Briney was sentenced on July 26, 1681, to receive nine stripes for violating this law and for missing Sabbath services.[357]

On May 9, 1682, Edward Cranfield was constituted lieutenant governor, and he assumed office on October 4, 1682.[358] Lieutenant Governor Cranfield and his council met at Great Island on December 10, 1683, and issued an order for the administration of the sacraments according to the mode of the Church of England.[359]

---

[353] Thorpe, IV, 2448.—". . . that by such examples ye infidels may be invited and desire to partake of ye Christian Religion, and for ye greater ease and satisfaction of our said loving subjects in matters of Religion We do hereby will, require and commend that liberty of conscience shall be allowed unto all protestants; and that such especially shall be comformable to ye rites of ye Church of England shall be particularly countenanced and encouraged."

[354] *Collections of the New Hampshire Historical Society* (11 vols., Concord, 1824-1915), VIII, *Provincial Records and Court Papers from 1680-1692*, p. 10.

[355] *Collections of the New Hampshire Historical Society*, VIII, 10. "If any Christian soe called be a witch, that is, hath or consulted with a familiar spirit, he or they shall be put to death."

[356] *Collections of the New Hampshire Historical Society*, VIII, pp. 15, 66. The assembly of 1682 passed a similar law. Cf. *ibid.*, pp. 91-92.

[357] *Collections of the New Hampshire Historical Society*, VIII, 15, 66, 67.

[358] Thorpe, IV, 2523.

[359] *Collections of the New Hampshire Historical Society*, VIII, 163.

As is evident, this act was destined to stir up much opposition, for the order attempted to change the character of the colonial churches and to assert the supremacy of the Church of England. After January 1, all the ministers of the colony were required to admit all persons of a suitable age to the Lord's supper and to admit children of such persons to baptism. "If any person desires the same according to the liturgy of the Church of England, that it be done accordingly, in pursuance of the laws of the realm of England, and His Majesty's command to the Massachusetts government."[360] When a minister refused to comply with this order, he incurred the penalties of the statutes relevant to the case, and the inhabitants were no longer obliged to support him.

But the ministers ignored the government's order, so the lieutenant governor and his council set out to make an example of the most prominent clergyman in Portsmouth, Joshua Moody. On February 6, 1683/4, a warrant was issued for his arrest. Cranfield had commanded Moody to read his order for conformity in his meeting house on the Sabbath. Moody stubbornly refused to pay any attention to this order. On January 15, 1683/4, James Serlock gave Moody a notice in writing to the effect that Cranfield, Barefoot, Chamberlain and Hincks would appear on the following Sunday to receive the sacrament from his hands according to the liturgy of the Church of England. When the lieutenant governor and his friends came to the services, Moody would not give them the sacrament as they had previously requested. Irked by this rebuff Cranfield set the legal machinery into motion whereby Moody was arrested in February.[361]

At the trial two charges were lodged against Moody: first, that he refused to administer the sacrament according to the rites of the Church of England, and second, that he administered the sacrament contrary to the rites of this Church. What followed could hardly be considered a model procedure of justice, because Barefoot was the judge and the minister pleaded his own defense. However, Moody proved equal to the task, for he clearly demonstrated that the laws of England forbade the use of the rites of

---

[360] *Collections of the New Hampshire Historical Society,* VIII, 163.
[361] *Collections of the New Hampshire Historical Society,* VIII, 164-165.

the Church of England to those who were not ordained in that Church. Therefore, he reasoned, he could not possibly use the liturgy of the Church of England without violating the law. Moody's logic failed to convince the judge who found Moody guilty as charged. Barefoot imposed a sentence of imprisonment or exile, and it is not clear whether Moody was actually exiled or that he fled of his own accord to Boston.[362]

Although the government succeeded in its efforts with Moody, the entire plan was not successful, because the ministers continued to resist Cranfield's efforts to force them to conform to the Church of England. What was more important, he failed to gain popular support for his behavior, and the people's opposition grew openly hostile. They "antagonized him in every possible way, and by denying him a legislature and refusing him supplies, compelled him to abandon his government," which he had administered for about two and a half years.[363]

Matters did not improve very much when his deputy, Walter Barefoot, succeeded him. On May 25, 1686, he was replaced by Joseph Dooley and a Council, "this being the prelude to the administration of Sir Edmund Andros (1637-1714) in the establishment of the Dominion of New England as undertaken by James II."[364]

Between April 18, 1689, and February 20, 1690, New Hampshire was without a colonial government. The colony was united for a second time with Massachusetts, and this union lasted until 1692. Then Samuel Allen was appointed to establish a separate government for New Hampshire. His efforts were strongly opposed by many of the colonists, and his rule was a stormy one. Richard, Earl of Bellomont (Beaumont), was commissioned as the new governor on June 18, 1697, but did not come to the colony and assume his office until July 31, 1699.[365] He remained

---

[362] *Collections of the New Hampshire Historical Society*, VIII, 165, 237.

[363] Thorpe, IV, 2523.

[364] Thorpe, IV, 2523-2526.

[365] Thorpe, IV, 2526-2527. The administration of New Hampshire under all of the succeeding governors until 1775 is discussed in Thorpe, IV, 2528-2531.

only eighteen days, and died on March 5, 1701-02. The Lieutenant Governor, William Partridge, administered the government in his absence and continued to do so until Joseph Dudley assumed the rule of the government under his own commission July 13, 1702. Beginning with the Earl of Bellomont (Beaumont) the same governor was appointed for Massachusetts and New Hampshire, and this situation persisted until 1741.

Years of governmental instability and popular dissatisfaction explain the almost complete lack of legislation in the area of Church and State. Various enactments confirmed "the Church, under the old Congregational order, as a *town* establishment."[366] The laws of 1692, 1702, and 1714 determined that the freeholders in each town should choose the minister of the town Church and agree upon a salary with him. The selectmen were to assess this salary upon the town, and the constable was directed to collect the said tax. Only those who constantly attended the public worship of their own faith were to be excused from this tax.[367]

The laws made no provision for the support of dissenting ministers, nor did they prohibit any arrangement for the support of the latter by their followers. An exemption from the general church support tax could be obtained, but only upon proof of the conscientious dissent, of the regular attendance at public worship, and of payment for its support. The State carefully examined all claims for exemption.

## C. The Statehood Period

A general condition of legal toleration and town establishment existed side by side during the eighteenth century. The constitution of 1776 was silent on matters of religion.[368] The Constitution of New Hampshire, 1784, granted complete freedom of worship to each individual, "provided he doth not disturb the public peace, or disturb others, in their religious worship."[369] This instrument

[366] Cobb, p. 298.

[367] Cobb, p. 298 citing the *Provincial Papers of New Hampshire,* III; IV, 226, 391, 414.

[368] Thorpe, IV, 2451.

[369] Thorpe, IV, 2454, Art. V.

stated that "no subordination, of any one sect or denomination to another, shall ever be established by law."[370] These two guarantees could seem to have disestablished the old town establishments, but they did not. Article VI also empowered towns, parishes, bodies-corporate or religious societies "to make adequate provision at their own expense, for the support and maintenance of public Protestant teachers of piety, religion and morality." The said bodies were given "the exclusive right of electing their own public teachers, and of contracting with them for their support." Towns could still elect ministers and levy a tax for their support, but "no portion of any one particular religious sect, or denomination, shall ever be compelled to pay toward the support of the teacher or teachers of another persuasion, sect or denomination."[371]

There remained, at least in the wide sense, the town establishment of the Protestant religion. Non-Protestant religions could not be so established. The one noticeable difference between the constitutional provision and the colonial law was that proof of dissent and support of this dissenting religion was not required for an escape from the payment of a tax supporting the town ministers. The new law only obliged those who adhered to the town religion to support it.

The religious provisions of the 1784 Constitution were retained in two articles of the Constitution of 1792.[372] These two articles were retained in the Constitution of New Hampshire (Amended) 1902.[373]

---

[370] Thorpe, IV, 2454, Art. VI, *in fine*.

[371] Thorpe, IV, 2454, Art. VI.

[372] Thorpe, IV, 2471, Arts. V, VI.

[373] Thorpe, IV, pp. 2494-2495, Arts. V, VI. Cf. Howe, *Cases on Church and State in the United States*, pp. 55-78. He reports a case involving the congregation and the church wardens. The wardens of the Unitarian church were permitting a renegade Unitarian, Francis E. Abbott, to preach non-Unitarian doctrines in the meeting house of the Society. The majority of the New Hampshire Supreme Court granted the congregation injunctive relief, and forbade the wardens to permit anyone to preach doctrines contrary to the fundamental beliefs of the Unitarians. Howe notes that the majority opinion covered eighty-four pages of the reports, and the dissent ran some one hundred and forty-three pages. The case was decided by the New Hampshire Supreme Court in 1868.

## ARTICLE IV. NON-ESTABLISHED COLONIES

Three colonies refused to adopt the principle of union of Church and State. They were Rhode Island, Pennsylvania and Delaware. In Rhode Island the separation of Church and State was absolute in theory and in practice. Pennsylvania rejected any form of religious establishment, but, in theory at least, it demanded a belief in the existence of God as a prerequisite for citizenship and permanent residence. Delaware, originally a part of Pennsylvania, retained the same sentiments of separation of Church and State as the parent colony.

### *Section 1. Rhode Island*

#### A. The Formative Period of Church-State Relations

The Puritan heretics, Anne Hutchinson (1591-1643) and Roger Williams (1603?-1683), who were banished from the Massachusetts Bay Colony, founded settlements along Narragansett Bay. These were federated in 1644 as Rhode Island and Providence Plantations. The religious character of this new colony was summed up by Morison and Commager in their description of Williams:

> Anywhere else in Christendom toleration of dissenters might or might not be allowed as a political concession, while one "true" church was always established. Revolutionary Williams believed in the individual's God-given right to worship as he chose, or not at all; and that right was enforced in Rhode Island.[374]

Some important documents preceded the federation of 1644. The Plantation Agreement of Providence, August 27-September 6, 1640, guaranteed liberty of conscience.[375] The Patent for the Providence Plantations (1643) made no mention of religious worship.[376] Cobb expressed the view that Williams did not wish

---

[374] Morison and Commager, I, 58-59.

[375] Thorpe, VI, 3206, § 2—"We agree, as formerly hath bin the liberties of the town, so still, to hould forth liberty of conscience."

[376] Thorpe, VI, 3209.

to raise the issue of religious freedom with the English authorities during the formative years.[377] There is on record an instance when a person was punished for interfering with the worship of his wife.[378]

Rhode Island proved to be a haven for Quakers. When they came to Rhode Island, the commissioners of the united colonies wrote a letter to the government of Rhode Island (Sept. 12, 1657), in which they requested that the Quakers be banished from Rhode Island and be forbidden to dwell there.[379] In a reply dated October 13, 1657, they answered that the Quakers then in the colony could not be persecuted because "we have no law among us, whereby to punish anyone for only declaring by words, etc., their mindes and understanding concerning the things and the ways of God, as to salvation and eternal condition."[380] They further noted that the Quakers seemed to thrive best under persecution. In Rhode Island, where they were tolerated, the Quakers were gaining fewer adherents than in those places where they were being persecuted. The reply conceded, however, that the Quaker doctrine tended to undermine the civil government, if it was generally received, and so the entire Quaker matter would be proposed for discussion at the next General Assembly with the hope that the assembly would be able to prevent the bad effects of Quaker activities and doctrines.[381]

After they had considered the matter, the General Assembly of Providence replied to the Commissioners with respect to the Quaker issue on March 13, 1658. The letter stated that freedom

---

377 Cobb, p. 431.

378 *Records of the Colony of Rhode Island and Providence Plantations in New England, 1636-1792* (ed. J. R. Bartlett, 10 vols., Providence, R. I., 1856-1858), I, 16.—May, 1637: "It was agreed that Joshua Verin upon the breach of a covenant for restraining the libertie of conscience, shall be withheld from the libertie of voting till he shall declare the contrarie." Verin had refused to allow his wife to attend Mr. Williams' services. Some of the colonists objected to the censure of Verin. Verin left Providence and moved to Salem (hereafter cited *Records of R. I.*).

379 *Records of R. I.*, I, 374-376.

380 *Records of R. I.*, I, 377.

381 *Records of R. I.*, I, 377.

of different consciences was the basic principle of the Charter of their colony and that it was still highly valued.[382] Nevertheless, the assembly wished to preserve civil peace and order. In the colony everyone was required to perform his duties toward his Highness and the colonial government. If the Quakers refused to conform in these matters like the other citizens, they would present the matter to the Supreme Authority in England to obtain advice as to how they should act towards these people. The assembly was taking the course of action outlined, so that "noe damage, or infringement of the chief principle in our charter concerning freedom of consciences" follow.[383]

In accordance with this promise the assembly of Providence dispatched a letter to His Highness dated November 5, 1658. This communication spoke of the ill feeling which the Quaker situation had engendered. If the assembly did not take immediate action against the Quakers, the letter continued, it was feared that the other colonies might secretly have agreed to place an embargo upon all shipping to the colony. The legislators asked His Highness and Council to help them with respect to the pressure being applied by the other colonies, "as wee may no be compelled to exercise any civil power over men's consciences, soe longe as humane orders in point of civility are not corrupted or violated, which our neighbors about us doe frequently practice. . . ."[384]

This exchange of correspondence demonstrates that equal treatment of all religions was in practice in Rhode Island in the early years of its formation. Despite great moral and threatened economic pressures from the neighboring colonies, the assembly clung to its principles of toleration and disestablishment.

---

[382] *Records of R. I.*, I, 378-379. "Freedom of different consciences, to be protected from inforcements was the principle ground of our charter, both with respect to our humble sute for it, as also to the true intent of the Honourable and renouned parleiment of England in grauntinge of the same unto us; which freedom we still prize as the greatest hapines that men can possess in the world."

[383] *Records of R. I.*, I, 378.

[384] *Records of R. I.*, I, 398. The assembly also forwarded a copy of the letter which the Commissioners had sent to Rhode Island.

B. The Colonial Period

A short time after the Providence charter was granted, the Colonies of Providence and Rhode Island desired to merge under one charter. However, the governor of Rhode Island was strongly opposed to this move, and he journeyed to England to frustrate the plan. He succeeded in obtaining an order for a separate government for Rhode Island.[385] A few months after he had returned from England, his subjects turned against him and united with Williams in the charter movement. John Clark and Williams went to England in 1651 to win the favor of Cromwell for the merger. They failed to persuade Cromwell, so Williams returned home in 1654, but left Clark behind to carry on the fight. The death of Cromwell (+ 1658) and the Restoration proved to be a happy turn of events. Charles II (1660-1685) not only approved the plan, but made the experiment his own.

Charles II granted the Charter of Rhode Island and Providence Plantations in 1663.[386] The king stated that the people of Rhode Island and Providence petitioned to conduct an experiment, viz., "that a most flourishing civill state may stand and best bee maintained, and that among our English subjects, with a full libertie in religious concernments. . . ."[387]

Charles II said that he willingly encouraged this undertaking of his subjects who, to secure the free exercise of their civil and religious rights, and to preserve their liberty of Christian faith and worship, because they could not conform to the public exercise of worship according to the Church of England nor take the prescribed oaths, desired to live under a charter granting full religious liberty. He declared that no one should be "molested, punished, disquieted, or called in question, for any differences in opinione in our said colony. . . ."[388] The inhabitants of Rhode Island were to enjoy full freedom of conscience and were not to use this liberty to cause civil injury or outward of others; any law or custom to

[385] Cobb, pp. 433-434.

[386] Thorpe, VI, 3211-3222; *Records of Rhode Island,* I, 1 ff.

[387] Thorpe, VI, 3212.

[388] "Charter of Rhode Island and Providence Plantations, 1663," Thorpe, V, 3213.

the contrary notwithstanding. These charter pronouncements continued to be the fundamental law of the land for more than a century.

The records contain a statute, claimed by some to have been passed in 1644, which denies citizenship to Roman Catholics.[389] In the original proceedings for March, 1664, no such act appears. It was undoubtedly the work of the committee appointed to prepare the digest of colonial laws. The exceptive clause added by this group was permitted to remain on the books. It appeared in the printed digests of 1719, 1731, 1767.[390] Cobb has a discussion of this act, and his facts are at variance with those of the *Colonial Records of Rhode Island.* He agrees that the exceptive clause is an interpolation, but, following Bancroft's *History of the United States,* he says that the interpolation was made by the revisory commission of 1774, whose members were motivated by English politics.[391]

The General Assembly of 1673 reiterated the charter guarantee of freedom of conscience for all those not disturbing the civil peace and affirmed that no one could be forced to worship God.[392]

---

[389] *Records of R. I.,* II, 36-37.—"That all men professing Christianity and of competent estates, and of civil conversation, who acknowledge and are obedient to the civil magistrates, though of different judgments in religious affairs (Roman Catholics only excepted), shall be admitted freemen, and shall have liberty to choose and be chosen officers of the Colony, both military and civil."

[390] Cf. *Records of R. I.,* II, 36-37, note 2. The editor is of the same opinion, because this act with an exceptive clause is opposed to the uniform policy of the colony, the attitude of the early settlers, and the principles of the newly granted charter (1663).

[391] George Bancroft, *History of the United States* (2 vols., New York, 1888), II, 65. Cobb, pp. 437-438. Cobb added that, even if this law had been passed by the assembly, there were no Roman Catholics in the colony until the time of the Revolution, when the French navy came to assist the colonists. At that time the law was expunged from the record.

Gustavus Myers, *History of Bigotry in the United States* (New York: Random House, 1943), p. 81. In his interpretation of this act, he believes that it was accepted as law.

[392] *Records of R. I.,* II, 503-504. Public order and civil peace were the only restraints placed upon this free exercise of religion. However, the assembly did pass some Sunday blue laws.

### C. The Statehood Period

Church establishments were shattered in the wake of the Revolution. This necessitated the formulation of new constitutions to adjust the fundamental law of the land in several of the colonies. Rhode Island needed no such change. She passed into the new era under the original charter of Charles II, and did not draw up a new constitution until 1842.[393]

## *Section 2. Pennsylvania*

### A. The Formative Period of Church-State Relations

Delaware and Pennsylvania were one colony until 1702. What is stated concerning Pennsylvania applies with equal force to Delaware until that year. There is a separate treatment of Delaware from 1702.

William Penn (1644-1718) was converted to Quakerism in 1667. Fourteen years later he obtained a tract of land from the Duke of York. Charles II implemented this grant by means of a charter.[394] The charter neither established a Church, nor did it make any provision for liberty of conscience. It did provide for freedom of action of a minister of the Church of England, if the colonists desired one.[395]

### B. The Colonial Period

In 1682 Penn brought to America some laws which he had composed in England. One article contained a free exercise

---

[393] "Constitution of Rhode Island, 1842," Thorpe, VI, 3233, Art. I, § 3. Disestablishment and free exercise of religion clauses.

[394] For a history of Penn's conversion and his successful attempt to start a colony cf. Morison and Commager, I, 74-76.

[395] Thorpe, V, 3043—". . . if any of the inhabitants of the said Province, to the number of Twenty, shall at any time hereafter be desirous, and shall by any writing, or by any person deputed for them, signify such their desire to the Bishop of London for the time being that any preacher or preachers, to be approved of by the said Bishop, may be sent unto them for their instruction, that then said preacher or preachers shall and may be and reside within the said Province, without any denial or molestation whatsoever."

clause.[396] Penn's grant of freedom was not as extensive as the one which existed in Rhode Island. Atheists were excluded by Article 35, and Article 34 required a profession of faith in Christ from one who was to hold public office. This discriminated against all non-Christians.[397]

The first colonial assembly met at Chester in 1682 and enacted The Great Law or Body of Laws. The first chapter was concerned with religion, and it substantially re-enacted the freedoms guaranteed by Penn's laws.[398] The assembly declared these laws to be fundamental. William and Mary annulled them in 1693, but the assembly immediately re-enacted them. Both Penn's Frame of Government and the assembly laws are significant because they granted Roman Catholics free exercise of worship and complete enfranchisement.

James II, Penn's patron, was exiled from England, and Penn himself fell under suspicion because of his close friendship with James. Penn's enemies succeeded in having the Charter of Pennsylvania set aside, and Pennsylvania was reduced to a royal province in 1693. The colony was placed under the jurisdiction of the governor of New York, and its citizens were obliged to take the test oath.[399] Although the oath requirement was repealed in 1701, Queen Anne's government re-enacted it in 1703.[400] Jews, Unitarians, and Roman Catholics felt the discrimination of this oath which required a belief in the Trinity, the divine inspiration of the Scriptures, and an abjuration of the Roman Catholic doctrines of transubstantiation, and of the veneration of Mary and the Saints, and of the belief in the sacrifice of the mass.[401]

---

[396] Thorpe, V, 3063, Art. 35.—All those who acknowledge one God and Creator and Ruler of the world "and that hold themselves obliged in conscience to live peaceably and justly in civil society, shall, in no ways, be molested or prejudiced for their religious persuasion, or practice in matters of faith and worship, nor shall they be compelled, at any time, to frequent or maintain any religious worship, place or ministry whatever."

[397] Thorpe, V, 3062-3063; Article 36 imposed the duty of Sunday rest.

[398] Cf. Cobb, p. 443.

[399] Cf. Morison and Commager, I, 76-77; Cobb, pp. 445-446.

[400] Cf. *Colonial Records of Pennsylvania* (16 vols., Philadelphia, 1852; Harrisburg, 1851-1853), II, 68, 89-96. Penn was in England at the time.

[401] *Church and State*, pp. 213-219.

Penn successfully petitioned the government of William and Mary in 1694 to rescind the order which reduced Pennsylvania to a royal province. The assembly was granted legislative power, and Penn's cousin, William Markham (1635-1704), was appointed governor. The first assembly under Markham in 1696 passed a law which required the religious tests of the Toleration Act for all officeholders.[402]

Penn returned to the colony in 1700, and he tried to remedy the harm done. He issued a Charter of Privileges and also passed a series of laws. The first article of this charter restored the exercise of religion to its original state, and this charter norm remained the fundamental law until 1776.[403]

At Penn's insistence two acts were passed by the assembly in November, 1700. The Law Concerning Liberty of Conscience granted freedom "to practice religion, and anyone who abuses or derides another for his different persuasion and practice in religious matters will be punished as a disturber of the peace."[404] The second law removed certain tests for offices.

England did not like this assembly action. The Queen in Council annulled this legislation in 1702, and ordered the religious tests to be restored. Present officeholders were to be removed, if they refused to take the oath. Contrary to the desires of Penn, the colonial officials gradually submitted to this ruling. He travelled to England in an attempt to stop this order of the Queen, but he was unsuccessful. In Penn's absence the entire assembly subscribed to the test, and in 1705 they passed an act requiring all the religious tests demanded by Queen Anne. They remained in force until 1776.[405] The assembly of 1705-1706 also passed a "Liberty

---

[402] Cf. Cobb, p. 446. "Frame of Government of Pennsylvania, 1696," Thorpe, V, 3070.

[403] Cf. Morison and Commager, I, 77; Cobb, pp. 446-447. "Charter and Privileges Granted by William Penn, Esq., to the Inhabitants of Pennsylvania and territories, 1701," Thorpe, V, 3077.

[404] *The Statutes at Large of Pennsylvania from 1682-1801* (XIII vols., Philadelphia: Clarence M. Busch, publisher, 1896), II, pp. 1-2, § 1 (hereafter cited *Statutes of Penna.*).

[405] For a detailed discussion of the history of the test act with reference to Quakers and Roman Catholics, cf. Cobb, pp. 447-449.

of Conscience Act."[406] The act granted to all those believing in the Trinity and in the inspiration of Scripture, and professing to live quietly under civil government, full liberty of conscience without molestation or interruption.

### C. The Statehood Period

Full religious freedom was finally granted in the Declaration of Rights of the Pennsylvania Constitution of 1776. It recognized that "all men have a natural and unalienable right to worship God according to the dictates of their own consciences and understanding."[407] The Constitution of Pennsylvania, 1790, repeated all these guarantees and explicitly said that there were to be no establishments preferred in law.[408]

At no time did Pennsylvania have a legal establishment. The policy of the early days of the colony was equal religious liberty for all, except atheists.[409] The religious intolerance which found its way into Pennsylvania was not the product of the settlers, but the work of Penn's enemies in England. Penn was partially successful in remedying the harm they inflicted upon the consciences of Pennsylvanians. Discrimination in the form of a religious test for office, which the Queen imposed upon the colony and the assembly seconded in 1705, remained until the Revolution. The Constitution of 1776 granted full and complete religious freedom to all in the State of Pennsylvania.

## *Section 3. Delaware*

### A. The Colonial Period

The three Lower Counties obtained by Penn from the Duke of

---

[406] *Statutes of Penna.*, II, 171.

[407] Thorpe, V, 3028, § 2; Churches of several denominations were incorporated after this constitution. Cf. *Statutes of Penna.*, XII, 6, 142, 182, 236, 244, 250; XIII, 12, 16, 20, 70, 130, 165, 392, 432.

[408] Thorpe, V, 3100, Art. IX, § 3. The 1790 guarantees were repeated in the 1838 Constitution. Cf. Thorpe, V, 3113.

[409] In the wide sense there was additional denial of religious liberty. Non-Christians could not hold office.

York became the Colony of Delaware.[410] The Lower Counties acquired an assembly in 1702, but Penn's Charter of Privileges remained their fundamental law and the governor of Pennsylvania was their governor.[411]

The records of Delaware show far less concern about matters of religion than the parent colony. There was a very modified form of the test act passed in 1704, and this was further modified by an act in 1719. Cobb stated that he found only one instance of discrimination against Romanists, and this was passed under pressure from England. It was an act empowering Protestant Churches and societies to receive and hold real estate.[412] The original fundamental law requirement that voters and officeholders believe in Jesus Christ remained in force after Delaware became a separate colony.

B. The Statehood Period

The Constitution of Delaware, 1776, stated "there shall be no establishment of any one religious sect in this State in preference to another."[413] Disestablishment and free exercise were clearly stated in the new Constitution of 1792, and religious tests for offices were forbidden.[414]

The writer has found three points of special significance reflected in the legal literature of the colonial period. The Toleration Act of William and Mary, 1689, effected as much intolerance in the colonies as tolerance. In Puritan Establishments and in Virginia it secured a greater breadth of freedom for Protestant dissenters, but in a number of other colonies the act provoked an intolerance and a discrimination against Roman Catholics and other dissenters hitherto non-existent or abrogated sometime prior to 1689.

Although the Puritan colonies retained some form of Estab-

---

[410] Delaware has some early history of religious matters, when it was under the jurisdiction of the Dutch Reform Government of New Netherland. Cf. Zwierlein, *Religion in New Netherlands,* Chapter IV, "Religion in New Sweden Before and After the Dutch Conquest," pp. 106-135.

[411] Morison and Commager, I, 77.

[412] Cobb, p. 452.

[413] Thorpe, I, 567.

[414] Thorpe, I, 568. This was repeated in the Constitutions of 1831 and 1897. Cf. *ibid.,* pp. 582, 600-601.

lishment beyond 1800, the general tenor of feeling among the colonists during the final quarter of the eighteenth century was for legal disestablishment. However, little legal evidence has been discovered in support of the contention that these colonists equated disestablishment with absolute separation of Church and State. On the contrary, there exists ample evidence in the constitutions, state statutes, and court practice, to demonstrate that they desired some form or union or co-operation, but less than legal establishment (except in the cases cited in Part I where legal establishment was continued after the adoption of the First Amendment to the Federal Constitution). Some manifestations of this desire are the retaining of religious tests and loyalty oaths, the tax support of Protestant ministers and teachers of religion, the support of missionaries in the Northwestern part of the United States, and various legal guarantees to safeguard the free exercise of worship by the police power of the State.[415]

The third significant point is that the colonists did not consider the right to the free exercise of worship and preaching to be an absolute right. Almost invariably the guarantee of this right, whether it was granted by a charter, an instruction, a colonial enactment, a constitution, or a statute in the seventeenth and eighteenth centuries, was conditioned by the clause "provided this exercise does not disrupt civil peace and public order," or some equivalent phrase. The State was the party competent to decide when this danger or violation existed.[416]

---

[415] For a study of religious and loyalty oaths in this country, cf. Harold M. Hyman, *To Try Men's Souls: Loyalty Tests in American History* (Berkeley, California: University of California Press, 1959).

[416] Rommen gives an excellent analysis of the form of "tolerance" extended in the established colonies: "Only against Catholics was tolerance not much exercised either in England or in the New England colonies. For these 'national' democrats, the pope was a foreign sovereign; the Catholic who recognized the pope's spiritual authority was considered a political enemy incapable of civil rights. This is understandable only if by this word 'tolerance' was meant, not a genuine freedom of conscience, but rather a practical principle in politics. Tolerance meant, therefore, adherence to religious individualism, and implied theologically the rejection of the Catholic Church, so that a Catholic adhering to an 'intolerant' dogmatic faith could not himself claim 'tolerance.'"—H. Rommen, *The State in Catholic Thought* (St. Louis: The Herder Book Co., 1950), p. 564.

## PART II

### Establishment and the Right to Preach Under the Federal Constitution

The primary purpose of this chapter is to determine the present constitutional status of the right to preach in the United States of America. A quest of this nature leads to an investigation of Supreme Court cases, because the answer lies in the Court's interpretation of the Constitution. The right to preach embraces two basic freedoms: freedom of religion and freedom of speech. These two freedoms are guaranteed in the First Amendment of the Federal Constitution by the free exercise clause and the free speech clause. To complete this inquiry into the status of the right to preach, at least a cursory consideration must be given to the "disestablishment" clause and the clause guaranteeing the right to peaceable assembly. In the final analysis, this means a study of the greater portion of the First Amendment.[1]

The substantive personal rights of freedom of religion, speech, press, and assembly were eventually protected on the federal and state levels by the absorption of the First Amendment liberties into the Fourteenth Amendment.[2] This process of absorption was

[1] For the historical background of the Constitution and the Bill of Rights consult: Merril Jensen, *The New Nation: a History of the United States during the Confederation, 1781-1789* (New York: Knopf, 1950, and Carl Van Doren, *The Great Rehearsal: the story of the making and ratifying of the Constitution of the United States* (New York: Viking Press, 1948).

[2] Edward Corwin, *The Constitution and What It Means Today* (11th ed. rev., Princeton, New Jersey: Princeton University Press, 1954), pp. 186-187—The Supreme Court in several decisions held that the first ten amendments bound only the National government, and were in no way a limitation to the powers of the States of their own independent force. Corwin cited Marshall's decision in Barron v. Balt., & Pet. 243 (1833). He also cited Warren, "The New Liberty Under the Fourteenth Amendment," *Harvard Law Review*, XXXIX (1926), 431, 436, who wrote that the courts had reaffirmed Marshall's decision of 1833 at least twenty times between 1877 and 1907. Consult also Milton R. Konvitz, *Fundamental Liberties of a Free People: Religion, Speech, Press, Assembly* (Ithaca, New York: Cornell

initiated in a most casual manner. The Supreme Court effected this far-reaching shift in point of view in Gitlow *v.* New York, 1925.[3] While upholding the conviction of Gitlow for violating a New York statute prohibiting the advocacy of criminal anarchy, the Court declared: "For the purposes we may and do presume that freedom of speech and of press—which are protected by the First Amendment from abridgment by Congress—are among the fundamental rights and 'liberties' protected by the due process clause of the Fourteenth Amendment from impairment by the States."[4]

"This dictum," Corwin commented, "became, two years later, accepted doctrine when the court invalidated a State law on the grounds that it abridged freedom of speech contrary to the due process clause of the Amendment XIV."[5] Freedom of the press was read into the due process clause of the Fourteenth Amendment in 1931.[6] Subsequent decisions brought the right to peaceable assembly and freedom of religion within the purview of the Fourteenth Amendment.[7] These Supreme Court rulings have continued to serve as the basis for much litigation involving alleged violations of personal liberties by State action. Several of these cases are considered below under the disestablishment clause, the free exercise of religion clause, the free speech clause, and the right of peaceable assembly clause.

---

University Press, 1957), pp. 34-39; John Raeburn Green, "The Bill of Rights, The Fourteenth Amendment and the Supreme Court," *Michigan Law Review,* XLVI (1948), 868; William Anderson, "The Bill of Rights, the Fourteenth Amendment, and the Liberty of Conscience," *Aspects of Liberty, Essays Presented to Robert Cushman* (Ithaca, New York: Cornell University Press, 1958), pp. 287-307; Robert J. White, "The Legal Status of the Church," *The Jurist,* I (1941), 20-49.

[3] 268 U.S. 652 (1925).

[4] Gitlow *v.* New York, 268 U.S. 652, 666 (1925).

[5] *Constitution and What It Means Today,* p. 188; Fiske *v.* Kansas, 274 U.S. 380 (1927).

[6] Near *v.* Minn., 283 U.S. 697 (1931). This case is discussed in detail later in the chapter.

[7] De Jonge *v.* Ore., 299 U.S. 353 (1937) and Cantwell *v.* Conn., 310 U.S. 296 (1940), respectively. Both of these cases are discussed in some detail during the course of this chapter.

## ARTICLE I. DISESTABLISHMENT OF RELIGION

The meaning of the First Amendment clause, "Congress shall make no law respecting an establishment of religion . . ." has bedeviled the courts since 1947.[8] Prior to this time the Court had not expounded at any great length the full meaning of these words. Two theories have vied for first position in recent court decisions. In their most digested form they are known as the "No Preference Doctrine" and the "Wall of Separation Doctrine."[9]

According to the "no preference doctrine" the clause prohibits the preferential treatment of any particular religion or sect by the government. Joseph Story (1779-1845) supported this theory in his commentary on the Constitution. The purpose of the First Amendment was not to discredit the then existing establishments of religion, he commented, but "to exclude from the National government all power to act on the subject."[10] The clause forbidding establishment prohibited Congress from preferring one denomination of the Christian faith, but it did not intend to withdraw the Christian religion as a whole from the protection of Congress. Story was of the opinion that:

> Probably at the time of the adoption of the Constitution, and of the amendment to it now under consideration, the

[8] For an earlier treatment of this matter consult: Carl Zollman, *American Church Law,* and George Torpey, *Judicial Doctrines of Religious Rights in America.* For an extensive historical treatment of both separation of Church and State and religious liberty consult: Anson Phelps Stokes, *Church and State in the United States* (3 vols., New York: Harper, 1950). Professor Mark De Wolfe Howe, professor of law in Harvard University, has compiled several cases in Church and State relations concerning Education, Police Powers, Church Corporations, Effect of Ecclesiastical Adjudication, in addition to a treatment of disestablishment in Virginia and Massachusetts in *Cases on Church and State in the United States.* Cf. also Alvin W. Johnson and Frank H. Yost, *Separation of Church and State in the United States* (Minneapolis: University of Minnesota Press, 1948).

[9] Cf. Everson *v.* Board of Education, 330 U.S. 1 (1947); McCollum *v.* Board of Education, 333 U.S. 203 (1948); Zorach *v.* Clauson, 343 U.S. 306 (1952).

[10] *The Constitution of the United States of America, Analysis and Interpretation* (ed. Edward S. Corwin, Washington, D. C.: The United States Government Printing Office, 1953), p. 758 (hereafter cited as *Constitution of the United States*).

> general if not the universal sentiment in America was, that Christianity ought to receive encouragement from the state so far as was not incompatible with the private rights of conscience and the freedom of religious worship. An attempt to level all religions, and to make it a matter of state policy to hold all in utter indifference, would have created universal disapprobation, if not universal indignation.[11]

This opinion also was supported by Cooley (1824-1898) in his *Principles of Constitutional Law,* in which he said: "It was never intended by the Constitution that the government should be prohibited from recognizing religion, . . . where it might be done without drawing any invidious distinctions between different religious beliefs, organizations, or sects."[12]

The second theory originated with Thomas Jefferson (1743-1826). He first expounded it in a letter which he addressed to a group of Baptists in Danbury, Connecticut, in 1802, in which he asserted that the purpose of the First Amendment was to build "a wall of separation between Church and State."[13] Seventy-two years later this interpretation reappeared in the Mormon Church case, in which the Court upheld the right of Congress to forbid polygamy in the territories. Chief Justice Waite (1816-1888), writing for a unanimous bench, cited Jefferson's "wall of separation" doctrine. After quoting from this letter to the Danbury Baptists, he declared: "Coming as this does from an acknowledged leader of the advocates of this measure, it may be accepted as almost an authoritative declaration of the scope and effect of the amendment thus secured."[14] Corwin notes that Jefferson expressed in his second Inaugural Address "a very different and presumably more

---

[11] The writer is compelled to agree with Story in the light of his research in the previous part on the colonies. Story, *Commentaries on the Constitution,* art. 1874 (1833) as cited by Corwin in *Constitution of the United States,* p. 759.

[12] *Principles of Constitutional Law,* pp. 224-225, 3d ed. (1898), as cited by Corwin in *Constitution of the United States,* p. 759.

[13] Cf. Saul K. Padover, *The Complete Jefferson* (New York: Tudor, 1943), pp. 518-519.

[14] Rynolds *v.* United States, 98 U.S. 145, 164 (1879).

carefully considered opinion upon the purpose of Amendment I: 'In matters of religion, I have considered that its free exercise is placed by the Constitution independent of the powers of the general government.' "[15]

William F. O'Brien points out the utter state of confusion now existing about the real mind and intent of the framers of the First Amendment. Corwin castigates Judge Rutledge (1894-1949) for his deception in his dissenting opinion in the Everson case. Leo Pfeffer disagrees with Corwin's interpretation and scolds certain authors for omitting what he considers relevant facts in the debate. Wilber B. Katz accuses Pfeffer of the same scholarship defect which he, Pfeffer, has charged against others. The writer pursues what is perhaps the more cowardly, but the most judicious, course of action in abandoning the field of the present battle, and leaving others more competent than himself to resolve the conflict. He places his feet on firmer ground by turning his attention to what the courts say the First Amendment means.[16]

The judicial meaning of the "no establishment" clause received considerable attention on February 10, 1947, when the Court handed down its decision in the Everson *v.* Board of Education case.[17] The facts of the case are as follows: A new Jersey school board, in compliance with a state statute, reimbursed the parents who had expended transportation money to send their children to public or to parochial schools. Everson challenged the right of the school board to reimburse the parents whose children attended Catholic schools. His contention was that such a procedure violated the due process clause of the Fourteenth Amendment, in so far as

---

[15] *Constitution and What It Means Today,* p. 189, note 11. This message was delivered three years after the letter to the Danbury Baptist Association. Corwin quoted from Richardson, *Messages and Papers of the Presidents,* p. 379 (ed. of 1909).

[16] The writer reports this difference of views as recorded in O'Brien, *Justice Reed and the First Amendment, The Religion Clause* (Washington, D. C.: Georgetown University Press, 1958), pp. 138-139 (hereafter cited O'Brien, *Justice Reed and the First Amendment*). Corwin outlined two basic theories in: *Constitution and What It Means Today,* pp. 188-189, and *Constitution of the United States,* pp. 758-759.

[17] 330 U.S. 1 (1947).

public taxes were being used for private purposes, viz., religious education. He entered a second contention: the New Jersey statute was a law respecting an establishment of religion.[18]

The Court upheld the statute on the ground that the school board used the money for a public purpose. The majority took the view that the New Jersey legislature had decided the public purpose was served by using the tax-raised funds to assist all children in riding to and from school.[19] No violation of the establishment clause existed because the state contributed nothing to a Church or Church school. The government merely aided the parents to get "their children, regardless of their religion, safely and expeditiously to and from accredited schools."[20]

During the course of delivering the opinion of the Court, Justice Black formulated a judicial definition of the "no establishment" clause, adopting Justice Waite's reasoning and confirming, as authoritative, Jefferson's notion of the scope of the freedom of religion clause in the First Amendment. He went even further than Waite, for he omitted the qualifying term "almost":

> The "establishment of religion clause of the First Amendment" means at least this: Neither a state nor the Federal Government can set up a church. Neither can pass laws which aid one religion, aid all religions, or prefer one religion over the other. Neither can force nor influence a person to go or to remain away from church against his will or force him to profess a belief or disbelief in any religion. No person can be punished for entertaining or professing religious beliefs or disbeliefs, for church attendance or nonattendance. No tax in any amount, large or small, can be levied to support any religious activities or institutions, whatever they be called, or whatever form they may adopt to teach or practice religion. Neither a state nor the Federal Government can, openly or secretly, participate in affairs of any religious organization or groups or *vice versa*. In the words of Jefferson, the clause against establishment of religion was intended to erect 'a wall of separation between

[18] 330 U.S. 1, 5 (1947).
[19] 330 U.S. 1, 6 (1947).
[20] 330 U.S. 1, 18 (1947).

> church and State.' Reynolds *v.* United States, *supra,* 98 U.S. at page 164." (25 L.Ed. 244.)[21]

Black concluded his opinion with the words: "The First Amendment has erected a wall between church and state. That wall must be kept high and impregnable. We could not approve the slightest breach. New Jersey has not breached it here."[22]

This case aroused a storm of criticism. One of the most outspoken critics is John Courtney Murray.[23] Father Murray, S.J., contends that the essence of the "Everson line" laid down "both by the Court and by the dissent, is that James Madison's concept of the relations between religion and government, together with the philosophy on which it rests, became in 1791 the fundamental law of the land by act of the states ratifying the First Amendment."[24] This raises two questions in Murray's mind: 1. Is this a historical fact? 2. Could it have been the historical fact? To both he replies quite flatly, no. The writer will present Murray's argument by which he seeks to substantiate his "no" to the second question.

Murray states that "for Madison . . . religion could not by law be made a concern of the commonwealth as such, deserving in any degree public recognition or aid, for the essentially theological reason that religion is of its nature a personal, private, interior matter of individual conscience, having no relevance to the public concerns of the state."[25] The state should interest itself in the freedom of religion, "as a matter of individual 'natural right' that it is bound to guarantee, and as a means to social harmony amid conflicting creeds that it is bound to protect."[26] But by Madison's own definition religion has no rank among social and civil interests

---

[21] *Ibid.,* 15, 16.

[22] Everson *v.* Board of Education, 330 U.S. 1, 18 (1947).

[23] "Law or Prepossessions," *Essays in Constitutional Law,* ed. with an introduction by Robert McCloskey (New York: Alfred A. Knopf, 1957), pp. 316-347. This essay originally appeared in *Law and Contemporary Problems,* XIV, 23.

[24] "Law or Prepossessions," *Essays in Constitutional Law,* pp. 322-323.

[25] *Ibid.,* p. 325.

[26] *Ibid.,* p. 326.

which may claim the help of government. "Legislation, therefore, whose purposes or effects would be in the slightest degree an aid to religion, would *ipso facto* be legislation for private purposes and therefore illegitimate." Religion is a completely private interest and it lies behind a wall, or as Judge Rutledge says, "the kingdom of the individual man and his God."[27] Pursuing the analogy, Murray says, "It is the single duty of government to halt its armies on the threshold of that kingdom, encircling it with legal force, to keep it (in Justice Rutledge's extraordinary phrase) absolutely 'free from sustenance, as also from other interference, by the state.' "[28] Any aid to religion is a form of political interference with what is theologically a private interest. Therefore, aid to religion is absolutely forbidden.

In Murray's analysis this is the Madisonian concept of separation of Church and State. Murray then argues:

> Its ultimate ground is a religious absolute, a sectarian idea of religion. The separation is therefore absolute in itself. And no other grounds may be assigned for its absoluteness but its theological premise. I should add too that Madison's principle of separation stands as an absolute in its own right. It need not be sustained by any functional relationship to "free exercise." It forbids all governmental aid to religion even in the demonstrable absence of any coercion of conscience, any inhibition of full religious liberty, any violation of civil equality, any disruption of social harmony. These considerations are secondary, and irrelevant to the principle in as much as it is an absolute. They prop the wall, if you will, with some flying buttresses; but the wall itself is built, not by any idea of liberty, but by an idea of religion.[29]

---

[27] *Ibid.*, p. 326, citing Everson *v.* Board of Education, 330 U.S. 1, 57-58 (1947). Murray adds in a note, "I take it that atheism is analogously the kingdom of the individual man and his Infinite Blank or Ultimate Doubt or whatever inhabits that kingdom, and has a similar sacredness."

[28] *Loc. cit.*, citing Everson *v.* Board of Education, 330 U.S. 1, 53 (1947).

[29] *Essays in Constitutional Law*, p. 326. In a note Murray rejects the "wedge argument" on the grounds that it is fallacious: 1) It begs the question: is the wall an absolute? 2) It proves too much. "Would the wedge argument be admitted, for instance, in a labor dispute or in any other case where the question is one of rights (as it is here)?" 3) "It has the same

Murray maintains that "this is the philosophy of separation advanced by the Court in the Everson case, implicitly by the Court's opinion, explicitly by the dissent, on which the Court fell back in the McCollum case."[30] Murray finds this philosophy absolutely unacceptable. It could not be the philosophy of 1791, and it cannot be read into the First Amendment in 1948: "The simple reason is that it is an irredeemable piece of sectarian dogmatism. And if there is one thing that the First Amendment forbids with resounding force it is the intrusion of a sectarian philosophy of religion into the fundamental law of the land."[31]

As Murray points out, we have a paradox that would be laughable were its consequences not so serious. The Supreme Court, in an effort to prove that "no establishment of religion" means "no aid to religion," has successfully proceeded to establish a religion —James Madison's. "In order to make separation of church and state an absolute, it united the state to a 'religion without a church' —a deistic version of fundamental Protestantism." Murray continues: "In the name of freedom of religion it decrees that the relations of the government to religion are to be controlled by the fundamental tenet of secularism—the social irrelevance of religion, its exclusion from the secular affairs of the city and its educational system, its relegation to the private forum of conscience or at best to the hushed confines of the sacristy."[32]

As a result of his personal investigation of colonial legislation, the writer is forced to agree with Father Murray that this could not have been the philosophy of the majority at the time of the adoption of the First Amendment. And if it could not have been the philosophy of that time, the sheer force of logic, as demon-

---

legal fallaciousness that Holmes recognized when he swept away Marshall's famous dictum in his Panhandle dissent: 'The power to tax is not the power to destroy while this court sits.' Panhandle Oil Co. *v.* Knox, 277 U.S. 218, at 223 (1928)."

[30] *Essays in Constitutional Law,* p. 327.

[31] *Ibid.,* p. 327. He cites part of Justice Frankfurter's opinion in the McCollum case to prove his point. Cf. *ibid.,* note 32.

[32] *Ibid.,* pp. 327-328. Cf. a more recent article by Murray: "Freedom, Responsibility and the Law," *Catholic Lawyer,* II, 214-223 (July, 1956).

strated by Murray, tells the writer that it cannot be poured into the First Amendment today.

A year later the Supreme Court, on the basis of the Everson dicta, declared a "release time" program unconstitutional.[33] A local school board in Illinois agreed to provide religious education for children attending public schools. The parents were required to sign a request card, which released the children from class to attend religious instruction given by outside teachers. These religion classes were conducted in public school classrooms during the regular school day. A religious council representing several faiths supplied the religion teachers, who had to be approved by the school superintendent and were subject to his supervision. The children or their parents selected the teacher of their religious persuasion and regular attendance records were kept. Children whose parents did not sign a request card continued with regular classes according to the secular curriculum. Terry McCollum preferred not to attend, and his mother, a professed atheist, challenged the constitutionality of the school board arrangement on the ground that it violated the no establishment clause of the First Amendment.

The Court held that this was a violation of the First Amendment made applicable to the states by the Fourteenth Amendment. Justice Black, speaking for the majority, said: "Here not only are the State's tax-supported public school buildings used for the dissemination of religious doctrine. The State also affords sectarian groups an invaluable aid in that it helps to provide pupils for their religious classes through use of the State's compulsory public school machinery. This is not separation of Church and State."[34]

A lone dissenting voice was raised in the McCollum case, which was eventually to triumph.[35] Reed's dissent was of considerable length, but perhaps the most significant passage is the one in which he indicates that the main supporter of the First Amend-

---

[33] McCollum *v.* Board of Education, 333 U.S. 203 (1948).

[34] *Ibid.,* 333 U.S. 203, 212 (1948).

[35] For a thorough discussion and evaluation of Reed's dissent consult: O'Brien, *Justice Reed and the First Amendment,* pp. 130-153.

ment by no means interpreted it as prohibiting Congress from encouraging religion:

> The phrase "an establishment of religion" may have been intended by Congress to be aimed only at a state church. When the First Amendment was pending in Congress in substantially the present form, "Mr. Madison said, he apprehended the meaning of the words to be, that Congress should not establish a religion, and enforce the legal observance of it by law, nor compel men to worship God in any manner contrary to their conscience." Passing years, however, have brought about acceptance of a broader meaning, although never until today, I believe, has this Court widened its interpretation to any such degree as holding that recognition of the interest of our nation in religion, through the granting, to qualified representatives of the principal faiths, of opportunity to present religion as an optional, extracurricular subject during released school time in public school buildings, was equivalent to an establishment of religion.[36]

Reed pointed out how daily practice was at variance with the majority's decision. Congress has a chaplain who invokes divine blessings for each day of the session. From the early days of our nation the armed forces have had chaplains, who conduct public services, each according to his own liturgy, on government owned property dedicated to the services of religion. The District of Columbia schools have opening exercises with Bible reading and the Lord's prayer.[37] "Though he convinced none of his colleagues on the Bench in 1948," O'Brien comments, "his arguments were calculated to cause embarrassment, soul searching, and . . . ultimately partial conversion of the Court to his persuasion."[38]

Reed's dissent triumphed in the 1952 case of Zorach *v.* Clauson.[39]

---

[36] *Ibid.*, 333 U.S. 203, 244 (1948).

[37] *Ibid.*, 333 U.S. 203, 253, 254. Cf. also 255, which discusses compulsory Church attendance at the Naval and Military Academies.

[38] *Justice Reed and the First Amendment*, p. 14. Reed also mentioned the compulsory Church attendance regulation at the Naval and Military Academies.—333 U.S. 203, 255.

[39] 343 U.S. 306 (1952). The groundwork for this victory was laid in a decision rendered by the Court some weeks earlier in Doremus *v.* Board

The Supreme Court by a six to three vote sustained a New York City "release time" program. The statute permitted the public schools to release the children during school hours, upon the written request of their parents, to attend religious instructions conducted off public school premises. Those who were not released remained in school.

Justice Douglas, delivering the opinion of the Court, reduced the issues in the case to two: ". . . whether New York by this system has either prohibited the 'free exercise' of religion, or has made a law 'respecting an establishment of religion' within the meaning of the First Amendment."[40] To the question of free exercise he replied: "It is obtuse reasoning to inject any issue of the 'free exercise' of religion into the present case. No one is forced to go to the religious classroom and no religious exercise or instruction is brought to the classroom of the public schools. A student need not take religious instruction. He is left to his own desires as to the manner or time of his religious devotions, if any."[41] Douglas referred to the charge that coercion was employed to force public school children to attend these classes. He retorted that no such evidence was in the record to support such a conclusion. If there were coercion, it would be an entirely different case.

Taking up the second issue, the Justice commented: ". . . we do not see how New York by this type of 'released time' program has made a law respecting an establishment of religion within the meaning of the First Amendment."[42] Douglas supported this observation by launching into a discussion of the philosophy underlying the First Amendment:

> There cannot be the slightest doubt that the First Amendment reflects the philosophy that Church and State should be separated. And so far as interference with the

---

of Education, 342 U.S. 429-435 (1952) 5 N.J. 435, 7 A 2d 880 (1950). For a development of this point consult O'Brien, *Justice Reed and the First Amendment*, pp. 161-170.

[40] Zorach *v.* Clauson, 343 U.S. 306, 310 (1952).

[41] *Ibid.*, 343 U.S. 306, 311 (1952).

[42] *Ibid.*, 343 U.S. 306, 312 (1952).

> "free exercise" of religion and an "establishment" of religion are concerned, the separation must be complete and unequivocal. The First Amendment within the scope of its coverage permits no exception; the prohibition is absolute.[43]

However, he was quick to draw a significant distinction, which only Justice Reed had perceived in the Everson case: "The First Amendment, however, does not say that in every and all respects there shall be a separation of Church and State. Rather, it studiously defines the manner, the specific ways, in which there shall be no concert or union or dependency one on the other."[44]

All this is a matter of common sense, the Court says, because to hold the contrary would be ridiculous. The majority opinion employs a *reductio ad absurdum* argument to demonstrate this contention: "Otherwise the state and religion would be aliens to each other—hostile, suspicious, and even unfriendly. Churches could not be required to pay even property tax. Municipalities would not be permitted to render police or fire protection to religious groups. Policemen who helped parishioners in their places of worship would violate the Constitution." This farce would extend even to the courtroom and the Congress: "Prayers in our legislative halls; the appeals to the Almighty in messages of the Chief Executive; the proclamations making Thanksgiving Day a holiday; 'so help me God' in our courtroom oaths—these and all other references to the Almighty that run through our laws, our public rituals, our ceremonies, would be flouting the First Amendment."[45] If the contrary view were valid, so that the First Amendment spelled out separation and opposition, this very Bench would be guilty of violating the Constitution it has sworn to uphold, for as Douglas says, "A fastidious atheist or agnostic could even object to the supplication with which the Court opens each session: 'God save the United States and this Honorable Court.' "[46] The majority believed that the Court would be forced to "press the

---

[43] *Ibid.,* 342 U.S. 306, 312 (1952).

[44] *Loc. cit.*

[45] *Ibid.,* 342 U.S. 306, 312, 313 (1952).

[46] *Ibid.,* 343 U.S. 306, 313 (1952).

concept of separation of Church and State to these extremes to condemn the present law on constitutional grounds. The nullification of this law would have wide and profound effects."[47]

The Court then touched upon the heart of the matter, and this dictum has echoed and reechoed across the land, producing salutary effects:

> We are a religious people whose institutions presuppose a Supreme Being. We guarantee the freedom to worship as one chooses. We make room for as wide a variety of beliefs and creeds as the spiritual needs of man deem necessary. We sponsor an attitude on the part of the government that shows no partiality to any one group and lets each flourish according to the zeal of its adherents and the appeal of its dogma. When the state encourages religious instruction or cooperates with religious authorities by adjusting the schedule of public events to sectarian needs, it follows the best of our traditions. For it then respects the religious nature of our people and accommodates the public service to their spiritual needs. To hold that it may not would be to find in the Constitution a requirement that the government show a callous indifference to religious groups. That would be preferring those who believe in no religion over those who do believe.[48]

In their annual statement the Catholic bishops of the United States usually turn their attention to current problems. The McCollum decision of 1948 caused such a dismay among intelligent and hard-thinking Americans that the bishops felt obliged to

---

[47] *Ibid.,* 313. The Court gave additional examples: A Catholic student could not be excused during school hours to attend a holyday mass; nor a Jew to participate in Yom Kippur; nor a Protestant for a family baptismal ceremony in the afternoon.

[48] Zorach *v.* Clauson, 343 U.S. 306, 313-314 (1952). The opinion went on to say that the constitution does not require the government to be hostile to religion and throw its weight against efforts to widen the scope of religious influence. It cannot compel anyone to join a sect, nor can the government favor one sect over the other, nor make religious observance compulsory. "But it can close its doors or suspend its operations as to those who want to repair to their religious sanctuary for worship or instruction. No more than that is undertaken here."

discuss the matter.[49] Arguing from the intent of the legislator, the bishops reasoned that establishment of religion in the First Amendment meant "no preferment of one religion over another by the federal government—at the same time no interference by the federal government in the Church-State relations of the individual states."[50]

They expressed the hope "that the novel interpretation of the First Amendment recently adopted by the Supreme Court [in the McCollum case] will in due process be revised." The bishops entertained the deep conviction "that for the sake of both good citizenship and religion there should be a reaffirmation of our original American tradition of free co-operation between government and religious bodies—co-operation involving no special privilege to any group and no restriction on the religious liberty of any citizen."[51] Four years later the bishops witnessed their fond hope realized, as the Court reversed itself and once again returned to the traditional doctrine of co-operation between government and religion.

Konvitz has coined a felicitous phrase which succinctly states the present mind of the Court: "The Principle as a Rule of Reason, or Co-operative Separation." In these cases, he commented, the Court upheld the principle of separation, but only a minority of the Justices "interpret the principle in absolute terms and apply it as to bar any form of state aid to religion." The majority of the Court

---

[49] "The Christian in Action, November 21, 1948," *Our Bishops Speak, 1919-1951* (ed. by Raphael M. Huber, Milwaukee: Bruce Publishing Co., 1952), pp. 149-153.

[50] *Ibid.*, pp. 152-153.

[51] *Ibid.*, p. 153. The bishops expressed their opinion on the content of the no establishment clause in Jefferson's metaphor a few paragraphs earlier, when they said: "This metaphor of Jefferson's [the wall of separation between Church and State] specifies nothing except that there shall be no "established Church," no state religion. All the rest of the content depends on the letter of the law that sets it up and can in the concrete imply anything from the impartial co-operation between government and free religious bodies (as in Holland and traditionally in our own country) all the way down to bitter persecution of religion (as in France at the turn of the century). As was pointedly remarked in a dissenting opinion: 'A rule of law cannot be drawn from a metaphor.' "—*Ibid.*, p. 152.

have now "whittled down the principle to a point where it has become a rule of reason."[52]

Theoretically the members of the Court, so Konvitz maintains, adhere to the principle of separation; "practically they tend in the direction of the principle of co-operation. They try to steer a middle course, but a middle course between separation and co-operation can only mean—co-operation." However, he warns that here is "a significant difference between the all-out co-operation urged by some churchmen and the restrained co-operation approved by these Justices of the Supreme Court. The latter position may be spoken of as 'co-operative separation.' "[53]

The new trend established by the Zorack case is one of *co-operation*. What has been the impact of this new formula? Frank J. Sorauf recently undertook a study to answer this question.[54] It is impossible to reduplicate here the findings of his investigation; the writer will restrict his considerations to stating some of Sorauf's conclusions:

> 1. Initially, the precedent such as Zorach *v.* Clauson legalizes certain policies within the states, and interested parties and officials of the state apply the precedent to identical or similar programs. This much is the immediate and intended result of the Court's action, and it can be measured in terms of the growth of the program.[55]
> 2. In effect, the Zorach precedent represents a continuation and extension, rather than a resolution, of conflicts in the arena of church-state relations. . . . Released time programs are sanctioned and grow modestly with greatly diminished opposition, and their proponents take a cue from Zorach to press for new policies in the area of lenience the Court appears to

[52] *Fundamental Liberties of a Free People,* p. 66.

[53] *Loc. cit.*

[54] "Zorach *v.* Clauson: The Impact of a Supreme Court Decision," *The American Political Science Review,* LIII, 777-791 (September, 1959).

[55] *Ibid.,* p. 790. From pages 782-784 he analyzes the impact on the release time programs and concludes: ". . . the impact of Zorach on local policy decisions has been a tonic to the movement, although it has hardly revolutionized the pattern of religious education."

open up in the decision. So a decision such as this . . . creates a popular and constitutional climate which encourages new goals and further innovations in aid of religion, thereby leading to new test cases. . . .[56]

3. Sorauf found evidence of both the McCollum and the Zorach rulings being ignored by the populace and by some courts.[57]
4. Finally, the analysis of the impact of Zorach *v.* Clauson illustrates once again that the doctrines of sociological jurisprudence cut two ways. Doubtless the Court felt forced by the prevailing values to retreat in the Zorach case from its earlier absolutist position on the separation of church and state. But in so accommodating the mores of the times, it has created a symbol and an endorsement—the Zorach precedent—that it is at the moment reshaping and molding the very values which the Court will have to attend to in later decisions.[58]

Zorach *v.* Clauson and the Everson and McCollum cases clearly show the problem a court is faced with in trying to formulate an adequate standard to apply to concrete cases. The Supreme Court has been grappling with this same problem in its efforts to arrive at a standard which will protect the liberty of free speech and

---

[56] *Ibid.,* p. 791. Cf. also *ibid.,* pp. 787-790.

[57] *Ibid.,* pp. 790-791.

[58] *Ibid.,* p. 791. The writer has a question for Sorauf. Did the "mores" of the times change so appreciably from 1948 to 1952 as to cause the Court to do an "about face"? It seems to the writer that the so called "mores" were essentially the same in 1948 and 1952. The only thing that changed in the McCollum case and the Zorach case was the measuring rod. As Konvitz so correctly observed, the Court returned to a rule of reason in the Zorach case. The writer holds no great love for some of the tenets of the School of Sociological Jurisprudence, but if they manage to arrive at a sound, or at least a constructive decision, despite the shortcomings in their jurisprudence, fine. The rule of reason, which the Zorach Court has attempted to apply, ultimately is rooted not in sociological jurisprudence, but in natural law jurisprudence. To avoid any misunderstanding, the writer wishes to make it clear that he agrees with Sorauf's judgment that "sociological jurisprudence cuts two ways." Happy will be the day when the Court adopts a natural law jurisprudence in which the principles are absolute and the application of these principles adjusts with the varying factual situations of changing times.

guard against the abuse of license, which at times masquerades under the guise of liberty.

### ARTICLE II. PROBLEM OF A STANDARD

Whenever freedom of speech, and especially speech associated with the free exercise of worship, comes into conflict with the claims of the police power of the State, there is a very delicate problem of a standard by which the relative value of one may be weighed against the demands of the other.[59] In an attempt to solve this problem, the Supreme Court in 1919 applied the "clear and present danger" doctrine. This norm requires that, before some utterance may be penalized by the government, it must ordinarily have occurred in such circumstances or have been of such a nature as to create a clear and present danger that would bring about substantive evils which the government is competent to prevent. Mr. Justice Holmes (1841-1935), expressing the opinion of a unanimous court, formulated this doctrine:

> The question in every case is whether the words are used in such circumstances and are of such a nature as to create a clear and present danger that they will bring about the substantive evils that Congress has the right to prevent. It is a question of proximity and degree.[60]

The principle embodied in this formula has become the measuring rod for allowing state and federal interference in the areas of free speech, press, assembly, and religious liberty.[61] Final judgment as to whether these conditions exist is left to the Supreme Court.[62]

---

[59] For a treatment of the history of this problem consult: Konvitz, *Fundamentals Liberties of a Free People,* pp. 275-341. Cf. also Corwin, *Constitution and What It Means Today,* pp. 194-196.

[60] Schenck *v.* United States, 249 U.S. 47, 52 (1919).

[61] Cf. Abrams *v.* U.S. 250 U.S. 616 (1919); Debs *v.* United States, 249 U.S. 211 (1919); Bridges *v.* California, 314 U.S. 252 (1941); Douglas *v.* Jeanette, 319 U.S. 157 (1943); Thomas *v.* Collins, 323 U.S. 516 (1945). For a treatment of the standard between 1919 and 1948 consult: Francis J. Powers, *Religious Liberty and the Police Power of the State* (Washington, D. C.: The Catholic University Press, 1948), pp. 137-157 (hereafter cited *Religious Liberty and the Police Power*).

[62] Cf. Whitney *v.* California, 274 U.S. 357 (1927); Fiske *v.* Kansas, 274 U.S. 380 (1927); and, in general, the cases cited or discussed in this section

In the Schenck case the clear and present danger standard was applied to situations in which the police power sought to curtail utterances designed to overthrow the government, or utterances which threatened serious and proximate injury to the state itself. Justice Holmes attempted to apply the Schenck test of clear and present danger to the Abrams case, in which the utterances of the defendants advocating a munitions' slowdown were alleged to have created a clear and present danger of substantive evil. Holmes was unsuccessful, for the majority of the Bench refused to adopt his opinion.[63]

In the famous Gitlow case of 1925 the Court did not appeal to the clear and present danger doctrine; it looked to the constitutionality of the statute rather than to the immediate effect of the specific utterance:

> In other words, when the legislative body has determined generally, in the constitutional exercise of its discretion, that the utterances of a certain kind involve such danger of substantive evil that they may be punished, the question whether any specific utterance coming within the prohibited class is likely, in and of itself, to bring about the substantive evil, is not open to consideration. It is sufficient that the statute itself be constitutional and that the use of the language comes within its prohibition.[64]

From this section and other areas of the dicta it is evident that the Court adopted the common law test of dangerous tendency, rather than clear and present danger. The fact that the Communist manifesto circulated by Gitlow had a bad tendency was sufficient to sustain the conviction of the lower court.

Two years later the case of Whitney *v.* California was decided by the Court and the majority refused to apply the clear and present danger standard. Miss Whitney had been convicted of

---

and the two succeeding sections of Part II. For a contrast between the operation of this clear and present danger rule and the common law rule consult: Corwin, *Constitution of the United States*, pp. 772-773.

[63] 250 U.S. 616 (1919).

[64] 268 U.S. 652, 670 (1925).

violating a California Criminal Syndicalism Act. Justice Sanford (1865-1930) delivered the opinion of the Court, which found Whitney guilty as charged. The pertinent provisions of the Act are:

> Section 1. The term "criminal syndicalism" as used in this act is hereby defined as any doctrine or precept advocating, teaching or aiding and abetting the commission of crime, sabotage (which word is hereby defined as meaning wilful and malicious physical damage or injury to physical property), or unlawful acts of force and violence or unlawful methods of terrorism as a means of accomplishing a change in industrial ownership or control, or effecting any political change.
>
> Section 2. Any person who: . . . 4. Organizes or assists in organizing, or is or knowingly becomes a member of, any organization, society, group or assemblage of persons organized or assembled to advocate, teach or aid or abet criminal syndicalism . . . is guilty of felony and punishable by imprisonment.[65]

The Communist Party in California, which Miss Whitney helped to organize, was formed to advocate, teach, aid and abet criminal syndicalism as defined in the Act. She was a member of the Executive Committee, but she claimed not to approve unlawful means. However, she never dissociated herself from the Communist Labor Party, nor did she relinquish her position on the Committee.

Sanford, during the course of his opinion, held that "what the legislature has prohibited" is the test. The State through its legislative body declared "that to knowingly be a member, or to become a member of, or assist in the organization of an association to advocate, teach, aid and abet crimes or unlawful acts of force, violence or terrorism as a means of accomplishing industrial or political changes, involves such a danger to the public peace and security to the State, that these should be penalized in the exercise

---

[65] Whitney *v.* California, 274 U.S. 357, 359-360 (1927).

of police power."[66] "That determination," he continued, "must be given great weight."

The Court was unable to find any unconstitutionality in this State statute or in its application to this case: "The essence of the offense denounced by the Act is the combining with others in an association for the accomplishment of the desired ends and the use of criminal and unlawful means. It partakes of the nature of criminal conspiracy. . . . That such united and joint action involves even greater danger to public peace and security than isolated utterances and acts of individuals, is clear."[67] The Court did not look to the clear and present danger standard, but rather to the "utterance and bad tendency" doctrine.

Justice Brandeis (1856-1941) wrote a concurring opinion in which Holmes joined. Brandeis restated the clear and present danger standard so as to include the intent to create the danger. The rights of free speech and assembly are fundamental, but not in their nature absolute. "Their exercise is subject to restriction, if the particular restriction proposed is required to protect the State from destruction or from serious injury, political, economic or moral. That the necessity which is essential to be a valid restriction does not exist unless speech would produce, or is intended to produce, a clear and imminent danger of some substantive evil which the State constitutionally may seek to prevent has been settled. See Schenck *v.* United States, 249 U.S. 47, 52."[68]

If Miss Whitney had only been a common member, the clear and present danger standard probably would have been applied. But since she was a high official in the organization she fell under the statute, and hence under the Whitney test—the "utterance and bad tendency" doctrine.

Ten years later the Supreme Court returned to the clear and present danger doctrine and applied it in its original connotation —a threatened danger to the State.[69] The invalidation of a negro Communist's conviction for the dissemination of inflammatory

---

[66] 274 U.S. 357, 371 (1927).
[67] 274 U.S. 357, 371, 372 (1927).
[68] Whitney *v.* California, 274 U.S. 357, 373 (1927).
[69] Herndon *v.* Lowry, 301 U.S. 242 (1937).

political literature rested mainly upon a denial of due process, yet the Court did appeal to the clear and present danger doctrine. In the words of Corwin, ". . . a narrowly divided Court drew a distinction between the prohibition by law of specific utterances which the legislators have determined have a 'dangerous tendency' to produce substantive evil and the finding by a jury to that effect, and on this basis reversed the conviction of a communist organizer . . . , with the intimation that, were it left to a jury to determine whether particular utterances are unlawful, the test of the clear and present danger must be applied."[70]

The clear and present danger standard has been mentioned or relied upon by the Court in several decisions since the Herndon case. The original connotation of the doctrine concerned a danger threatening the State. Beginning with the Thornhill *v.* Alabama and the Cantwell *v.* Connecticut decisions in 1940 the doctrine embraced a wider meaning.[71]

The Thornhill case declared a state anti-picketing statute invalid, and formulated the principle that peaceful picketing is a legitimate method of communicating information to the public in a labor dispute. In this instance there was no direct threat to the State, and yet the Court applied the clear and present danger rule. The majority found that the state's restraint of the right of free expression in this labor dispute was illegal on the ground that "the danger to an industrial concern is neither so serious nor so imminent as to justify the sweeping proscriptions of freedom of discussion" contained in the Act. This decision implicitly acknowledged the right of the State to employ its police power to restrict the free exercise of expression in a situation other than when a threat to the State itself is involved.[72]

The Cantwell decision maintained that the activities of Jehovah's Witnesses in a predominantly Catholic neighborhood were legitimate, because they did not constitute a clear and present danger

[70] *Constitution of the United States,* p. 777. Whitney *v.* California, 301 U.S. 242, 261-263 (1937) ; cf. also Powers, *Religious Liberty and the Police Power,* p. 139.

[71] Thornhill *v.* Alabama, 310 U.S. 88 (1940) ; Cantwell *v.* Connecticut, 310 U.S. 296 (1940) ; also Bridges *v.* California, 314 U.S. 252 (1941).

[72] 310 U.S. 88, 105-106.

of a common law breach of the peace. This case extended the principle of valid state restriction of the freedom of expression. The Court acknowledged the right of the State to exercise its police power to restrain such expression when a "clear and present danger of a riot, disorder, interference with traffic upon the streets, or the immediate threat to public safety, peace or order appears. . . ."[73]

In an attempt to solve some of the difficult cases involving state restrictions of free expression in religious matters, the courts, as Powers commented, have "relied heavily on the readily available, extensive and fairly well established formula of clear and present danger."[74] Religious expression had to present a serious and proximate threat to the welfare of the community before it could be curtailed.[75] Clear and present danger has not been the exclusive test for deciding the validity of police action in the area of religious expression. A supplementary standard has been adopted, which Powers termed "the principle of avoidability of clash."[76]

C. W. Summers has formulated a descriptive definition of the principle of avoidability of clash which Powers accepted:

> A religious activity is beyond the limit of judicial protection only when it creates a substantive danger which is extremely serious and the imminence of which is extremely high, and when the danger cannot be avoided by some other method which will leave religious freedom unrestrained.[77]

---

[73] Cantwell *v.* Connecticut, 310 U.S. 296, 308 (1940).

[74] Powers, *Religious Liberty and the Police Power,* p. 140.

[75] To illustrate this point, Powers cited Barnette *v.* West Virginia State Board of Education, 47 F. Supp. (D.C., W.Va.) 251 (1942):

> To justify the overriding of religious scruples, however, there must be a clear justification thereof in the necessities of national or community life. Like the right of free speech, it is not to be overborne by the police power, unless its exercise presents a clear and present danger to the community.

[76] *Religious Liberty and the Police Power,* p. 141.

[77] C. W. Summers, "The Sources and Limits of Religious Freedom," *Illinois Law Review,* XLI (1946), 79; Powers, *Religious Liberty and the Police Power,* p. 141. For additional discussion of this doctrine and its application in concrete cases cf. Summers, *art. cit.,* pp. 76-79, and Powers, *op. cit.,* pp. 141-142.

The importance of this supplementary test is that "restrictions of fundamental constitutional liberties will not be upheld if any other means of avoiding a clash between public order and the exercise of freedom in question are available."[78]

Konvitz made some significant observations about the Thornhill and Cantwell cases.[79] In the Thornhill case Justice Murphy (1890-1949) cited the opinions of Holmes in the Schenck and Abrams cases. In the Cantwell case Justice Roberts (1875-1955) implicitly relied upon Herndon and Thornhill for his conclusion: ". . . in the absence of a statute narrowly drawn to define and punish specific conduct as constituting a clear and present danger to a substantial interest of the State, the petitioner's communication, considered in the light of the constitutional guarantees, raised no such clear and present menace to public peace and order as to render him liable to conviction."[80] The Cantwell decision was a unanimous one, as was the Schenck case of 1919, which first enunciated the clear and present danger formula that served as basis for the Cantwell test. Speaking of the formula's dormant existence, Konvitz remarked:

> Thus twenty-one years passed between the first acceptance, if one may call it that, of the doctrine by a unanimous Court—a very uneven career, to say the least, for a constitutional doctrine—and in both the *Thornhill* and *Cantwell,* unlike *Schenck,* the decision was for the defendants.[81]

To plot the course of the clear and present danger standard during the next eleven years would be for a layman a nightmare. This sentiment is shared by Konvitz, who prefers to phrase it this way: "Between the *Cantwell* and the *Dennis* cases the doctrine wove itself into and out of majority and dissenting opinions. Only the specialist can have the patience to follow the path of the doctrine in detail in the intermediate cases."[82] These years witnessed

[78] Powers, *Religious Liberty and the Police Power,* p. 141.

[79] *Fundamental Liberties of a Free People,* pp. 304-305.

[80] Cantwell *v.* Connecticut, 310 U.S. 296, 311 (1940).

[81] *Fundamental Liberties of a Free People,* p. 304.

[82] *Ibid.,* p. 305.

the development of the "preferred position" doctrine. As Corwin so cleverly described the situation: "Then suddenly in 1940, the stone rejected of the builders suddenly appeared at the head of the column, and along with it the further tenet that freedom of speech and press occupied 'a preferred position' in the scale of constitutional values."[83]

The "preferred position" school of thought claimed that Holmes definitely intended to supplant the reasonable-man test by the clear and present danger formula whenever legislative enactments invaded the field of civil liberties. The reasonable-man test was still appropriate for other fields, but where the freedoms of the First Amendment were at stake, the Court had to hold itself and the legislature to a higher standard.[84]

According to Pritchett, Justice Stone (1872-1946) is usually credited with the invention of the concept of the "preferred position" in 1938.[85] The precise phrase "preferred position" was apparently employed by Justice Stone in his dissent in Jones *v.* Opelika.[86] The next year, as Pritchett noted, Justice Douglas re-

---

[83] *Constitution and What It Means Today,* p. 198.

[84] Pritchett, *Civil Liberties and the Vinson Court,* pp. 32-33. The reasonableman theory: ". . . legislative conclusions embodied in the statutes must be upheld by the courts if there is any basis on which a 'reasonable man' could have reached the same conclusion as the legislature."—*Ibid.,* p. 28. Justice Frankfurter was a sharp opponent of those who sought to expand the clear and present danger standard beyond the reasonable-man rule to a "preferred position" status. Pritchett summarized his arguments under three points: "1. that the test was being used for the purpose other than Holmes intended—namely, to determine the constitutionality of legislation; 2. that it was being applied in much different areas than Holmes contemplated, including contempt of court proceedings and violation of petty police regulations; and 3. that the *spirit* of its use was much different than Holmes would have approved."—*Ibid.,* p. 31. Cf. also Konvitz, *Fundamental Liberties of a Free People,* p. 305, for a discussion of Frankfurter's dissenting opinions in this matter.

[85] *Civil Liberties and the Vinson Court,* p. 33.

[86] 316 U.S. 584, 608 (1942): The First Amendment is not confined to safeguarding freedom of speech and freedom of religion against discriminatory attempts to wipe them out. On the contrary the Constitution, by virtue of the First and Fourteenth Amendments, has put those freedoms in a preferred position. Their commands are not restricted to cases where the

stated this opinion for the majority of the Court in Murdock *v.* Pennsylvania, which overruled Jones *v.* Opelika: "Freedom of press, freedom of speech, freedom of religion are in a preferred position."[87] The preferred position standard was adopted in a number of subsequent cases.[88]

Pritchett synthesized the various standards as follows:

> The reasonable-man test placed the burden of proof of unconstitutionality on any person attacking a legislative conclusion. The clear-and-present danger test shifted the burden of proof to the defenders of any legislation which limited First Amendment freedoms. The preferred-position argument reinforced the clear-and-present danger test and supplied its reason for being.[89]

A landmark decision was made in 1951 in the Dennis case.[90] Eleven Communists were indicted on charges of conspiracy by teaching and organization under the Smith Act of 1940. There were no overt acts other than teaching and advocation. These eleven persons had organized clubs, schools, etc., to teach and advocate the overthrow of the government.

The Court was divided on whether the Gitlow or the Schenck ruling should be the standard. The majority opinion delivered by Justice Vinson (1890-1953) adopted the compromise ruling formulated by the lower court. The clear and present danger standard of Schenck was modified to "clear and probable danger." The new test was to be "grave and probable danger."

Judge Hand of the Circuit Court held that the first and most important issue was "whether the evidence was sufficient to sup-

---

protected privilege is sought out for attack. They extend at least to every form of taxation which, because it is a condition of the exercise of the privilege, is capable of being used to control or suppress it.

[87] 319 U.S. 105, 115 (1943); *Civil Liberties and the Vinson Court,* p. 35. The Court declared that the non-discriminatory nature of the ordinance was immaterial and could not save it.

[88] Prince *v.* Massachusetts, 321 U.S. 158 (1944); Follett *v.* Town of McCormick, 321 U.S. 573 (1944); Marsh *v.* Alabama, 326 U.S. 501 (1946); Saia *v.* New York, 334 U.S. 558 (1948).

[89] *Civil Liberties and the Vinson Court,* p. 36.

[90] Dennis *et al. v.* United States, 341 U.S. 494 (1951).

port the jury's verdict that the defendants were guilty of the crime charged in the indictment?"[91] On this issue of fact, the court found that the government had clearly established that the defendants made concerted efforts to advocate and teach the overthrow and destruction of the government by forceful and violent means.

The second question entertained by Hand was: Can such activities be penalized without an abridging of the First Amendment?[92] Hand believed that they could be, and he adopted a middle of the road position between Gitlow and Schenck. The new test was to be "a clear and probable danger."[93]

All the essential points made by Judge Hand were adopted by Chief Justice Vinson.[94] Vinson firmly believed that the Court was faced with the problem of applying the clear and present danger test to particular circumstances and of deciding the precise meaning of this phrase. "Obviously," he reasoned, "the words cannot mean that before the Government may act, it must wait until the ***putsch*** is about to be executed, the plans have been laid and the signal is awaited."[95] Nor do chances of success enter into the question: "Certainly an attempt to overthrow the Government by force, even though doomed from the outset because of inadequate numbers or power of the revolutionists, is a sufficient evil for Congress to prevent."[96] Vinson concluded that the phrase as interpreted by Judge Hand was the interpretation acceptable to the majority of the Court:

> Chief Judge Leonard Hand, writing for the majority below, interpreted the phrase as follows: "In each case [courts] must ask whether the gravity of the 'evil,' discounted by its improbability, justifies such invasion of

---

[91] Konvitz, *Fundamental Liberties of a Free People,* pp. 309-310.

[92] It is significant to note that the particular section of the Smith Act under discussion in this case is directed at advocacy, not discussion.

[93] Cf. Konvitz, *Fundamental Liberties of Free People,* pp. 311-314, for a discussion of Hand's opinion.

[94] Justices Reed, Burton, and Minton (1890- ) concurred and joined with Vinson. Clark did not participate in the case. Frankfurter wrote a concurring opinion, as did Jackson. Black and Douglas dissented.

[95] Dennis *et al., v.* United States, 341 U.S. 494, 509 (1951).

[96] *Ibid.,* 341 U.S. 494, 509 (1951).

> free speech as is necessary to avoid the danger." 183 F. 2d at 212. We adopt this statement of the rule. As articulated by Chief Judge Hand, it is as succinct and inclusive as any other we might devise at this time. It takes into consideration those factors which we deem relevant, and relates their significances. More we cannot expect from words.[97]

In Corwin's opinion, Vinson's final position seems to be that, after all, the question is one for judicial discretion:

> When facts are found that establish the violation of a statute the protection against conviction afforded by the First Amendment is a matter of law. The doctrine that there must be a clear and present danger of a substantive evil that Congress has a right to prevent is a judicial rule to be applied as a matter of law by the courts.[98]

Black and Douglas dissented. They clung to the clear and present danger formula. Freedom of expression is wrong only when the danger is both clear and imminent. In Corwin's opinion "both dissenters, in fact, ignore the conspiracy element" of the case.[99]

What is the status of the "clear and present danger" formula in the light of the Dennis decision? Corwin attempts to answer this question in his *Constitution and What It Means Today*:[100]

> It probably can be safely said, on the basis of the Dennis holding, that the "clear and present danger" formula will never be successfully invoked in behalf of persons shown to have conspired to incite to a breach of a federal law. On the other hand, as Justice Jackson suggests, the formula may still be applicable in cases es-

---

[97] *Ibid.*, 341 U.S. 494, 510 (1951).

[98] *Constitution of the United States*, p. 797. Corwin cited Dennis *et al. v.* United States, 341 U.S. 494, 513 (1951).

[99] *Constitution and What It Means Today*, p. 801. This work of Corwin's has a treatment of the clear and present danger standard under topic headings such as Public Morals, Picketing, Contempt of Court, etc., in addition to a historical development of the doctrine.—*Ibid.*, pp. 773-801.

[100] Page 200.

> sentially trivial, and in cases where the intent of the speaker is innocent or ambiguous, but other circumstances create a real danger of violence or substantive evil.[101]

Corwin's final remark in this connection was: "The common law, properly charged, would probably do quite as well in such cases without an assist from 'clear and present danger.' "

The clear and present danger test has had a strange existence. Justice Holmes first formulated it in the Schenck case of 1919, and there it had a restrictive application. The formula referred only to a substantive evil threatening the State. The majority of the Court did not adopt this standard again for several years. During the interim the Bench applied a different test—the "bad tendency" doctrine.[102]

The dormant doctrine was revived in 1937 in Herndon *v.* Lowry and applied with its original connotation—a threatened danger to the State. Three years later the clear and present danger formula was expanded not only to encompass a danger of harm to the State, but also to restrain freedom of expression when it constituted a clear and present danger of riot, interference with traffic regulations, or an immediate threat to safety, peace or order.

For determining the validity of police action in the area of religious expression, a subsidiary standard was added—the principle of avoidability of a clash. Under this supplementary norm restrictions of fundamental liberties would not be upheld, if some other means was available to avoid the clash between public order and the exercise of freedom.

The nineteen forties witnessed the development of a "preferred position" for the liberties guaranteed in the First Amendment. This meant more than "reasonable" protection. The reasonable

---

[101] Cf. 341 U.S. 494, at 568-569 (1951). *Constitution and What It Means Today,* p. 200.

[102] The Supreme Court utilized this in the Gitlow case of 1925. Two years later in the Whitney *v.* California case the majority looked to the "utterance and bad tendency" doctrine. In this same case Brandeis and Holmes restated the clear and present danger standard, so that it embraced the intent to create a danger, i.e., a clear and imminent danger of some substantive evil which the State is constitutionally empowered to prevent.

test placed the burden of proof of unconstitutionality upon the party attacking the legislative conclusion. The clear and present danger test shifted the burden of proof to the defenders of any legislative enactment which limited the First Amendment freedoms. The preferred position reinforced the clear and present danger standard.

Nineteen forty-nine and the early nineteen fifties marked the return to the reasonable protection formula for the four freedoms, e.g., Beauharnais *v.* Illinois, although the Court has not completely abandoned its protective role.[103] The Dennis case of 1951 reflected the conservative spirit being ushered in during this period. It proposed the "clear and probable danger" test. However, the formula of clear and present danger may still be employed as the standard in trivial cases, or when the intent of the speaker is innocent or ambiguous, but circumstances generate a real danger of violence or substantive evil.

The application of these tests will be seen more clearly in the following two sections which consider the police power of the State and freedom of expression under two aspects—prior restraint and subsequent punishment, respectively.

### ARTICLE III. FREEDOM OF EXPRESSION AND PRIOR RESTRAINT

In the opinion of Pritchett the Supreme Court's first great anticensorship decision of modern times was the case of Near *v.* Minnesota, 1931.[104] The statute in question provided for a "padlock injunction." The injunction could be invoked against a newspaper whose printing matter was found to be scandalous, malicious, defamatory, or obscene, and it could be removed only upon a convincing of the judge that the said publication would be unobjectionable in the future (Chapter 285 of the Session Laws of Minn., 1925). In delivering the opinion of the Court Mr. Chief Justice Hughes (1862-1848) stated that this amounted to prior restraint. The State could not authorize a previous restraint upon scandalous

---

[103] Beauharnais *v.* Illinois, 343 U.S. 250 (1952).

[104] *Civil Liberties and the Vinson Court,* p. 38. Near *v.* Minn., 283 U.S. 697 (1931).

and defamatory publications by the method outlined in the statute, viz., by authorizing its courts to enjoin them as nuisances. This was arbitrary state action and a form of prior restraint clearly unconstitutional.[105]

In 1938 the Court, following the decision of Near *v.* Minnesota, ruled that a city ordinance which required the permission of the City Manager before handbills, circulars, or other forms of literature could be distributed within the city limits was an unlawful abridgment of freedom of the press.[106] The following year the Supreme Court declared that a city ordinance which forbade, without exception, the distribution of handbills on the street was unconstitutional.[107]

A Connecticut statute prohibiting house-to-house canvassing for religious or philanthropic purposes without the prior approval of a county welfare official was declared unconstitutional on the ground that it constituted "a censorship of religion."[108] In Cox *v.* New Hampshire, 1941, a unanimous court upheld an ordinance that required a permit to be obtained from a license board in order to parade in the streets.[109] A group of Jehovah's Witnesses were convicted for marching single file along the downtown streets of Manchester, New Hampshire, and carrying placards announcing a forthcoming meeting. They had failed to apply for the license required by law to parade or march on the streets. Chief Justice Hughes made it clear that the Court viewed the license, which

---

[105] The Court recognized some restrictions in the form of prior restraint as constitutional: ". . . the protection even as to previous restraint is not absolutely unlimited. But the limitation has been recognized only in exceptional cases: 'When a nation is at war many things that might be said in time of peace are such a hindrance to its effort that their utterance will not be endured so long as men fight, and that no court could regard them as protected by any constitutional right.' Schenck *v.* United States, 249 U.S. 47. . . ."—Near *v.* Minn., 283 U.S. 697, 716. Cf. also Corwin, *Constitution of the U. S.*, p. 786, under Censorship.

[106] Lovell *v.* Griffin, 303 U.S. 444 (1938).

[107] Schneider *v.* Town of Irvington (State), 308 U.S. 147 (1939); cf. also Jamison *v.* Texas, 318 U.S. 413 (1943).

[108] Cantwell *v.* Connecticut, 310 U.S. 296 (1940). This case is discussed in detail in the next section, Speech and Public Order.

[109] Cox *v.* New Hampshire, 312 U.S. 569 (1941).

was demonstrated to be non-discriminatory, merely as a traffic regulation, and not as a restraint upon gathering for a meeting or conveying information. It was not a prior restraint of speech, press, or assembly.

In 1943 there were three companion cases involving the propagation of religion and the invasion of private property.[110] The Murdock case was decided on the basis of an invalid tax. A fee was required for the distributing of things on the street. The Court held the ordinance unlawful on the ground that it is unconstitutional to tax the right to preach or to disseminate religion. You may tax the income of the person, but you may not tax his right to preach.[111] The Douglas decision was arrived at on the basis of prior censorship. Jeannette, Pennsylvania, was a town of about sixteen thousand people, and over one-third were Roman Catholics. On Palm Sunday one hundred Witnesses swarmed on the place and completely canvassed the entire town, ringing door bells, attempting to sell literature, and playing phonograph records highly offensive to several religious bodies, especially the Roman Catholic Church. The police and fire departments could not cope with the

---

[110] Murdock *v.* Pennsylvania, 319 U.S. 105 (1943); Douglas *v.* Jeannette, 319 U.S. 157 (1953); Martin *v.* Struthers, 319 U.S. 141 (1943).

[111] Corwin seems to have lost patience with the Court in this case. He says:

> The Court, one suspects, has not thought its problem quite through, if indeed most of these cases present a problem. In this connection a statement by Justice Douglas in Murdock *v.* Pennsylvania appears to be especially significant. "This form of religious activity," that is, proselytizing by the distribution of tracts, etc., he asserts there, "occupies the same estate under the First Amendment as do worship in churches and preaching from the pulpits." In other words, the right of religious enthusiasts to solicit funds and peddle their doctrinal wares in the street, to ring doorbells and disturb householders, and to accost passersby and insult them in *their* religious beliefs stands on the same constitutional level as the right of people to resort to their own places of worship and listen to their chosen teachers! If, as is generally understood, one man's right to swing his fist stops just short of where another man's nose begins, a somewhat similar rule must be presumed in the field of religious activities. As Justice Jackson sensibly suggested, the Court ought to ask itself what would be the effect "if the right given these Witnesses should be exercised by all sects and denominations."

*Constitution and What It Means Today,* pp. 257-258; Opinion of Douglas —Murdock *v.* Penn., 319 U.S. 105, 109 (1943); Opinion of Jackson— Douglas *v.* Jeannette, 319 U.S. 157, 180. Powers is equally critical of these decisions. Cf. *Religious Liberty and the Police Power,* pp. 101-110.

disturbances which the Witnesses created.[112] Justice Douglas, in writing the majority opinion, declared the ordinance was an abridgment of the liberties of the Witnesses.

Martin *v.* Struthers concerned a city ordinance of Struthers, Ohio, which prohibited distributors of handbills from summoning residents to their doors to receive such handbills and circulars.[113] Justice Black, who wrote the majority opinion, did not deny that individual tenants and home owners could post signs to prohibit Witnesses from summoning them to the door, but a city council exceeded its bounds when it attempted to establish a prohibition for an entire city.[114]

Cushman made an observation concerning the opinion of the Murdock case which has a bearing upon the present section under discussion. The opinion in the Murdock case "strongly indicates that religious speech and press enjoy a protection against restraint and regulation which may be denied to secular or commercial speech and press."[115] He found support for this doctrine in a 1951 case, in which the Supreme Court denied this liberty to those soliciting magazines of a secular nature. In upholding a city ordinance which forbade such door-to-door solicitation without the prior consent of those solicited, the Court distinguished this from the Martin *v.* Struthers' case on the ground that "no element of the commercial entered into the free solicitation, and this opinion was narrowly limited to the precise fact of the free distribution of an invitation to religious services. . . ."[116] "Secular books," Cushman concluded, "enjoy a broad range of freedom of the press; but it is not as broad as that enjoyed by religious literature."[117]

The Court extended the right of religious propagandizing even further in Marsh *v.* Alabama.[118] Mrs. Marsh, a Jehovah's Witness, entered the private property of a company-owned town and began

---

[112] Douglas *v.* Jeannette, 319 U.S. 157, 167-171.

[113] 319 U.S. 141 (1943).

[114] 319 U.S. 141, 143, 146-147 (1943).

[115] Robert F. and Robert E. Cushman, *Cases in Constitutional Law* (New York: Appleton-Century-Crofts, Inc., 1958), p. 730.

[116] Cushman quoting from Beard *v.* Alexandria, 341 U.S. 622, 643 (1951).

[117] *Cases in Constitutional Law, loc. cit.*

[118] 326 U.S. 501 (1946).

to distribute the literature of her sect in the manner usual with this religious body. The managers of the town had prohibited the distribution of literature on its streets. An officer told her of this prohibition and requested that she leave the property. She ignored the request and was arrested. Mrs. Marsh was convicted on the ground that she had violated a state statute which makes it unlawful to remain on private property, after the party has been warned to leave.

The Court reversed the conviction because the prohibition infringed upon the freedom of religion and press. Black wrote in the majority opinion that the company-town had lost its claim to privacy by permitting the public to shop in the company-stores. This latter action on the part of the owners made their company property subject to the same constitutional restrictions which govern other municipalities.[119]

The Saia *v.* New York and Kovacs *v.* Cooper cases involved ordinances regulating the use of loud-speakers.[120] In the former case a Jehovah's Witness minister challenged an ordinance of Lockport, New York, which prohibited the use of loud-speaker, except for announcement of news, matters of public concern, and athletics. Permission for the use of this sound equipment had to be obtained from the Chief of Police. Saia gave lectures at a definite place in a public park on designated Sundays. He had a permit from the Chief of Police and used sound equipment mounted on a car to reach a greater audience. When his permit expired, he applied for another, but he was refused because the Chief had received several complaints. The Witness minister continued to use his loud-speakers without a permit, and he was arrested and convicted for violating the Lockport ordinance. Douglas and four other Justices found the law unconstitutional.

Douglas, writing in the majority opinion, believed that the

---

[119] Marsh *v.* Alabama, 326 U.S. 501, 506 (1946). This principle of the town being open to the public was extended to government-owned housing projects in Tucker *v.* Texas, 326 U.S. 517 (1946). For a discussion of the merits of the majority opinions in these cases and the strong points made in the dissents, cf. O'Brien, *Justice Reed and the First Amendment,* pp. 36-40.

[120] Saia *v.* New York, 334 U.S. 558 (1948); Kovacs *v.* Cooper, 336 U.S. 77 (1949).

statute did not establish a definite enough standard for the administrative official to follow. The ordinance on its face was a prior restraint of the right to free speech. He allowed an administrative official the power simply to control loud-speaking equipment by regulating the volume, the hours, and the place for discussion. This would have to be spelled out clearly in a narrowly defined statute.[121]

The facts of the case indicated that Douglas' fear, that the free exercise of speech or religion would be unduly abridged under the Lockport statute, was almost unfounded. The ordinance itself did not place any limitation on the days or the hours for religious gatherings in public places, provided that loud-speakers were not used.[122] As was noted above, the park was intended primarily for recreational purposes. Nevertheless, the Chief of Police had permitted the Witnesses for a period of time to use the park for their meetings, even with the use of amplifiers.[123]

Both Frankfurter and Jackson wrote dissenting opinions in which they stressed the "right of privacy" for the people who came to the park for quiet conversation and meditation.[124] Eleven months later, the Court decided the case of Kovacs *v.* Cooper, which virtually reversed the Saia decision.[125] The state courts interpreted the prohibition contained in a Trenton, New Jersey, ordinance to be of a broader nature than did Justice Reed. Reed read the ordinance as prohibiting only "loud and raucous" sound trucks.

There were two differences in the Lockport and the Trenton ordinances, which are of some significance for the present consideration of religious liberty: The Trenton statute required no license or permit to conduct religious services with the aid of an amplifier, and indicated no prior need of permission to operate even "loud and raucous" amplifiers in the city parks.[126]

---

[121] Saia *v.* New York, 334 U.S. 558, 559, 560, 562 (1948).

[122] *Ibid.*, 334 U.S. 558 (1948).

[123] *Ibid.*, 334 U.S. 558, 566, 570 (1948).

[124] *Ibid.*, 334 U.S. 558, 563, 571 (1948).

[125] Kovacs *v.* Cooper, 336 U.S. 77 (1949).

[126] Kovacs *v.* Cooper, 336 U.S. 77, 78, 85 (1949). Cf. O'Brien, *Justice Reed and the First Amendment*, pp. 61-68. He has an excellent discussion of Reed's

The Kovacs' ruling seems to sustain the constitutionality of ordinances prohibiting "loud and raucous" noises from sound trucks on public streets. But the Court finds no unconstitutional activity in the action of a privately owned transportation system playing news, music, and advertisement over loud-speakers located in its passenger cars.[127]

A custom or practice of requiring a permit to use a park was declared unconstitutional in a decision made in 1951.[128]

This was an unusually clear-cut case and none of the judges of the Court dissented. A group of Jehovah's Witnesses wished to use the park in Havre de Grace, Maryland, for a series of Sunday Bible talks. There was no ordinance requiring a permit, but a long-standing custom ruled that a permit must be obtained from the Park Commission. The Witnesses came to the city council and asked for permission to conduct their Sunday series in the park. They were questioned about their refusal to salute the flag and also about their views on the Bible. Upon their replies, the permit was refused. The Witnesses proceeded to conduct their meeting without a license, and their speaker was promptly arrested and convicted of disorderly conduct.

Chief Justice Vinson, speaking for the Court, ruled that this practice was an invalid prior restraint in which censorship could be exercised without fixed standards or narrowly drawn and reasonable limitations.[129] In a number of cases between 1938 and 1953 the Court has ruled that a person may absolutely disregard a law

---

majority opinion, and it is O'Brien's conclusion that "it is not certain whether the *Saia* decision has been virtually overruled and cities are now permitted to ban all loud-speakers from their streets." His note indicates that his doubt is shared by others.—*Ibid.*, p. 67, note 82.

[127] Public Utilities Commission *v.* Pollak, 343 U.S. 451 (1952). The aftermath of this case is amusing. As one writer phrased it, "The law of economics accomplished what the law of liberties could not." The transportation company discontinued the broadcasting a short time later for financial reasons.

[128] Niemoko *v.* Maryland, 340 U.S. 268 (1951).

[129] 340 U.S. 268, 271, 272 (1951). There was a similar case, Kunz *v.* New York, 340 U.S. 290 (1951), before the Court at that time. It is discussed under the next section, Speech and Public Order. The majority ruled prior restraint.

regarding the First Amendment freedoms which is unconstitutional on its face. If he is arrested for holding a religious gathering or for delivering a speech contrary to the said law, the very unconstitutionality will constitute a complete defense.[130] May a person follow such a course of action when the statute is constitutional on its face, but unconstitutional in its application? In a word, may he defy the refusal of administrative officials to give him a license to speak in a public place on the ground that such a denial is unconstitutional? The majority of the Supreme Court said no, he may not, in the Poulos *v.* New Hampshire ruling in 1953.[131] The burden is placed upon the citizen to exhaust all the possible legal remedies. Poulos should have filed a civil suit in the courts to compel the granting of the license.

The ordinance in question reads:

> No theatrical or dramatic representation shall be performed or exhibited and no parade or procession upon any public street or way, and no open air public meeting shall be permitted unless a license therefor shall first be obtained from the City Council.[132]

In compliance with this law, William Poulos, a Jehovah's Witness, applied for a license to speak in Goodwin Park in Portsmouth, New Hampshire, during June and July. He promised to pay the fee, but was refused on the ground that the council had never received a request from a religious body to use the public parks. The council was afraid that a disturbance might follow, if it permitted the Witnesses to hold their meetings in Goodwin Park. Poulos made no further effort to have the council's decision reversed; he simply addressed his group in Goodwin Park. His arrest and conviction followed on the ground that he spoke in the park without a license. The conviction was upheld by the New Hampshire Supreme Court.

A seven to two majority in the United States Supreme Court

---

[130] E.g., Lovell *v.* Griffin, 303 U.S. 444 (1938); Cantwell *v.* Connecticut, 310 U.S. 296 (1940); Schneider *v.* Town of Irvington (State), 308 U.S. 147 (1939).

[131] 345 U.S. 395.

[132] Poulos *v.* New Hampshire, 345 U.S. 395, 397, n. 2. This is Section 22 of the statute.

found the ordinance constitutional on its face and upheld the conviction, contrary to the appellant's contention that his constitutional rights under the First and Fourteenth Amendments had been violated. The state supreme court interpreted the statute as requiring impartiality of treatment and uniformity. Reed, writing in the majority opinion, concurred in this view. He said that the officials were given non-discriminatory authority to grant permits to speak in the park, but were given "no power to discriminate, and no control over speech." The ordinance simply called "for the adjustment of the unrestrained exercise of religions within the reasonable comfort and convenience of the whole city."[133]

The ordinance was constitutional, only its application to Poulos was invalid. Poulos had no right to flout the law by taking things into his own hands in the opinion of the majority; although the dissenters, Douglas and Black, held that he did.[134] Seven Justices believed that the proper remedy for administrative arbitrariness was judicial redress. Justice Reed was cognizant of the burden this recourse placed upon the injured party, but felt that the common good outweighed the particular interest in this situation.[135]

O'Brien seeks to defend the Court against those who charge it with inconsistency. He does not deny the charge, but sees in the Court's retreat from its previous position a striving to reach stability. In reviewing the Murdock case, Corwin said, "The Court,

---

[133] 345 U.S. 395, 404-405 (1953).

[134] Cf. 345 U.S. 395, 421-423 (1953).

[135] *Ibid.*, 345 U.S. 395, 409.—"It must be admitted that judicial correction of arbitrary refusal by administrators to perform official duties under valid laws is exulcerating and costly. But to allow applicants to proceed without the required permits to run businesses, erect structures, purchase firearms, transport or store explosives or other inflammatory products, hold public meetings without prior safety arrangements, or take other unauthorized action, is apt to cause breaches of the peace or create public dangers. The valid requirements of license are for the good of the applicants and the public. It would be unreal to say that such official failures to act in accordance with state law, redressable by state judicial procedures, are state acts violative of the Federal Constitution. Delay is unfortunate, but the expense and annoyance of litigation is a price citizens must pay for life in an orderly society where the rights of the First Amendment have a real and abiding meaning. Nor can we say that a state's requirement that redress must be sought through appropriate judicial procedure violates due process."

one suspects, has not thought its problem through. . . ."[136] O'Brien believes that is what the Court is trying to do ten years later in the Poulos case—think the problem through.[137]

Pritchett has summed up very well the present position of prior restraint in the eyes of the Court: ". . . it would seem that seven years of the Vinson Court left prior restraint still suspect, but no longer unconstitutional on its face." He finds that the 1953 rule is one of reasonableness "as stated by Justice Reed in the Poulos case: 'Regulation and suppression are not the same thing, either in purpose or result, and courts of justice can tell the difference.' "[138]

The Supreme Court has continued to strike down statutes permitting administrative officials to refuse arbitrarily licenses to speak. In Staub *v.* Baxley a salaried union organizer was convicted of violating an ordinance of the City of Baxley, Georgia, which provided that no person could solicit membership in any organization or union which required the payment of dues, unless he first obtained a permit from the Mayor and the Council of the City.[139]

The Mayor and his Council were given the option to grant or to refuse a permit "after considering the character of the applicant, the nature of the . . . organization for which members are desired to be solicited, and its effect upon the general welfare of [the] citizens of the City of Baxley."[140]

---

[136] *Constitution and What It Means Today,* p. 257.

[137] *Justice Reed and the First Amendment,* p. 99.—"As for charges of inconsistency, it may be said that inconsistency is at times hard to avoid in judicial review under a written Constitution. In reviewing legislation, the Court must strive to give a semblance of stability. This could never have been done if decisions were not frequently reversed. Justice Reed appears to be particularly conscious of this duty of the Court, and thus he at times strains for distinctions when a blunt notice of a reversal would appear to be called for. As has been pointed out, the Kovacs opinion can thus be explained. Likewise, the Breard and the Poulos argumentations seem to represent an effort to map a strategic retreat for the beleaguered Court, entangled in its own previous errors. Had he been a political essayist, unfettered by the restraints that bind justices, Reed might well have penned an argument impervious to the thrusts of strict logicians."

[138] *Civil Liberties and the Vinson Court,* p. 49.

[139] Staub *v.* Baxley, 355 U.S. 313 (1957).

[140] *Ibid.,* 355 U.S. 313, 321. Sections I to IV of the ordinance.

The appellant contended "that the ordinance was invalid on its face because it makes enjoyment of the constitutionally guaranteed freedom of speech contingent upon the will of the Mayor and Council of the City, and thereby constitutes a prior restraint upon, and abridges, that freedom." The Court agreed with the appellant, and restricted itself to that particular consideration.[141]

This ordinance attempted to establish some policy, but the Court believed that "these criteria are without a semblance of definite standards or other controlling guides governing the action of the Mayor and Council in granting or withholding a permit. Cf. Niemotko *v.* Maryland, 340 U.S. 268, 271, 273. It is thus plain that they acted in this respect in their uncontrolled discretion."[142]

The Majority of the Bench held that "the ordinance, on its face, imposes an unconstitutional prior restraint upon the enjoyment of the First Amendment freedoms and lays a forbidden burden upon the exercise of liberty protected by the Constitution. Cantwell *v.* Connecticut, *supra* at 307."[143]

The Court has been comparatively consistent in its doctrine of

---

[141] *Ibid.,* 321.

[142] *Ibid.,* 355 U.S. 313, 322 (1957). The Court also cited Cantwell *v.* Conn., 319 U.S. at 296, 305, 307; Lovell *v.* Griffin, 303 U.S. 444, at 451, 452; Hague *v.* C.I.O., 307 U.S. 496, 516; Schneider *v.* Town of Irvington (State), 308 U.S. 147, 163, 164; Kunz *v.* New York, 340 U.S. 290, 293, to support its judgment. Cantwell *v.* Connecticut was referred to more than the others during the course of the opinion.—*Ibid.,* 322-324.

[143] *Ibid.,* 355 U.S. 313, 325 (1957). In 1958 the Court entertained a case dealing with "advocacy of ideas." (Kingsley Pictures Corp. *v.* Regents of New York University, 360 U.S. 684.) Mr. Justice Stewart delivered the majority opinion, and there were a few concurring opinions. Kingsley Corp. had applied to the Regents for a permit to show "Lady Chatterley's Lover." The Regents denied the license on the ground that the film was immoral, "for the theme is the presentation of adultery as a desirable, acceptable and proper pattern of behaviour" (*ibid.,* 685). The majority held that the New York Educational Law "as thus construed and applied . . . violates the freedom to advocate ideas which is guaranteed by the First Amendment and protected by the Fourteenth from infringement by the States." This case and others decided earlier in the nineteen fifties about censorship of films reflects the limited area in which the court will permit the State to exercise prior restraint over the communication of ideas and of its demand for a very clear and narrowly defined censorship statute.

prior restraint. However, the years between 1930 and 1953 have witnessed a transition in the attitude of the Court regarding prior censorship. Initially, the Court tended to regard prior censorship as unconstitutional on its face. By 1953 prior restraint was still suspect, but no longer unconstitutional on its face.

In Near *v.* Minn. the Court declared prior censorship of newsprint to be unconstitutional. During the course of the majority opinion the Judges admitted that the restriction on prior restraint was not absolute. Certain extreme forms of free expression, which would normally be tolerated, could be suppressed in time of war.

The Supreme Court refused to uphold any form of blanket prohibition. A statute containing an absolute prohibition to disseminate handbills was declared unconstitutional on its face. Another general prohibition, this one preventing door-to-door canvassing for religious and philanthropic purposes without prior county approval, was condemned as an unconstitutional censorship of religion. The Court went so far as to allow a town to be invaded on a Sunday morning by a large body of almost fanatical religious zealots. Justice Black graciously conceded that the residents could post signs prohibiting distributors of handbills, etc., from summoning them to the door to receive this material, but denied that a city council could establish such a prohibition for an entire city, no matter how worthy the motives. Individual privacy and peace and quiet of a small town was of less value, in the eyes of the majority of the Court, than the liberties guaranteed by the First Amendment.

The Court extended the right of religious propagandizing even further in 1946. It argued that once a company-owned town had opened its stores to the general public, the town lost its claim to privacy. The owners caused their private property to be subject to the same restrictions which govern municipalities. They could not appeal to trespass laws to prevent religious proselytizing on the streets. This principle of a town being open to the public was expanded in Tucker *v.* Texas (1946) to include government-owned housing projects.

A custom requiring permission from local officials to use public parks was declared an invalid prior restraint, in which censorship could be exercised without fixed standards or narrowly drawn and reasonable limitations. It was likewise held unconstitutional to tax the right to preach.

Where traffic on streets and highways was concerned, the Court was prone to look more benignly upon state control. The requirement in a clearly drawn and non-discriminatory statute that a permit be first obtained to parade in the streets, even for religious purposes, was found to be a legitimate exercise of police power.

The Court was faced with a special problem in park preaching—the employment of an amplification system. It ruled that an ordinance regulating the use of loud-speakers must be clearly and narrowly drawn in order to provide an adequate standard for administrative judgment. The Kovacs case (1949) upheld the constitutionality of prohibiting "loud and raucous" noises from sound trucks on public thoroughfares. This ruling mitigated the Saia decision of the previous year, but it did not completely reverse it. In the Kovacs case there was no question of requiring a permit for the use of loud-speakers during religious services in a park.

A citizen, the Court has ruled, may absolutely disregard a statute restraining the First Amendment Freedoms, when it is unconstitutional on its face. If the violator is arrested for conducting a religious service or delivering a speech contrary to the law, the statute's unconstitutionality will constitute a complete defense. However, as the Supreme Court declared in Poulos *v.* N. H. (1953), if the law is constitutional on its face, but the administrative application of it is unconstitutional, the citizen may not flout the law. He must exhaust all possible legal remedies. This decision marked a return to the reasonable standard as applied to the constitutional protections given to personal rights.

The norms formulated by the Court between 1930 and recent times, which have just been summarized in the preceding paragraphs, apply to both religious and secular forms of expression. However, added protection seems to be given to religious expression. Both the Murdock case and Breard *v.* Alexandria (1951) give the impression that secular literature and speech enjoy a wide range of freedom, but not as broad as that enjoyed by religious expression.

ARTICLE IV. SPEECH AND PUBLIC ORDER

How far may oral expression be permitted to disturb the peace before a civil official is legally justified in arresting the speaker? The Supreme Court was obliged to answer this question in Cantwell *v.* Connecticut.[144] The Court upset the conviction of two Jehovah Witnesses for the common law offense of breach of peace. The Witnesses were engaged in distributing religious pamphlets and playing phonograph records in a predominantly Catholic neighborhood in New Haven. Their materials presented a bitter attack on religious groups in general, and the tracts and records especially directed vile charges against the Catholic Church. One of the Witnesses, Jesse Cantwell, met two Catholics on the street and received their permission to play one of his records. Both men were highly incensed by the derogatory content of the phonograph record and were tempted to strike Cantwell. They told him to move on and he did so. There was no evidence that he was personally offensive or that he engaged in any argument with the men. Cantwell and his companions were later arrested on the street, and Cantwell was convicted on a charge, not of assault or breach of peace or threats personally uttered, but on the grounds of invoking or inciting others to breach the peace.

The Supreme Court held the statute, as construed and applied to the appellants, deprived them of their liberty without due process of law of the Fourteenth Amendment. This Amendment rendered the state legislatures as incompetent as the Congress to legislate such laws. It forbade any compulsion by law to accept or practice any creed or practice of worship. "On the other hand, it safeguards the free exercise of the chosen form of religion. Thus the Amendment embraces two concepts—freedom to believe and freedom to act. The first is absolute but, in the nature of things, the second cannot be. Conduct remains subject to regulation for the protection of society." Mr. Justice Roberts (1875-1955), delivering the opinion of the Court, said that regulation must not be such as to unduly infringe the protected freedom. However, the State may "by general and non-discriminatory legislation regulate the times,

[144] 310 U.S. 296, 309 (1940).

the places and the manner of soliciting on its street, and of holding meetings thereon; and may in other respects safeguard the peace, good order and comfort of the community, without unconstitutionally invading the liberties protected by the Fourteenth Amendment."[145]

The court proceeded to apply the "clear and present danger" test: "No one would have the hardihood to suggest that the principle of freedom of speech sanctions incitement to riot or that religious liberty connotes the privilege to exhort others to physical attack upon those belonging to another sect. When clear and present danger of riot, disorder, interference with traffic upon the public streets, or other immediate threat to public safety, peace, or order appears, the power of the State to prevent or punish is obvious."[146]

In the view of the Court, Cantwell's conduct did not amount to a breach of the peace. "We find in the instant case no assault or threatening of bodily harm, no truculent bearing, no intentional discourtesy, no personal abuse. On the contrary, we find only an effort to persuade a willing listener to buy a book or to contribute money in the interest of what Cantwell, however misguided others may think him, conceived to be true religion."[147]

The Court admitted that, though the record's content of its nature aroused animosity, "in the absence of a statute narrowly drawn to define and punish specific conduct as constituting a clear and present danger to a substantial interest of the State, the petitioner's communication, considered in the light of the constitutional guarantees, raised no such clear and present menace to public peace and order as to render him liable to conviction of common law offense in question."

In the following year the Supreme Court was again called upon to review a case involving a Witness convicted of violating a statute aimed at the preservation of the peace. This time the Court upheld the conviction by the lower court.[148] Chaplinsky was convicted of

---

[145] Cantwell *v.* Conn., 310 U.S. 296, 304 (1940).
[146] 310 U.S. 296, 308 (1940).
[147] 310 U.S. 296, 310.
[148] Chaplinsky *v.* New Hampshire, 315 U.S. 568 (1942).

breaking the law, which provided that "no person shall address any offensive, derisive or annoying word to any other person who is lawfully in any street or other public place, nor call him any offensive or derisive name, nor make any noise or exclamation in his presence and hearing with the intent to deride, offend or annoy him."[149] The appellant denounced religion as a racket and created a disturbance when the police led him off to jail as a protective measure. He called the officer "a god-damned racketeer," "a damned Fascist," and went so far as to declare that "the whole government of Rochester are Fascists or agents of Fascists."

In the Cantwell case the Court had established as one of the criteria for lawful State action a "statute narrowly drawn to define and punish specific conduct as constituting a clear and present danger to a substantial interest of the State." In sustaining the constitutionality of the New Hampshire statute, the Court propounded that "a statute punishing verbal acts, carefully drawn so as not unduly to impair liberty of expression, is not too vague for a criminal law."[150] The New Hampshire supreme court interpreted the statute as prohibiting words clearly provocative of a breach of peace. Its purpose was to forbid words "such as have a direct tendency to cause acts of violence by the person to whom, individually, the remark is addressed." Words which would have this tendency were enumerated by the court: fighting classical words, and words of a less classical usage but equally apt to stir up violence, and other remarks, including profanity and threats. The Supreme Court adopted this interpretation of the New Hampshire court and found that a breach of peace, so defined, existed in this case. A "resort to epithets or personal abuse," the Court continued, "is not in any proper sense communication of information or opinion safeguarded by the Constitution." The Court also clarified the religious issue involved: "But even if the activities of the appellant which preceded the incident could be viewed as religious in character, and therefore entitled to the protection of the Fourteenth Amendment, they could not cloak him with im-

[149] *New Hampshire Public Laws,* Chapter 378, Sec. 2 (1926). Cf. 315 U.S. 568, 569 (1942).

[150] Chaplinsky *v.* New Hampshire, 315 U.S. 568, 574 (1942).

munity from legal consequences for consummated acts in violation of a valid criminal statute."[151]

Moreover, the Supreme Court found that a clear and present danger of such a breach did exist: ". . . the appellations 'damned racketeer' and 'damned Fascist' are epithets likely to provoke the average person to retaliation, and thereby cause a breach of the peace."[152] The Chaplinsky case definitely established that lewd, obscene, profane, libelous, or other fighting words, i.e., those words tending to incite to an immediate breach of the peace, do not fall under the protection of the Constitution, even if uttered under the guise of religious expression. Public peace and harmony far outweigh the social value of these expressions.[153]

Terminiello *v.* Chicago, a case still extremely controversial, reflects the impact of the clear and present danger test. A sharply divided court held that punishment for breach of peace by speech which "stirs up the public to anger, invites disputes, [or] brings about a condition of unrest" was an unlawful restriction of the right to free speech.[154] In short, the court underwrote a near riot.

Under the sponsorship of the Christian Veterans of America, Terminiello was introduced by Gerald L. K. Smith and spoke to a crowd of about eight hundred people packed into a Chicago auditorium. A crowd of about one thousand milled around outside, yelling and smashing windows. Despite the tumultuous mob, Terminiello delivered a speech filled with race hatred and other provocative subjects. The speaker needed police protection both to enter and to leave the building.

---

[151] *Ibid.*, 315 U.S. 568, 571-573.

[152] *Ibid.*, 315 U.S. 568, 574.

[153] Powers, *Religious Liberty and the Police Power,* p. 100. He is of the opinion that, "if the test used in the Chaplinski case is applied here, the remarks addressed to the specific auditors in the Cantwell situation amounted to language which would cause an average addressee to fight. More realistic is the Court's treatment of the *Chaplinsky* case, striking as it does a reasonable balance between the obvious need of local government both to preserve the peace and to insure reasonable individual free expression." In Youngdahl *v.* Rainfair, Inc., 355 U.S. 131 (1957), the Court included the word "scab" among the words inciting to violence, and, therefore, outside the constitutional protection.

[154] Terminiello *v.* Chicago, 337 U.S. 1 (1949).

Terminiello was found guilty of disorderly conduct under a Chicago ordinance covering "all persons who shall make, aid, countenance, or assist in making any improper noise, riot, disturbance, breach of peace, or diversion tending to a breach of the peace." The Supreme Court reversed the conviction. Justice Douglas wrote that "a function of free speech under our system of government is to invite dispute. It may indeed best serve its high purpose when it induces a condition of unrest, creates dissatisfaction with conditions as they are, or even stirs people to anger." He admitted that speech is often provocative and challenging, striking at prejudices and producing profoundly unsettling effects. "That is why freedom of speech, though not an absolute . . . is nevertheless protected against censorship and punishment, unless shown likely to produce a clear and present danger of a serious substantive evil that rises far above public inconvenience, annoyance, or unrest."[155] Declaring the ordinance to be unconstitutional, the majority of the Supreme Court did not enter into a consideration of the facts of the particular case.

Justice Jackson was numbered among the dissenters. The dicta of his dissent were later to become the ruling norm in Feiner *v.* New York (1951).[156] He considered the evidence, which clearly demonstrated that a riot had actually occurred. Terminiello's speech provoked a hostile crowd and stirred up a friendly one, and brought both to the point of mob violence. He conceded that a topic may be legally arguable, but that its advocacy may not be tolerated under certain conditions. Many speeches like this one may be legally permissible, but in given surroundings may be "a menace to peace and order. When conditions show the speaker that this is the case, as it did here, there certainly comes a point beyond which he cannot indulge in provocations to violence without being answerable to society."[157]

---

[155] Terminiello *v.* Chicago, 337 U.S. 1, 4 (1949). Citing Chaplinsky *v.* N. H., 315 U.S. 568, 571-572 (1942).

[156] 340 U.S. 315 (1951).

[157] Terminiello *v.* Chicago, 337 U.S. 1, 33. Cf. Pritchett, *Civil Liberties and the Vinson Court,* pp. 59-61. He examines Jackson's dissent in some detail and finds that "Jackson's rhetoric was persuasive, but, in fact, he was battling a straw man." Pritchett also believes that Douglas could have

Several months later, the Court was called upon to resolve a problem far less acute than the Terminiello outbreak.[158] Feiner, a university student, addressed a crowd of Negro and white persons through a public address system on the sidewalk. Pedestrians were forced to walk in the street to circumvent the crowd. Feiner's inflammatory remarks called upon the Negroes to "rise up in arms and fight for their rights" and his derogatory statements included calling President Truman and Mayor O'Dwyer of New York "bums" and the American Legion a Nazi Gestapo. Two policemen were attracted to the scene by the traffic problem caused by the crowd. As they mingled with the crowd they became aware of angry mutterings, restlessness, and shoving around. One man in the gathering told the police that if they didn't take that S-O-B off the box, he would. The officers approached Feiner, and one of them asked him to get off the box. He continued to speak, so he was told to get down. When all their efforts failed, the officers demanded that he come with them, telling him that he was under arrest. When Feiner asked what was the charge, the officer said "unlawful assembly." This charge was later changed to that of disorderly conduct.

Mr. Chief Justice Vinson (1890-1953) delivered the opinion of the Court. He noted that the "petitioner was accorded a full, fair trial." The state court had "heard evidence both supporting and contradicting the judgment of the police officers that a clear danger of disorder was threatened. After weighing this contradictory evidence, the trial judge reached the conclusion that the police officers were justified in taking action to prevent the breach of peace."[159] The lower courts, Vinson commented, recognized Feiner's right to hold a street meeting in the particular locality, to use loudspeaking equipment, and to make derogatory remarks about public officials and the American Legion. They found that the arrest

---

made a real contribution to the civil liberties theory, "by arguing for the right of the speaker to address willing listeners in a private hall and by examining the nature of the community's obligation to defend that right against violent interruptions from outsiders." *Ibid.*, p. 61. This Douglas does in the Feiner case two years later.

[158] Feiner *v.* New York, 340 U.S. 315 (1951).

[159] Feiner *v.* New York, 340 U.S. 315, 319 (1951).

was motivated solely "by a proper concern for the preservation of order and protection of the general welfare, and that there was no evidence which could lend color to a claim that the acts of the police were a cover for suppression of the petitioner's views and opinions."[160] After these observations, Vinson concluded that the "petitioner was thus neither arrested nor convicted for the making or the content of his speech. Rather, it was the reaction which it actually engendered."

The Court appealed to the language of Cantwell *v.* Connecticut, 301 U.S. 296 (1940): "When clear and present danger of riot, disorder, interference with traffic upon the public streets, or other immediate threat to public safety, peace, or order, appears, the power of the State to prevent or punish it is obvious." The record of this case showed that the traffic hazard created by the gathering, the rumblings of the crowd, and the unwillingness of the petitioner to co-operate with the police request created such a situation. These conditions persuaded the Court "that the conviction of the petitioner for violation of public peace, order and authority does not exceed the bounds of proper state action."[161]

The Supreme Court had to decide between conflicting interests: the interest of the community in maintaining peace and order on the street, and the interest of the petitioner's right to free speech. In this particular case the Court placed free speech below public order. The majority realized the inherent danger in such a choice.[162] They applied the test of a clear and imminent substantive

---

[160] Feiner *v.* New York, 340 U.S. 315, 319.

[161] Feiner *v.* New York, 340 U.S. 315, 320, 321 (1951).

[162] We are well aware that ordinary murmurings and objections of a hostile audience cannot be allowed to silence a speaker and are also mindful of the possible danger of giving overzealous police officials complete discretion to break up otherwise lawful public meetings. "A State may not unduly suppress free communication of views, religious or other, under the guise of conserving desirable conditions."

But we are not faced here with such a situation. It is one thing to say that police cannot be used as an instrument for the suppression of unpopular views, and another thing to say that, when as here the speaker passes the bounds of argument and persuasion and undertakes incitement to riot, they are powerless to prevent a breach of the peace.—*Ibid.*, 340 U.S. 315, 320, 321.

evil to the State: "The findings of the state courts as to the existing situation and the imminence of greater disorder coupled with the petitioner's deliberate defiance of the police officers convince us that we should not reverse this conviction in the name of free speech."[163]

Douglas, in his dissenting opinion, stressed the duty of the public officials "to protect lawful gatherings, so that the speakers may exercise their constitutional rights." When the police support those who break up such meetings, "the police become the new censors of speech. Police censorship has all the vices of censorship from city halls which we have repeatedly struck down."[164] Black, in his dissent, was equally pessimistic: ". . . today's holding means that, as a practical matter, minority speakers can be silenced in any city. Hereafter, despite the First and Fourteenth Amendments, the policeman's club can take heavy toll of current administration's public critics. Criticism of public officials will be too dangerous for all but the most courageous. . . ."[165]

In both the Terminiello case and the Feiner case there were arrests of the speakers on account of the disorder their addresses engendered. The Court upheld the conviction of Feiner, but not of Terminiello. In the Terminiello case the Court only looked to the constitutionality of the statute, and not to the facts of the case. In the Feiner case the majority opinion gave serious consideration to the facts, and decided upon the facts. The facts in the two cases differed to some degree. Terminiello lectured in a hall; Feiner employed the sidewalk dedicated to the use of the pedestrians. Both used speech tending to incite riot, but only Feiner was requested to desist. The police granted Terminiello safe escort to and from the hall. Two policemen were attracted to the scene of Feiner's gathering because of the traffic problem it was engendering. Pedestrians were obliged to risk life and limb by walking in the street at a busy traffic hour. Feiner was interfering with the

[163] *Ibid.*, 340 U.S. 315, 321.

[164] *Ibid.*, 340 U.S. 315, 330-331.

[165] *Ibid.*, 340 U.S. 315, 328. Cf. Pritchett, *Civil Liberties and the Vinson Court*, pp. 62-63. He seems to share their views concerning the majority opinion.

right of the safety to citizens by using the busy thoroughfare for his meeting place. He was directly responsible for obstructing traffic, which the police have a duty to keep moving. Had he held his gathering in a hall, he would have been only indirectly responsible for interfering with traffic and could have continued to address at least a limited audience. The primary reason why the police requested Feiner to stop his speech was the danger to life and limb which his monopoly of the street was causing. He was silenced and convicted not because of his provocative speech, but because he violated the more primary right of the citizens to use the pavement dedicated to protect their life and limbs.

There is merit in the argument that such a decision opens the door to arbitrary police action. This danger is inherent in any administrative decision. But the protection against such arbitrariness must flow from the predictability contained in well written statutes and redress to the courts, where arbitrariness is ordinarily guarded against by procedural safeguards. The danger of arbitrary police action must not be prevented by permitting a greater evil, namely, the engendering of a riot and the loss of the pedestrian's right to the safeguard of life and limb afforded him by the public pavements. If the choice must be made, let the speaker move indoors, not the pedestrian out in the street.

The Kunz case was decided the same day.[166] New York City had adopted an ordinance which made it unlawful to hold public worship meetings on the streets without first obtaining a permit from the city police commissioner. Carl Jacob Kunz, the appellant, was convicted and fined ten dollars for holding a religious meeting without a permit.

In 1946, Kunz, a Baptist preacher, had applied for and received a permit, renewable each year, and no objection was raised at the time as to his right to preach. His permit was revoked after a hearing by the police commissioner in November, 1946. The basis for the revocation was evidence that he had ridiculed and denounced the religious beliefs of others at his street meetings. The city ordinances provided penalties for such activities, but among these there was not the revocation of the license. In fact,

[166] Kunz *v.* New York, 340 U.S. 290 (1951).

the ordinance made no mention of the reasons for the revocation.

Kunz applied for a permit in 1947, and again in 1948, and each time he was notified that his application was disapproved, but no reasons were given for the disapproval. On September 11, 1948, he was arrested at Columbus Circle, New York City, for speaking without a permit.

The issue in the case, Vinson stated in the opinion of the court, was "the propriety of the action of the police commissioner in refusing to issue the permit." The ordinance made no mention of the reasons for which a permit application could be rejected. "This interpretation allows the police commissioner, an administrative official, to exercise discretion in denying subsequent permit applications on the basis of his interpretation, at the time, of what is deemed to be conduct condemned by the ordinance."[167] The administrative official was given discretionary power "to control in advance the right of citizens to speak on religious matters on the streets of New York. As such, the ordinance is clearly invalid as a prior restraint on the exercise of First Amendment rights."[168]

Vinson proceeded to take the lower jurisdiction to task. In effect he said that they missed the issue of the case. The lower court passed judgment on the subsequent punishment. Something more fundamental was at issue—prior restraint. "We are here concerned with suppression—not punishment. It is sufficient to say that New York cannot vest restraining control over the right to speak on religious subjects in an administrative official where there are no appropriate standards to guide his action."[169]

This case did not disturb the doctrine of the Feiner case. As Milton Konvitz accurately observed: "This does not mean that Kunz has the constitutional right to make a speech which incites to disturbance or riot; for if he should make such a speech, he might be punished for the act. Because an act may not be prevented does not mean that it may not be subsequently punished."[170]

---

[167] Kunz *v.* New York, 340 U.S. 290, 293 (1951).

[168] *Ibid.*, 340 U.S. 290, 293.

[169] *Ibid.*, 340 U.S. 290, 294-295.

[170] *Fundamental Liberties of a Free People*, p. 181.

This was clearly a case where lack of a policy or standard in the ordinance made impossible the predictability necessary for a well-ordered society and opened the way for arbitrary administrative action. Had the ordinance contained a reasonable standard, it might have been declared constitutional.

Two years later the Supreme Court was called upon to decide two cases involving the exercise of speech, both with reference to Jehovah's Witnesses. Fowler, a Witness, addressed a meeting of some four hundred people, of whom about one hundred and fifty were Witnesses. Fowler spoke to his audience gathered in the park over two loud-speakers, and the meeting was quiet and orderly. He had hardly begun to speak when he was arrested for violating an ordinance of Pawtucket, Rhode Island. It provided that no one shall address a political or religious meeting in any park. He was convicted, but the Supreme Court unanimously reversed his conviction.[171]

In oral argument the State conceded that the ordinance did not apply to sermons delivered in conjunction with religious or church services, as distinguished from addresses to a religious meeting like the one for which Fowler was convicted. Justice Douglas, in his opinion for the Court, declared that public officials may not classify the speaking by the minister of one sect as preaching or a sermon, and that of another as an address, so as to permit the former and regulate the latter. For the Court to permit such discrimination would be to allow one religion to be preferred over another. Douglas commented that sermons are as much a part of religious services as are prayers, and no public official may undertake to "approve, disapprove, classify, regulate, or in any manner control sermons delivered at religious meetings."[172]

The second case involved the same ordinance as the Cox *v.* New Hampshire ruling, in which the statute section requiring a permit from a licensing board for street parades was upheld. Again it was the Witnesses who were involved in both cases.[173] The

---

[171] Fowler *v.* Rhode Island, 345 U.S. 67 (1953).

[172] *Ibid.*, 345 U.S. 67, 70 (1953).

[173] Cox *v.* New Hampshire, 312 U.S. 569 (1941); Poulos *v.* New Hampshire, 345 U.S. 395 (1953).

ordinance required that a license be obtained to hold a meeting in the park. Poulos, a Witness, was refused a license, and he then proceeded to flout the law. The Supreme Court held that the law was constitutional on its face and upheld the conviction of Poulos for preaching in public without a permit. Poulos should have sought judicial redress, instead of ignoring the ordinance, after the permit had been arbitrarily refused.[174]

Lewd, obscene, and other words of a profane or threatening nature do not fall within the area of protected speech. The Court made this clear in the Chaplinsky case: "A resort to epithets or personal abuse is not in any proper sense communication of information or opinion safeguarded by the Constitution. . . ."[175] In 1952 the Court sustained an Illinois statute which makes it a crime to display in a public place any kind of publication which portrays depravity, criminality, unchastity, or lack of virtue of a class of citizens, of any race, creed, color, or religion. It is likewise criminal to expose the citizens of any race, color, creed or religion to contempt, derision, or obloquy.[176]

The Illinois Supreme Court considered the act as a form of criminal libel, and so a defense by the truth of the utterance was not available under the Illinois law, unless the publication was demonstrated to have been made with good motives and justifiable

---

[174] This case is more properly one of prior restraint, therefore it has been given more detailed consideration in the previous section. In a recent case two Church groups refused to take an oath required, when they filed a property-tax exemption. According to the law, the applicant must swear that he does not advocate the overthrow of the government of the United States by force or violence or other unlawful means and does not advocate the support of a foreign government engaged in hostilities against the United States. The appellants declared this to be a violation of the due process clause, and also invalid under the Fourteenth Amendment as an abridgment of religious freedom and a violation of the principle of separation of Church and State. The Court decided the case in favor of the appellants on the ground of violation of due process, but refused to entertain the other two contentions.—First Unitarian Church *v.* Los Angeles, 357 U.S. 545, 546, 547 (1958).

[175] Chaplinshy *v.* New Hampshire, 315 U.S. 568, 571-574 (1942). Quote at 572 citing Cantwell *v.* Conn., 310 U.S. 296, 309-310.

[176] Beauharnais *v.* Illinois, 343 U.S. 250 (1952).

ends. The United States Supreme Court concurred in the judgment of the Illinois bench and maintained that the Act did not violate the freedom of speech and press guaranteed under the Fourteenth Amendment.

Justice Frankfurter reasoned that, "if an utterance directed at an individual may be the object of criminal sanctions, we cannot deny to a state power to punish the same utterances directed at a defined group, unless we can say that this is a wilful and purposeless restriction unrelated to the peace and well-being of the State."[177] Further on, he equivalently stated the same position: ". . . we are precluded from saying that speech concededly punishable when immediately directed at individuals cannot be outlawed if directed at groups with whose position and esteem in society the affiliated individual may be inextricably involved."[178] In effect, this decision of the Court placed group libel outside the protection of the Constitution.

The Court has continued to defend the right of the State to punish what is offensive to public morals and decency. The First Amendment was not intended to protect obscenity, and therefore the Court refused to apply any clear and present danger standard in the Roth case in 1957.[179]

---

[177] *Ibid.*, 343 U.S. 250, 258 (1952). Civil courts probably would not grant allegations in group libel, because damage is extremely difficult to prove. For recent cases concerning privileged communication: Howard *v.* Lyons, 360 U.S. 593 (1959). A navy captain enjoys an absolute privilege to send a defamatory report about his subordinates to his superiors and to Congressmen. Barr *v.* Matteo, 360 U.S. 564 (1959). The Court ruled that executive officials below the rank of cabinet officers in the Federal government enjoy a privileged position of speech in the fulfillment of their office.

[178] *Ibid.*, 343 U.S. 250, 263 (1952). This was a close decision with Justices Douglas, Black, Reed, and Jackson dissenting.

[179] Roth *v.* United States, 354 U.S. 476. Cf. also Kingsley Books *v.* Brown, 354 U.S. 436 (1957). However, the Court still demands that statutes be narrowly drawn, so that they restrict the evil purported to be dealt with in the said statute. In Butler *v.* Michigan, 352 U.S. 380 (1957), a Michigan law was declared unconstitutional because state police power could not restrict the reading of the general public merely to protect youths from harmful reading. Cf. also Youngdahl *v.* Rainfair, Inc., 355 U.S. 131 (1957).

ARTICLE V. FREEDOM OF ASSEMBLY

Inasmuch as freedom of assembly is intimately connected with the right to preach, a word must be said about the De Jonge *v.* Oregon case.[180] This case read the First Amendment right of assembly protection into the Fourteenth and protected the individual citizen against arbitrary state action. De Jonge's "sole offense as charged," Chief Justice Hughes (1862-1948) wrote in the opinion of the Court, "and for which he was convicted and sentenced to imprisonment for seven years, was that he had assisted in the conduct of a public meeting, albeit otherwise lawful, which was held under the auspices of the Communist Party."[181] Hughes said that the holding of meetings for peaceable political action cannot be proscribed. Those who participate in the conducting of such meetings cannot be branded criminals. "The question, if the rights of free speech and peaceable assembly are to be preserved, is not as to the auspices under which the meeting is held but to its purpose; not as to the relations of the speakers, but whether their utterances transcend the bounds of freedom of speech which the Constitution protects." If they have committed crimes of conspiracy or violated other laws elsewhere, let them be prosecuted under the laws punishing such crimes. "But it is a different matter when this State, instead of prosecuting them for such offenses, seizes upon mere participation in a peaceable assembly and a lawful public discussion as a basis for a criminal charge."[182]

Finally, the Court declared "that the Oregon statute as applied to the particular charge as defined by the state court is repugnant to the due process clause of the Fourteenth Amendment."[183]

Two years later the Court ruled that a Jersey City statute requiring a license for all public meetings violated the right of free assembly.[184] In a more recent case the Court defended the right of freedom of association for the advancement of ideas and beliefs. The NAACP refused to divulge its membership list and was fined

---

[180] 299 U.S. 353 (1937).
[181] *Ibid.*, 299 U.S. 353, 362 (1937).
[182] *Ibid.*, 299 U.S. 353, 365 (1937).
[183] *Ibid.*, 299 U.S. 353, 366 (1937).
[184] Hague *v.* CIO, 307 U.S. 496 (1939).

one hundred thousand dollars for contempt of court by the State. The Court in voiding the civil penalty declared that freedom of association for the advancement of ideas and beliefs was a part of the liberty protected by the due process clause of the Fourteenth Amendment.[185]

It should not be surprising that there are so few significant cases involving freedom of assembly specifically. This issue is usually an integral part of the freedom of speech cases. Therefore, it is to these cases that one must look for a more detailed doctrine on the right of assembly.

In a leading case the Court said that the Fourteenth Amendment embraces two things in the area of religion: freedom to believe, which is absolute, and freedom to act, which remains subject to regulation for the protection of society. This regulating must not unduly infringe upon the freedom of exercise. General and non-discriminatory regulation of times, places, and methods to safeguard peace and good order ordinarily does not unconstitutionally invade the liberties protected by the Fourteenth Amendment.

The Supreme Court frequently appealed to two norms—clear and present danger and a narrowly drawn statute. In the Cantwell case the Bench declared that "in the absence of a statute narrowly drawn to define and punish specific conduct constituting a clear and present danger to a substantial interest of the State, the petitioner's communication, considered in the light of the constitutional guarantees, raised no such clear and present menace to public peace and order as to render him liable to conviction of the common law offense in question." Two years later the Court again appealed to these two norms: clear and present danger and a narrowly drawn statute. This time, in the Chaplinsky case, they found both conditions satisfied and upheld both the statute and the conviction. "A statute punishing verbal acts," the Court said, "carefully drawn so as not to unduly impair liberty of expression, is not too vague for criminal law."

The Court sometimes went to great length to protect the right of free speech. In the Terminiello case of 1949 it stretched the

---

[185] NAACP *v.* Alabama, 357 U.S. 449 (1958). Two similar cases were decided on the same ground on February 23, 1960.

application of clear and present danger to such a degree that it underwrote a near riot. The majority stated in effect that it requires more than "reasonableness" to strike down free speech. Douglas admitted that freedom of speech is not an absolute, but it "is nevertheless protected against censorship and punishment, unless shown likely to produce a clear and present danger of a serious substantive evil that rises far above public inconvenience, annoyance, or unrest." This case clearly placed freedom of speech above public order.

Jackson's dissent became the guiding norm two years later in the Feiner case, which placed freedom of speech below public order. Jackson reasoned in the Terminiello case that, when circumstances are such that a speaker's words become a menace to public peace and order, "he cannot indulge in provocations to violence without being answerable to society."

Feiner was neither arrested nor convicted for making a speech, nor for the content of the speech, according to Justice Vinson, but for the reaction his activity engendered. The Court appealed to the language of Cantwell *v.* Connecticut: "When clear and present danger of riot, disorder, interference with traffic upon the public streets, or other immediate threat to public peace, safety, or order, appears, the power of the state to punish or prevent is obvious." The traffic hazard created by the crowd on the street corner, the rumblings of some of the group, and Feiner's failure to co-operate with the police, generated such a situation of disturbance of public peace and order. Had Feiner been indoors, instead of on a busy street corner, the case might have been decided in his favor.

The Court has consistently held that libel, profanity, obscenity, threats, fighting words apt to stir up violence, and this includes the term "scab," and other words of personal abuse, are not in any proper sense communication of information or opinion safeguarded by the Constitution. The right to utter other forms of speech does fall under the protection of the First and Fourteenth Amendments, and no public official may arbitrarily rule otherwise. Justice Douglas, delivering the opinion of the Court in the Fowler case in 1953, declared that public officials may not classify the speaking of a minister of one sect as preaching or a sermon, and that of another sect as an address, in order to freely permit the former and regulate the latter. Not only would this be preferring one religion over another, it would be unduly regulating speech. Douglas regarded sermons as much a part of a religious service as prayers, and no public official, he declared, may undertake to "approve, disapprove, classify, regulate, or in any manner control sermons delivered at religious meetings."[186]

Preachers may only subsequently be punished on indirect grounds, if their words are responsible for a serious disturbance of the public order, either by creating the danger of incitement to riot or by disrupting the flow of traffic as a result of the crowd which they attract. In the latter case preachers probably could not be penalized, unless they failed to heed the order of a peace officer to desist from preaching in this place. In a situation where the preacher is indoors, the police first have to try to remedy the traffic problem by dispersing the overflow crowd.

---

[186] 345 U.S. 67, 70 (1953).

# PART III

## Public Ecclesiastical Law and American Law

### ARTICLE I. PAPAL PRONOUNCEMENTS

This article is divided into two sections. One is concerned with the encyclicals of Pope Pius XI as occasioned by the violation of the rights of the Church and, in particular, the failure on the part of such nations as Germany and Italy to abide by the solemn conventions which guaranteed among other things the right of the Church to exercise its mission freely. The three encyclicals directed to Mexico and the one to Spain, in addition to his encyclical on Atheistic Communism, form an important segment of the discussion under the title of the free exercise of the ministry. The primary object of this discussion is to present the papal reaction to the violation of the right of the Church to fulfill its mission, especially when this right has been given juridic security in a concordat or a *modus vivendi.*

The second section treats of the juridic relations of Church and State. In discourses to jurists and other professional groups Pope Pius XII restates, and in some instances clarifies, the teaching of the Church on this matter. He also defines clearly the nature and the role of concordats in two of the allocutions. These considerations form the basis for the statement of a series of principles which serve as a guide or norm for judging how adequately the legal relationship between Church and State in a given nation conforms to the desires of the Holy See.

#### *Section 1. The Free Exercise of the Ministry*

The Political Constitution of the Federated Mexican States (1917) contained an article directed against the free exercise of the ministry of the Church.[1] In open violation of the Church's

[1] Cf. Joseph Husslein, *Social Wellsprings* (2 vols., Milwaukee: Bruce Publishing Co., 1940-1942), II, 280-281, for a complete reproduction of this infamous Article 130 in English translation.

divine mandate this Article held that "the federal authorities have exclusive power to exercise in matters of religious worship and outward ecclesiastical forms, such intervention as is by law authorized."[2] The Article denied the corporate existence of any Church, and "ministers of religious creeds shall be considered as persons exercising a profession and shall be subject to all the laws enacted on the subject."[3] Only those who were of Mexican birth could be ministers of religion, and they were forbidden to criticize the fundamental laws of the country. Places of worship could be erected with government permission only and were operated under the supervision of a lay commission responsible to the municipal authorities. Other restrictions of a "political nature" were placed upon ministers of religion.[4]

Article 130 was applied in full vigor in a law passed in 1926. The gravity of the situation was expressed clearly in Husslein's comment, "Not a shred had been left of religious liberty. The very exercise of the sacred ministry was made a capital crime, visited with dire punishment."[5]

Pius XI vigorously protested against this despotic action in his Encyclical, *Iniquis afflictisque,* of November 18, 1926.[6] He realized that the Church could not possibly function under these harassing conditions, and so he suspended all Church services. After three years a *modus vivendi* (1929) was concluded between the government and the hierarchy of Mexico. Mr. Dwight Morrow, the ambassador of the United States to Mexico, acted as mediator. Pius XI gave permission to the bishops to lift the ban on public worship. However, the government failed to honor the agreement and the persecution of the Church continued.[7] This villainous behavior led to the writing of a second encyclical, *Acerba animi,* of September 29, 1932.[8]

---

[2] *Ibid.,* p. 280, note 1.

[3] *Loc. cit.*

[4] *Ibid.,* pp. 280-281.

[5] *Social Wellsprings,* II, 278.

[6] *Acta Apostolicae Sedis,* XVIII (1926), 456 ff. (hereafter cited *AAS*).

[7] *Church and State,* p. 580.

[8] *AAS,* XXIV (1932), 321-332. For an analysis of this encyclical and for a discussion of the iniquitous role played by certain American citizens in the

In the encyclical Pius XI discussed the unjust Article 130, the protests which he lodged, the suspension of religious worship and its eventual restoration, and the perfidy of the Mexican government in violating the *modus vivendi* of 1929.[9] The pope charged gross interference on the part of the government in the exercise of the Church's ministry by its assignment of one priest for thirty-three thousand of the faithful in the State of Michoacan, one priest for sixty thousand in the State of Chiapas, and one priest for one hundred thousand in Vera Cruz.[10] Even though he urged the bishops of Mexico to exercise great prudence in these delicate matters, the pope did not hesitate to indict this state action as a grave violation of the fundamental rights of the Church:

> Nevertheless, since any restriction whatever of the matter of priests is a grave violation of divine rights, it will be necessary for the bishops, the clergy, and the Catholic laity to continue to protest with all their energy against such a violation, using every legitimate means. For even if these protests have no effect on those that govern the country, they will be effective in persuading the faithful, especially the uneducated, that by such action the state attacks the liberty of the Church. This liberty the Church can never renounce, no matter what may be the violence of the persecutors.[11]

Although these Mexican laws were iniquitous and derogated from the rights of God and His Church in the government of souls, Pius XI made it clear that it was not evil to co-operate with such laws.[12] The priest is compelled to seek government permission, because without this clearance "it would be impossible for him to exercise his sacred ministry for the good of souls. It is

---

Mexican persecution, cf. Wilfred Parsons, "There is a Persecution in Mexico," *America,* October 15, 1932; also consult Francis C. Kelly, *Blood-Drenched Altars* (2 ed. rev., Milwaukee: Bruce Publishing Co., 1935), Chapter XVIII, "The American Front," pp. 305 ff.

[9] *AAS,* XXIV (1932), 321 ff.; Husslein, *Social Wellsprings,* II, 280-284.

[10] *AAS,* XXIV (1932), 326; Husslein, *Social Wellsprings,* II, p. 285, § 14.

[11] Husslein, *Social Wellsprings,* II, p. 287, § 20; *AAS,* XXIV (1932), 328.

[12] Husslein, *Social Wellsprings,* II, pp. 287-288, §§ 22, 23. *AAS,* XXIV (1932), 329.

an imposition to which he is forced to submit to avoid a greater evil."[13] In such dire circumstances the pope permitted material co-operation with the unjust laws to prevent "a total cessation of worship, which would lead to exceedingly great harm to innumerable souls."[14] "Such," declared the pontiff, "is the certain and safe doctrine of the Church."[15]

Pius XI addressed a third encyclical to Mexico on March 28, 1937, entitled *Firmissimam constantiam*—Catholic Action Plan for Mexico.[16] By this time there had been a gradual lessening of tension between the Church and the State under the administration of General Cardenas. The encyclical was concerned with the role which Catholic action was to play in the Christian recovery of Mexico. In one section the pontiff alluded to the Church's need for liberty of action to fulfill its mission.[17]

In these three encyclicals to Mexico Pius XI re-echoed the constant teaching of his predecessors that the Church has a right to exercise its ministry independently of any civil regulation. When encroachments are made upon this right, every member of the Church must protest and use every licit means to remove this unjust transgression. The clergy may materially co-operate with the State when it regulates the ministry of the Church in order to avoid the greater evil of a complete cessation of worship and great harm to countless souls. This is certain and safe doctrine,

---

[13] Husslein, *Social Wellsprings,* II, p. 288, § 24; *AAS,* XXIV (1932), 329. In this same paragraph the pontiff compared such a priest to one who has been robbed and is then obliged to ask his despoiler for the use of the looted articles.

[14] Husslein, *Social Wellsprings,* II, p. 288, § 25; *AAS,* XXIV (1932), 330.

[15] Husslein, *Social Wellsprings,* II, p. 288, § 26; *AAS,* XXIV (1932), 330.

[16] *AAS,* XXIX (1937), 189-190; Husslein, *Social Wellsprings,* II, 376 ff.; *Church and State,* pp. 582 ff.

[17] . . . the Church being a society of men, cannot exist or develop, if it does not enjoy the liberty of action, and if its members have not the right to find in civil society the possibility of living according to the dictates of their consciences.

Consequently, it is quite natural that, when elementary religious and civil liberties are attacked, Catholic citizens must not resign thenselves passively to renouncing these liberties. Notwithstanding, the revindication of these rights and liberties can be, according to the circumstances, more or less opportune, more or less energetic. —Husslein, *Social Wellsprings,* II, p. 385, §§ 33-34; *AAS,* XXIX (1937), 196.

which however, can never be honestly construed to signify a capitulation to a more fundamental right of the State in matters of the ministry.

The Church suffered a similar persecution in Spain. On April 4, 1931, the monarchy was overthrown. This event cleared the way for a hostile persecution of the Church. Laws were enacted with the view to bringing about "the complete destruction of liberty: civil, domestic, educational, and religious."[18] Pius XI raised his voice in protest against this anti-Catholic action in the Encyclical, *Dilectissima nobis,* of June 3, 1933.[19]

The new Spanish constitution declared that the State professed no official religion, and it reaffirmed a separation of the Church and the State. Pius XI condemned this statement of public law:

> We shall not delay here to repeat that it is a serious error to affirm that this separation is licit and good in itself, especially in a nation almost totally Catholic. Separation, well considered, is only the baneful consequence—as We have so often declared, especially in our Encyclical *Quas primas*—on laicism, or rather the apostasy of society that today feigns to alienate itself from God and therefore from the Church.[20]

The pope likewise censured the usurpation of Church property and the obligation to pay taxes on the same buildings when the Catholic Church and its ministers used them for worship. He unmasked the true intent of the tax law—to render public worship impossible. The State had not only seized the ownership of Church property, but also had deprived the Church of every form of subsidy. "How can the Church pay these taxes," the pope queried.[21]

*De facto,* the Church was denied the right to private property and the free exercise of the ministry. The Church was permitted

---

[18] Husslein, *Social Wellsprings,* II, 291.

[19] *AAS,* XXV (1933), 261-274; Husslein, *Social Wellsprings,* II, 293 ff.

[20] Husslein, *Social Wellsprings,* II, p. 295, § 15; *AAS,* XXV (1933), 264-265.

[21] Husslein, *Social Wellsprings,* II, pp. 296-297, §§ 22-23; *AAS,* XXV (1933), 266-267.

to use only such properties as were necessary for religious services, and all places of public worship were declared by law to be public property. As Pius XI observed, "in this way the Church is compelled to submit to examination by the civil power for the fulfillment of its divine mission, and the State has constituted itself judge of what is necessary for purely spiritual functions."[22]

The pontiff enumerated the injustices of seizing shrines and Church chattels, the deplorable act of rejecting the authority of the Roman pontiff, the attacks upon religious orders, the prohibition against their teaching, and the establishment of godless schools.[23] He expostulated most vigorously against these godless schools which sought "to laicize all teaching which was hitherto inspired by religion and morality."[24]

In the face of legislation so harmful to ecclesiastical rights and liberties, Pius XI felt compelled by the duty of his Apostolic ministry to reprove and condemn this enactment: "Therefore, We do solemnly protest against the law itself, declaring that it cannot be invoked against the inalienable rights of the Church."[25] Once again this pontiff enunciated the traditional view that the Church has the right to fulfill its mission of teaching and preaching to all nations independently of civil regulation and interference.

A few years before the Spanish trouble the Holy See and Italy entered into negotiations which proved to be more a truce than a lasting peace. In 1929 Pius XI concluded a treaty, a concordat, and a financial convention with the Italian Fascist government.[26] These agreements were designed to resolve the "Roman Question," which arose in 1870 when the Kingdom of Italy annexed Rome, and also to ease tensions between the Catholic Church in

---

[22] Husslein, *Social Wellsprings,* II, p. 297, § 24; *AAS,* XXV (1933), 267.

[23] Husslein, *Social Wellsprings,* II, pp. 297-301, §§ 26-43; *AAS,* XXV (1933), 268-272.

[24] Husslein, *Social Wellsprings,* II, p. 301, § 43; *AAS,* XXV (1933), 272.

[25] Husslein, *Social Wellsprings,* II, p. 301, § 45; *AAS,* XXV (1933), 272.

[26] For the complete texts of these respective documents consult: *AAS,* XXI (1929), 209-221, 275-295, 273-274; *Church and State,* pp. 385-393, 393-406, 406-407; Angelus Perugini, *Concordata Vigentia* (Romae, 1934), pp. 96-111, 112-141, 111-112.

Italy and Benito Mussolini's Fascist Party.[27] Events demonstrated that the Fascists were not acting in good faith. The Fascist Party continued to attack the Catholic Church, and its leaders sought to suppress Catholic Action, which was guaranteed freedom of action in non-political spheres under the concordat of 1929.[28]

The basic question at issue was the education of Italian youth, and the controversy raged about an attempted state monopoly over schools and youth clubs.[29] In May, 1931, a decree of the Italian government ordered all the Catholic youth organization offices to be closed, and the Fascist Party initiated a campaign of intimidation and violence against the leaders and members of these Catholic organizations.[30] The Vatican wireless at that time was on a short-wave length and could not match the powerful transmission of Mussolini's Roman radio station. Therefore, Pius XI penned his defense in the Encyclical *Non abbiamo bisogno,* of June 29,

---

[27] These agreements are discussed within their historical context under the concordat section of this work.

[28] *Church and State,* p. 405, § 43:

> The Italian State recognizes the organizations connected with the Italian "Catholic Action" in so far as these shall—according to the instructions of the Holy See—carry out their activities outside any political Party, and under the immediate guidance of the Church's hierarchy for the diffusion and practical application of Catholic principles. . . .

[29] Cf. Edward Hales, *The Catholic Church in the Modern World* (London: Eyre and Spottiswoode, 1958), pp. 286-288; *Church and State,* pp. 457-458; Husslein, *Social Wellsprings,* II, 235-237.

[30] Husslein, *Social Wellsprings,* II, 237, quoting the London *Tablet,* of July 11, 1931, which clearly describes the tactics of this Fascist campaign:

> The Fascist pot suddenly boiled over last May, filling Italy with a steam and reek of NO Popery. . . . Vile cartoons appeared in the Roman newspapers chosen by Fascismo for this nasty job. A small Terror raged. Catholic printing presses were smashed, Catholic clubs were raided and wrecked, Catholic archives were impounded, Bishops' palaces were invaded, the premises of Catholic Action societies were locked up and the associations of Catholic young people were dissolved, amid assault and battery.
>
> These things were presumably done by Fascismo's bullies. But far more grave is the fact that the high Fascist authorities pounced upon the disturbances and outrages as an excuse for the stroke which they had long been planning: namely the disbanding and smashing of the Catholic social and cultural organizations, so as to secure all Italy and all Italians for the Totalitarian, omnivorous State.

1931.[31] The encyclical was smuggled out of Rome by the future Cardinal Spellman and published in Paris.[32]

A more violent conflict erupted between the Holy See and the government of Mussolini. However, the encyclical achieved its purpose. The statement of Pius XI received world-wide publicity, and an unfavorable reaction against the Italian government resulted. Mussolini made overtures to the Holy See and promised that the youth organizations of Catholic Action would not be disturbed. In return he received a renewed guarantee that the Catholic Action groups would remain neutral in politics, use only the banner of the State, and expel the few remaining political leaders from the ranks of Catholic Action.[33]

In *Non abbiamo bisogno,* Pius XI declared that Catholic Action in Italy was non-political by explicit orders of the Holy See. The government charges that Catholic youth organizations were a threat to the State were both unfounded and malicious. The pope deplored the false charge that the Vatican was a foreign power, whose existence was a real danger to the security of Italy.[34]

Pius XI unmasked the true aim of the Fascist government in its attack upon the Vatican and upon Catholic youth organizations—to wrest the youth of Italy away from the Church. This constituted a violation of the rights of souls and of the Church.[35]

---

[31] *AAS,* XXIII (1931), 285-312; *Church and State,* pp. 460-484; Husslein, *Social Wellsprings,* 238-254. Husslein does not give the full text.

[32] Cf. Thomas Harte, *Papal Social Principles* (Milwaukee: Bruce Publishing Co., 1956), p. 134.

[33] *Church and State,* p. 459; Harte, *Papal Social Principles,* p. 134.

[34] Husslein, *Social Wellsprings,* II, 238-241.

[35] *Ibid.,* pp. 243-244. Two paragraphs are especially pertinent:

> We repeat: "The sacred and inviolable rights of souls and of the Church"; because this matter concerns the rights of souls to procure for themselves the greatest spiritual good, according to the teaching and under the formative work of the Church, the divinely appointed and sole mandatory of this teaching and of this work in that supernatural order which is established in the blood of the Redeemer, and is necessary and obligatory for all of us if we are to share in the Divine Redemption. *It concerns the rights of souls, so formed, to share the treasures of the Redemption with other souls, thus participating in the activities of the Apostolic Hierarchy. . . .*
>
> *Besides, there is involved another right of the Church equally inviolable—the right to fulfill the imperative Divine Commission entrusted to her by her Divine Founder, to bring to souls, to bring to*

The pope acknowledged that the State has a right to educate youth, but he denied that this right was all inclusive. The State may not encroach upon the area where the Church alone is competent—the spiritual formation of youth.[36] In a word, the encyclical was a defense of the right and the duty of the Church to carry out her teaching and preaching mission independently of civil regulation.

This beleaguered pontiff was afforded no respite from the attacks of the enemies of the Church, for no sooner had he repelled the assaults of the godless leaders of one nation than he had to withstand fresh encounters from another quarter. The German Concordat of 1933 proved to be little more than a truce, because Adolf Hitler failed almost from the start to abide by the terms of this convention. The vigorous protests of the German hierarchy fell upon deaf ears. Pius XI realized that the hour had come for him to speak out. He carefully timed the publication of the Encyclical, *Mit brennender Sorge,* so that it could be delivered by the German pastors on Palm Sunday, March 21, 1937.[37] The text was smuggled into Germany, multigraphed there, and within three days distributed by private messenger to the clergy in every part of Germany. This plan was executed so efficiently that it escaped the notice of the infamous secret police.

Pope Pius XI berated the perfidious behavior of the Hitler regime. The Church had signed a treaty with Hitler, and as an international agreement it was solemnly binding upon both parties. The Holy See adhered to the agreement, whereas "anyone must acknowledge, not without surprise and reprobation, how the con-

---

*every soul, all the treasures of truth and of good, doctrinal and practical, which He Himself brought to the world.* "Go, therefore, and make disciples of all nations . . . teaching them to observe *all that* I have commanded you" (Matt. xxviii, 19, 20).

[36] Husslein, *Social Wellsprings,* II, 245. Pius XI also condemned the Fascism but permitted those who must remain in the Party for safety or sustenance of life to take it with certain reservations.—*Ibid.,* 249.

[37] For the text of the encyclical cf. *AAS,* XXIX (1937), 145-167; Husslein, *Social Wellsprings,* II, 318 ff.; *Church and State,* pp. 519-539. For an excellent account of the events leading up to the issuance of this encyclical and its decisive effect upon the attitude of the Nazi government toward the Catholic Church consult *Church and State,* pp. 516-519.

tracting party emasculated the terms of the treaty, distorted their meaning, and eventually considered its more or less official violation as normal policy."[38]

One of the gravest violations of the concordat consisted not simply in an interference with the right of the Church to teach, but in the usurpation of this right on the part of the State. Church doctrine was supplanted by teachings designed to destroy the Catholic faith. The encyclical denounced this State encroachment upon the rights of the Church.[39]

The pontiff longed for a peaceful settlement of these vital issues, but this did not slacken his determination to defend the position of the Church. He concluded his message with these sentiments:

> We have no greater desire than to see in Germany the restoration of true peace between Church and State. But if, without any fault of Ours, this peace is not to come, then the Church of God will defend its rights and its

[38] Husslein, *Social Wellsprings,* II, 319-320; *AAS,* XXIX (1937), 147.

[39] Documentary evidence of the destruction of Catholic youth organizations both by the direct method of legislation and indirect methods of defamation, opposition engendered by the State in the schools, economic pressures, and physical terrorism is presented in *The Persecution of the Catholic Church in the Third Reich: Facts and Documents Translated from the German* (London: Burns, Oates, 1940), pp. 82-114. This book also provides documentary evidence of the systematic attempt to exclude the Church from the work of education in the primary and secondary schools, and the efforts made to obstruct the Church's pastoral work. Convent schools were systematically suppressed. Teachers who belonged to religious congregations were dismissed, and members of religious congregations of men and women were dispersed. Lay teachers in Catholic elementary schools frequently taught religious doctrine incompatible with Catholic doctrine. Catholic elementary schools were closed by means of rigged elections. Religious instruction was eventually abolished, and denominational schools were transformed into community schools by governmental decree in 1938-1939.—*Ibid.,* pp. 115-233. The Catholic Church was denied legal protection, sacred places were desecrated, bishops and other members of the clergy were attacked, and the Church itself was defamed by songs and posters, at public exhibitions, in films, and by speeches of high-ranking Nazi officials. Clerics and religious were subjected to currency and immorality trials based upon "trumped up" evidence. Other modes of attack upon the Church and her members, and morality, itself, are documented in the remainder of the work. —*Ibid.,* 234-328.

> freedom in the name of the Almighty, whose arm has not been shortened.[40]

A few days after the release of the Encyclical *Mit brennender Sorge,* Pius XI addressed his famous encyclical on "Atheistic Communism" to the world.[41] He reiterated the claim of the Church to unrestricted freedom in the fulfillment of its mission, and pointed out the salutary effects which the unfettered exercise of its teaching and preaching would have upon the existing world crisis.[42]

The reaction of Pius XI to the violations of solemn treaties and of the fundamental rights of the Church by civil society may be summarized as follows:

1. The State has no right to interfere in the purely spiritual matters of the Church, or to deprive it of the material means necessary for its existence and the fulfillment of its mission.
2. In particular, the State has no right to reduce ministers of religion to the rank of lay professionals and to subject them to State regulations in the exercise of their ministry.
3. The assignment of priests to minister to the faithful and the determination of the spiritual needs of the faithful is absolutely outside the competency of the State.
4. Complete separation of Church and State is never licit in itself, especially in a nation which is predominantly Catholic.
5. The clergy and the faithful must denounce, and use every licit means to remove, these State incursions upon Church liberties; yet it is not immoral to co-operate materially with such State laws, if the spirit of tolerance will prevent a greater

---

[40] Husslein, *Social Wellsprings,* II, 338; *AAS,* XXIX (1937), 166-167.

[41] *"Divini Redemptoris,"* 19 Mart. 1937.—*AAS,* XXIX (1937), 65-106; Husslein, *Social Wellsprings,* II, 341-374.

[42] At the same time the State must allow the Church full liberty to fulfill its divine and spiritual mission, and that in itself will be an effectual contribution to the rescue of nations from the dread torment of the present hour. . . . We trust that those rulers of nations who are at all aware of the extreme danger threatening every people today may be more and more convinced of their supreme duty not to hinder the Church in the fulfillment of its mission. This is the more imperative since, while the mission has in view man's happiness in heaven, it cannot but promote his true felicity in time.

Cf. Husslein, *Social Wellsprings,* II, 372-373; *AAS,* XXIV (1937), 104-105.

evil—the total cessation of worship. This is certain and safe doctrine.

6. The Church desires peace and harmony with the State, but it will never cease to defend its rights when they are unjustly violated or usurped.

### *Section 2. Juridic Relations of Church and State*

In his encyclical on the Mystical Body, Pope Pius XII reiterates the constant teaching of the Holy See on the nature of the Church and the nature of the State. Both the Church and the State are perfect societies, but the Church "is not made up of merely moral and juridic elements and principles. It is far superior to all other human societies. . . ."[43] However, the pope promptly adds that "human societies, and in the first place civil society, are by no means to be dispensed with or belittled."[44]

Pope Pius XII returns to this theme in his address to the International Congress of Historical Sciences.[45] He says that Leo XIII has "condensed the specific nature of those relations [of Church and State] in one formula, of which he has given brilliant illustration in his Encyclical Letters *Diuturnum illud* (1881), *Immortale Dei* (1885), and *Sapientas Christianae* (1890)."[46] In brief, Leo XIII taught that the two powers are sovereign and that their

---

[43] Francis Powers, *Papal Pronouncements on the Political Order* (Westminster, Md.: The Newman Press, 1952), p. 106, n. 160; *AAS,* XXXV (1943), 223; *Encyclical Letter on the Mystical Body of Christ,* trans. of *Mystical Corporis Christi* of Pius XII by Gerald C. Treacy, with discussion club outline (New York: The Paulist Press, no date), p. 21, n. 67. Cf. Harte, *Papal Social Principles,* pp. 86-89, for an outline of this encyclical.

[44] Powers, *Papal Pronouncements on the Political Order, loc. cit.; Encyclical Letter on the Mystical Body,* Paulist Press edition, *loc. cit.; AAS, loc. cit.*

[45] *"Vous avez voulu,"* 7 Sept. 1955—*AAS,* ALVII (1955), 672-682; "The Church and History," *The Pope Speaks, Addresses and Publications of the Holy Father,* ed. Frederick Dyer and John O'Neil, II (1955), 205-215. For an outline of this discourse cf. Harte, *Papal Social Principles,* pp. 91-95.

[46] *The Pope Speaks,* II, 210; *AAS,* XLVII (1955), 677. *"Immortale Dei," ASS,* XVIII (1885), 161-180. "Diuturnum illud," *ASS,* XIV (1881), 3-14. *"Sapientiae Christianae," ASS,* XXII (1890), 385-404.

nature and aims define the limits within which they rule *iure proprio.*[47]

There are essential differences between the origin, nature and end of the authority of the Church and of the State. The State has its origin in the natural law and, as Pius XII declares in his allocution to the Roman Rota on October 2, 1945, "the Church owes its origin to a positive act of God, an act which is in perfect accord with the social nature of man, but which completely transcends it."[48] Hence, its authority transcends the authority of the State, since unlike the latter its authority is conferred directly by God, and not immediately by men.

Pius XII, citing *Immortale Dei* of Leo XIII, states that the Church, like the State, "possesses a sovereign right to all that it needs to obtain its objective, and this includes material things."[49] It is in keeping with nature and with the divine will that these two powers co-operate in mutual understanding. However, conflicts will occasionally arise. When conditions are such that "the laws of the State violate the divine law, the Church has a moral obligation to oppose them."[50]

The Holy See considers collaboration between Church and State as normal and "regards as ideal the unity of a people in the true

---

[47] For a treatise on the nature of the State, a Catholic philosophy of the State, and some notions on Church and State, consult: Rommen, *The State in Catholic Thought,* and John A. Ryan and Francis J. Boland, *Catholic Social Principles,* rev. ed. of *The State and the Catholic Church* (New York: The Macmillan Co., 1940).

[48] Powers, *Papal Pronouncements on the Political Order,* p. 108, n. 163; *Church and State,* p. 605; *"Dacchè piacque,"* 2 Oct. 1945—*AAS,* XXXVII (1945), 259. The topic of this discourse is "Authority, Civil and Ecclesiastical."

[49] *The Pope Speaks,* II, 210; *AAS,* XLVII (1955), 677.

[50] *The Pope Speaks,* II, *loc. cit.; AAS,* XLVII (1955), *loc. cit.* Pius XII made similar observations in his allocution to the Roman Rota on Authority—Civil and Ecclesiastical, October 29, 1947.—*"Ci torna," AAS,* XXXIX (1947), 493-498. These two societies have different ends, and this excludes any violent subjection of the Church to the State. However, it does not preclude every kind of union between these two societies. Cf. Rommen, *The State in Catholic Thought,* pp. 570-585. Rommen gives an excellent analysis of Pope Leo XIII's ideas on *Libertas Ecclesiae.*

religion and unanimity of action between itself and the State."[51] The Holy See is also cognizant of the fact that events have been unfolding in another direction, i.e., a condition exists in which religious pluralism flourishes in the same nation, and Catholics constitute a more or less strong minority. "It may be interesting, and even surprising," the pontiff comments, "for the historian to find in the United States of America one example among others of the way the Church succeeds in flourishing in the most varied conditions.[52]

In two other allocutions Pius XII discusses the question of freedom of conscience and religious toleration.[53] It may appear to the modern conscience, the pontiff declares, that the punishment of crimes against the faith in the past exceeded at times the bounds of justice. Today, the contrary tendency is operative, for in general society displays an excessive insensibility and indifference in these matters. The religiously pluralistic composition of modern nations has caused civil tribunals to adopt the principle of tolerance and liberty of conscience. Nevertheless, the pope observes, "there is a political tolerance, a civil tolerance, a social tolerance, in regard to adherents of other religious beliefs which, in circumstances such as these, is a moral duty for Catholics."[54]

It would be an unwarranted digression to discuss the entire notion of toleration, but a brief consideration of Catholic political and religious toleration is justified within the general framework of the present investigation of the juridic relations of Church and

---

[51] *The Pope Speaks,* II, 211; *AAS,* XLVII (1955), 679.

[52] *The Pope Speaks,* II, 211-212; *AAS,* XLVII (1955), 679.

[53] *"Ecco che già,"* 6 Oct. 1946—*AAS,* XXXVIII (1946), 391-397. *"Ci riesce,"* 6 Dec. 1953—*AAS,* XLV (1953), 794-802. In *Ecco che già,* his discourse to the Roman Rota on October 6, 1946, the pontiff made an observation similar to the comment of his predecessor, Leo XIII. Many who appeal to the principle of freedom of conscience, when they become ensconced in power, make it their first project to impose an oppressive burden on the Catholic population, especially in the area of rights of the parents over education of their children.—*AAS,* XXXVIII (1946), 392-393.

[54] Powers, *Papal Pronouncements on the Political Order,* p. 122, n. 181; *AAS,* XXXVIII (1946), 393. Italian and English versions of some sections of this allocution, including the foregoing selection, are contained in *The Clergy Review* (ed. G. D. Smith, London: Oates and Washbourne, July-December, 1948), XXX (new series), 244-246.

State. These principles of religious toleration are clearly formulated in the address of Pius XII to the participants of the Fifth National Convention of the Union of Italian Catholic Jurists on December 6, 1953.[55]

The Catholic attitude toward religious toleration in the international community may be briefly summarized under five points:

1. No human authority, municipal, regional, or international, "whatever be their religious character, can give a positive command or positive authorization to teach or to do that which would be contrary to religious truth or moral good."[56] Such a command or authorization has no binding effect because "it is contrary to nature to oblige the spirit and the will of man to error and evil, or to consider one or the other as indifferent."[57]
2. The hypothesis that religious error and moral error must be impeded whenever possible, "because toleration of them is in itself immoral, is not valid *absolutely and unconditionally.*"[58]
3. The ultimate norm of action is not "that of repressing moral and religious error whenever possible." This repression "must be subordinated to *higher and more general* norms, which *in some circumstances* permit, and even perhaps seem to indicate as the better policy, a toleration of error in order to promote *a greater good.*[59]
4. Two principles must be applied by the jurist, the statesman, and the sovereign Catholic State in concrete cases:
   (a) "that which does not correspond to truth or the norm of morality objectively has no right to exist, to be spread or to be activated."
   (b) "failure to impede this with civil laws and coercive measures can nevertheless be justified in the interests of a higher and more general good."[60]

---

[55] *"Ci riesce," AAS,* XLV (1953), 794-802. "International Community and Religious Tolerance," *The Pope Speaks,* I, 64-71.

[56] *The Pope Speaks,* I, 67; *AAS,* XLV (1953), 798.

[57] *The Pope Speaks,* I, 67-68; *AAS,* XLV (1953), 798.

[58] *The Pope Speaks,* I, 68; *AAS,* XLV (1953), 799.

[59] *The Pope Speaks,* I, 68; *AAS,* XLV (1953), 799.

[60] *The Pope Speaks,* I, 68-69; *AAS,* XLV (1953), 799.

5. The Catholic statesman in arriving at a decision must weigh the "dangerous consequences that stem from toleration against those from which the community of nations will be spared, if the formula of toleration be accepted."[61]

In that which concerns religion and morality, the Catholic statesman will seek the judgment of the Church. For the pope alone, "to whom Christ has entrusted the guidance of His whole Church is competent to speak in the last instance on vital questions, touching international life."[62]

Pius XII applies these principles to the Catholic Church, which in the fulfillment of its mission has had to cope with, and continues to be faced to a great extent with the same problems which the functioning of a community of sovereign states must overcome. The pontiff observes that the Church feels these problems more acutely, "for it is obligated to the purpose of its mission, determined by her Founder Himself, a purpose which penetrates to the very depths of the spirit and heart of man."[63] History shows that conflicts in this area are inevitable, and the Lord Himself predicted this would be so to the end of time.

One of the problems the Church must face is toleration of evil. It will never compromise or vacillate in the matter of doctrine or religious truth. However, the Church has and will continue to be tolerant of what is not objectively true and good, even at times when it could suppress it. The attitude of the Church in individual cases is determined "by what is demanded for the safeguarding and considering the *'bonum commune,'* on the one hand, the common good of the Church and the State in individual states, and on the other, the common good of the universal Church, the reign of God over the whole world."[64] In resolving these questions of fact, the norms cited above for the Catholic statesman and jurist are equally valid for the Church.

---

[61] *The Pope Speaks,* I, 69; *AAS,* XLV (1953), 799. He will also consider the good that will flow directly to the community of nations and indirectly to his own.

[62] *The Pope Speaks,* I, 69; *AAS,* XLV (1953), 779-780.

[63] *The Pope Speaks,* I, 69; *AAS,* XLV (1953), 800.

[64] *The Pope Speaks,* I, 70; *AAS,* XLV (1953), 801.

The Holy See frequently makes practical application of these principles in international agreements such as a concordat, treaty, *modus vivendi,* etc. "The Concordats are for her a practical expression of the collaboration between the Church and State."[65] Pius XII discusses both the purpose and the binding nature of Concordats. Primarily, they "must assure to the Church a stable condition in right and in fact in the state in which they are concluded, and must guarantee to her full independence in the fulfillment of her divine mission."[66] In his 1955 allocution (*"Vous avez voulu"*) to historians he sums up the purpose of concordats in these words: "In Concordats the Church seeks juridical security and the necessary independence for her mission."[67] From these papal statements it is evident that Concordats are a means employed by the Holy See to attain legal standing for the Church in the public law of the said State and to secure the free exercise of worship and of the ministry, which, of course, includes preaching independently of civil interference.

The degree of binding power of a concordat cannot be stated in one formula; each concordat must be examined within the circumstances surrounding its negotiation. Pius XII states its binding power as follows:

> When the Church has set her signature to a Concordat, it holds for everything contained therein. But, with the mutual acknowledgment of both high contracting parties, it may not hold in the same way for everything.[68]

Although the general purpose of concordats is that of securing a juridic stability and freedom of action for the Church, the specific purpose of a concordat within the general purpose may differ in individual concordats. A concordat with a given nation may solemnize a juridic establishment, i.e., "the Church and the State proclaim in a Concordat their common religious conviction."[69] It

[65] *The Pope Speaks,* I, 71; *AAS,* XLV (1953), 802.
[66] *The Pope Speaks,* I, 71; *AAS,* XLV (1953), 802.
[67] *The Pope Speaks,* II, 212; *AAS,* XLVII (1955), 679.
[68] *The Pope Speaks,* I, 71; *AAS,* XLV (1953), 802.
[69] *The Pope Speaks,* I, 71; *AAS,* XLV (1953), 802.

may simply seek to forestall "disputes with regard to questions of principle," and to remove "from the very beginning possible matters of conflict."[70] Finally, a concordat "may also mean a simple tolerance, according to those two principles which are the norm for co-existence (*convivenza*) of the Church and her faithful with the civil powers and with men of another belief."[71]

The concordats examined in the next article illustrate the purpose, both general and specific, as outlined by Pius XII. The general purpose of securing a juridic standing for the Church, be it establishment, preferred position, equal status, or inferior position at law, is present in most of the concordats, as well as the general purpose of securing freedom of action for the Church to fulfill its preaching and teaching mission. Some concordats seek to forestall possible conflict, and specific concordat articles reflect at times an overwhelming approval of a situation, whereas others mirror a simple tolerance of a given condition.

Pius XII was confident that the international community "can banish every danger of war and establish peace, and, as far as the Church is concerned, can guarantee to it freedom of action everywhere" to fulfill her mission—the establishment of the Kingdom of Christ.[72]

The chief desire of the Church is not that heresy be suppressed whenever and wherever possible, but that the Church be free to exercise its mission of preaching and saving souls everywhere in the world. It is the same freedom of action desired and demanded by Leo XIII, by Pius X, by Benedict XV, and by Pius XI, the predecessors of the pontiff who addressed the international community on the subject of religious tolerance. One of the means employed by these pontiffs to guarantee the free exercise of the ministry was the signing of concordats. These concordats, as Pius XII stated, may represent the ideal conditions of the union of Church and State and the establishment of religion, they may express less than complete approval, or even simple tolerance, of the Church-State relations in a given nation.

---

[70] *The Pope Speaks,* I, 71; *AAS,* XLV (1953), 802.
[71] *The Pope Speaks,* I, 71; *AAS,* XLV (1953), 802.
[72] *The Pope Speaks,* I, 71; *AAS,* XLV (1953), 802.

The present consideration of the more significant writings and discourses of Pius XII on subjects directly or indirectly connected with the juridic relations of Church and State demonstrates that his teachings are a re-echoing and, in some instances, a development or clarification of the position of Leo XII. Both pontiffs agree that the Church and the State are two powers, distinct in origin, nature and end. The formula of this relationship can be succinctly stated as "distinction and cooperation." Neither society may dominate the other, but there should exist a mutual spirit of collaboration. In his encyclical *Libertas* (on Human Liberty) Leo XII condemned the false liberal teaching of absolute separation of Church and State, and Pius XII stated that "in principle, she [the Church] cannot approve complete separation of the two powers."[73]

Toleration, provided that it is properly understood, is sanctioned by both pontiffs. In his encyclical *Libertas* (on Human Liberty), Leo XII countenanced an adaptation of Church policy in matters of Church and State to the requirements of the modern system of government, provided it was an equitable adjustment consistent with truth and justice. Pius XII reflected greater lucidity, and perhaps a more liberal frame of mind, in this matter. In his allocution to historians in 1955 and in his address to the Roman Rota in 1946, he maintained the ideal of one religion and the unanimity of action between Church and State, and yet he spoke of a political, a social and a religious tolerance in a religiously pluralistic society as "a moral duty for Catholics." He and his predecessor, Leo XIII, looked benignly upon the flourishing condition of the Church in the religiously pluralistic United States of America. They did not hail its juridic arrangements as ideal, and accordingly hoped for continued improvement in this area. Nevertheless, they were pleased with the freedom of action afforded to the Church in this nation.

## ARTICLE II. A SURVEY OF MODERN CONCORDATS

A new era of concordats was initiated by the Consistorial Al-

---

[73] *The Pope Speaks,* I, 71; *AAS,* XLV (1953), 802. *"Libertas," ASS,* XX (1887), 593-613.

locution of Benedict XV on November 21, 1921.[74] The pope let it be known that the Holy See no longer considered itself bound by the concordats made with States in which radical changes were effected by World War I. These States were no longer regarded by the Holy See as the same moral entities.[75]

The First World War not only reshaped old nations, it gave rise to new States, or, in some cases, a rebirth of old nations. Latvia was the first of these nations to conclude a concordat with the Holy See (1922). During the next few years two States which border on Latvia negotiated concordat agreements with the Holy See—Poland (1925) and Lithuania (1927). Other nations were soon added to the list, including Italy (1929), Rumania (1929), Germany (1933), and Austria (1934).[76] A survey of these and other concordats will follow under the headings of: (1) the juridic status of Church and State; (2) the free exercise of the ministry; (3) concessions made by the Church to negotiating nations.

### *Section 1. The Juridic Status of Church and State*

This concept is discussed under four titles: 1. establishment, 2. preferred position, 3. equal status, 4. inferior status in law.

---

[74] *"In hac quidem," AAS*, XIII (1921), 521-524; cf. Alaphridus Ottaviani, *Institutiones Iuris Publici Ecclesiastici* (2 vols., *Ius Publicum Internum et Ius Publicum Externum* (3rd ed. Romae: Typis Polyglottis Vaticanis, 1947), II, 309-315 (hereafter cited Ottaviani).

[75] This unilateral action by the Holy See has given rise to the question where the Holy See acted arbitrarily. Willabald M. Plöchl resolves this problem by stating that the action of Pope Benedict XV "is, in fact, another application of the clause, *rebus sic stantibus*. In serving notice to the States concerned, the Pope announced the principle that the Holy See desired to bring the relations between Church and State in accord with the new situation."—"Reflections on the Nature and Status of Concordats," *The Jurist*, VII (1947), 35-36. Cf. also Ottaviani, *op. cit.*, II, 349-350. For a discussion of the doctrine known as the *clausula rebus sic stantibus* consult: J. L. Brierly, *The Law of Nations* (4 ed., London: Oxford University Press, 1949), pp. 244-249.

[76] For an account of the events which helped to reshape the continent of Europe consult: A. J. P. Taylor, *The Struggle for Mastery in Europe, 1848-1918* (London: The Oxford University Press, 1954), and Charles D. Hazen, *Fifty Years of Europe* (New York, 1919).

Only three of the eighteen States under consideration in this section granted the Catholic Church legal establishment—Italy in 1929, Spain in 1953, and the Dominican Republic in 1954. This is not surprising, because the majority of the concordats negotiated since the First World War have been with non-Latin European States, most of which have been religiously pluralistic from the days of the Protestant Revolt.

## 1. Establishment of Religion

Rome was occupied by the Italian Monarchist forces in 1870. On May 13, 1871, the Italian parliament passed the Law of Guarantees. The first part of the law, which consisted of twelve articles, concerned the prerogatives of the pope and of the Holy See. The second part, which consisted of seven articles, legislated regarding the relations of the State with the Church.[77] The Holy See rejected these articles, and in the course of time a *modus vivendi* crystallized between the Church and the State.[78]

After the First World War there were three strong political parties in Italy—Mussolini's Fascists, Don Sturzo's *Populare,* and the communists who looked to Moscow for leadership. The Fascist Party led by Benito Mussolini (1883-1945) took control of the Italian government in 1922. By 1923 Mussolini's party had the communists under control. Mussolini then turned his attention to crushing the last pocket of resistance, the *Populare,* which was founded by Luigi Sturzo, a secular priest, in 1919.[79] An all-out

---

[77] *The Italian Law of Guarantees,* May 13, 1871, is reproduced in English translation in *Church and State,* pp. 287-291.

[78] *Church and State,* pp. 285-287. For a more detailed discussion of the question of Rome consult: *The History of Nations,* vol. IV, *Italy* (ed. J. Higginson Cabot, New York: 1928), pp. 387-411; Hales, *The Catholic Church in the Modern World,* pp. 141-156; Raymond Corrigan, *The Church and the Nineteenth Century* (Milwaukee: Bruce Publishing Co., 1948), pp. 231-237, especially pp. 235-236 where Corrigan discusses the suppression of religious houses, the confiscation of religious property, and the attempt to subject the Sacred Congregation of the Propaganda to the State.

[79] Hales sums up the objectives of the *Populare* as follows: "Their programme was partly religious and partly political. They wanted to see freedom for religious orders and for the schools, and a full return of Catholics

Fascist assault upon the Church was threatened. Don Sturzo resigned as party leader, and the *Populare* ceased to be a serious threat to the Fascists.[80]

Pope Pius XI desired to better Church-State relations in Italy and to find a solution to the "Roman Question," which had been a great source of Church-State agitation since Rome was annexed to the Kingdom of Italy in 1870. Both of these problems were "settled" by three conventions effected in 1929: The Lateran Treaty, The Concordat between the Holy See and Italy, and the Financial Convention.[81]

The first article of the Lateran Treaty reaffirms the establishment of the Catholic Church in Italy: "Italy recognizes and reaffirms the principle contained in Article I of the Statutes of the Kingdom of March 4, 1848, according to which the Catholic Apostolic and Roman Religion is the sole religion of the State."[82] The meaning of this essential treaty guarantee is elaborated upon in the concordat.

The second concession of the Lateran Treaty is the recognition

---

into political life on every front; they also wanted decentralization of the administrative system, with effective power for the different provinces of Italy, and proportional representation in the central parliament."—*The Catholic Church in the Modern World,* pp. 282-283.

[80] *Ibid.,* pp. 285-286; *History of Nations,* IV, *Italy,* pp. 425-436.

[81] For the complete texts of these respective documents consult: *AAS,* XXI (1929), 209-221; 275-295; 273-274; *Church and State,* pp. 385-393; 393-406; 406-407; Angelus Perugini, *Concordata Vigentia,* pp. 96-111; 112-141; 111-112.

For a brief historical treatment of the events preceding these agreements consult: *Church and State,* pp. 382-385; Hales, *The Catholic Church in the Modern World,* pp. 122-130, 234-257, 282 ff. Cf. also Ottaviani, *op. cit.,* II, 387-392, for a discussion of the Italian relations of Church and State.

[82] *Church and State,* p. 386; Art. 1; *AAS,* XXI (1929), 210, Art. 1; Perugini, *Concordata Vigentia,* p. 97, Art. 1. Perugini reproduces article one of the 1848 Constitution which states that the Catholic Apostolic Roman religion is the sole religion of the State and that all other sects are to be tolerated in conformity with the law. Cf. *ibid.,* p. 97, note 8. In this same note Perugini maintains that by force of the Penal Code and the Law Regarding Public Security (December 23, 1887, Art. 7) liberty and equality of religion were sanctioned.

of the sovereignty of the Holy See—The State of the Vatican. Italy recognizes the sovereignty of the Holy See in international matters as being inherent in its nature, in conformity with its tradition, and required by its mission in the world.[83]

The next nation to reinstate the establishment of the Catholic Church and to reëstablish rapport with the Holy See was Spain. General Franco emerged as the victor in the Spanish revolution of the nineteen thirties, and conditions were settled enough by 1941 for the Holy See to sign a convention with the Spanish government.[84] Both parties hoped eventually to negotiate a full-fledged concordat. Until this new concordat could be brought into being, Spain agreed to observe the dispositions contained in the first four articles of the Concordat of 1851.[85] Article I states that the Roman Catholic religion is the sole religion in Spain. Article II declares that instruction in all schools, public and private, from the elementary grades to the university inclusive, must conform to the doctrine of this religion. It further guarantees that the vigilance of the clergy concerning the purity of the faith, morals and religious education of youth, even in public schools, can be exercised unimpededly. Article III assures the sacred ministers that the State will not tolerate any opposition or interference on the part of anyone in the exercise of their sacred ministry and offices. Article IV completes these guarantees of free and unimpeded exercise of the ministry when it states that "in all other things which pertain to the right and the exercise of ecclesiastical authority and the ministry of sacred orders, the bishops and the

---

[83] *Church and State,* p. 386, Art. 2; *AAS,* XXI (1929), 210; Perugini, *Concordata Vigentia,* pp. 97-98. The extent of this guarantee is stated in detail in the remainder of the Lateran Treaty. The *AAS* contains maps of the lands, territorial and extra-territorial, which belong to the Vatican State.—*AAS,* XXI (1929), 223-271.

[84] "Conventio inter Sanctam Sedem et Guberium Hispanicam," *AAS,* XXXIII (1941), 480-481.

[85] *Ibid.,* p. 481, Art. 9; for the Concordat of 1851 cf. "Concordato fra Pio IX ed Isabella II Regina di Spagna," *Raccolta di Concordati su Materie Ecclesiastiche tra la Sancta Sede e le Authorita Civili,* a cura Angelo Mercati, nuova edizione anastatica con supplemento (2 vols., Romae: Tipografia Vaticana Poliglotta, 1954), I, 771 ff. (hereafter cited *Raccolta di Concordati*).

clergy dependent upon them shall enjoy the full liberty which the sacred canons establish."[86]

The projected concordat was ultimately negotiated and promulgated in 1953.[87] In the first article Spain grants a legal position which the Catholic Church has ceased to enjoy in a number of "Catholic" States—Establishment.[88] The Dominican Republic accorded the Church this same recognition of rights in identical terminology in the following year.[89]

## 2. Preferred Status in Law

Four nations recognized the Catholic religion as the preferred religion of the State after the First World War. Poland granted the Catholic Church this position in the Concordat of 1925, and Austria did the same in the Concordat of 1934. Ireland extended this position to the Church in its Constitution of 1937. Haiti simply renewed the status which it guaranteed the Church in the Concordat of 1860.[90]

Poland achieved its independence through the Treaty of Ver-

---

[86] *Raccolta di Concordati,* I, 771-772 (trans. by writer).

[87] "Concordato tra la Santa e la Spagna," *AAS,* XXXXV (1953), 625-655.

[88] *AAS,* XXXXV (1953), p. 626, Art. I: The Roman Catholic and Apostolic religion continues being the only religion of the Spanish nation and shall enjoy the rights and prerogatives that correspond to it in conformity with the Divine Law and Canon Law (trans. by writer).

[89] *AAS,* XXXXVI (1954), p. 434, Art. I. A number of South and Central American governments granted some form of establishment to the Catholic Church during the nineteenth century: Bolivia (1851)—*Raccolta di Concordati,* I, supplement [3], Art. I; Costa Rica (1852), *Raccolta di Concordati,* I, p. 800, Art. I; Guatemala (1852)—*ibid.,* I, p. 810, Art. I; Honduras (1861)—*ibid.,* I, p. 937, Art. I; Nicaragua (1861)—*ibid.,* I, p. 949, Art. I; San Salvador (1861)—*ibid.,* I, p. 960, Art. I; Venezuela (1862) —*ibid.,* I, p. 971, Art. I; Ecuador (1862)—*ibid.,* p. 984, Art. I. When this concordat renegotiated in 1881 the establishment clause remained unaltered. Cf. *ibid.,* I, pp. 1001-1002, Art. I. Columbia (1887)—*ibid.,* I, p. 1052, Art. I. For a discussion of the origins of diplomatic missions with these countries consult: Robert A. Graham, *Vatican Diplomacy: A Study of Church and State on the International Plane* (Princeton, N. J.: Princeton University Press, 1959), pp. 79-82.

[90] For the Concordat of 1860 consult: *Raccolta di Concordati,* I, p. 930, Art. I.

sailles, June 28, 1919. In 1795 Poland had been divided among three nations, and the ecclesiastical hierarchy of Poland was partly in Russia, partly in Prussia, and partly in Austria. Attempts had been made by means of concordats to insure the liberty of the Polish Church and its hierarchy.[91]

Vested with its newly gained sovereignty, Poland sought to negotiate a concordat with the Holy See. This desire was clearly manifested in the Polish Constitution, March 17, 1921, which envisioned such a permanent settlement with the Holy See.[92]

However, a long delay ensued before the concordat was finally approved. There was the delicate problem of Polish territorial boundaries. These lines were definitively established by the League of Nations in 1923. The second obstacle, the redistribution of lands, of which many were ecclesiastical, produced additional cause for procrastination. The land issue was finally settled on June 2, 1925, and the concordat went into effect on August 2 of the same year.[93]

The concordat contains a broad statement of freedom for the Catholic Church. The various rites of the Catholic Church are guaranteed full freedom in Poland. The State guarantees the Church the free exercise of its spiritual power and a free administration of its affairs and property in conformity with divine law and Canon Law.[94] Perugini notes that this article of the

---

[91] E.g., "Concordato fra Pio IX e Niccolo Imperatore delle Russie" (1847), *Raccolta di Concordati,* I, pp. 751 ff., and "Concordato fra Pio IX e Francesco Guiseppi I Imperatore d'Austria" (1855), *Raccolta di Concordati,* I, pp. 821 ff. For a brief treatment of the relations of the Holy See with Prussia and Russia in the eighteenth and nineteenth centuries consult: Graham, *Vatican Diplomacy,* pp. 37-68.

[92] Perugini, *Concordata Vigentia,* p. 32. Perugini reproduces a section of Article 114 of the Constitution, which says that the Roman Catholic Church is governed by its own laws, and that the relationship between Church and State will be defined through a convention to be negotiated with the Holy See. This concordat, the article adds, must meet with the approval of the parliament.

[93] *Loc. cit.*

[94] Cf. "Inter Sanctam Sedem et Poloniae Republicam Solemnis Conventio" in Perugini, *Concordata Vigentia,* p. 33, Art. 5. The text of the concordat also appears in *AAS,* XVII (1925), 273 ff.

concordat abrogates all the laws of the Civil Codes of Russia, Bavaria, and Austria, which are not in conformity with the divine law of the Canon Law, and which were still accepted as law in Poland. In his opinion the guarantees of this article with respect to the liberty of the Church are clearly broader and more defined than the guarantees of the Polish Constitution (Articles 111-116 and 102), which recognize and safeguard the Catholic religion as the dominant and preferred one among all the religious sects existing in Poland.[95]

Austria was the next nation to grant a preferred position in the public law of the State to the Church. In 1934 the Austrian government adopted a new constitution. About this time the Holy See and the government agreed to promulgate the concordat which had been under negotiation for some months.[96]

The Constitution guaranteed freedom of assembly, association, speech, religion, etc., but most of these freedoms were temporarily suspended because of the subversive elements operative in Austria at the time of the promulgation of the Constitution. The Catholic Church was granted a preferred position, which was not surpris-

---

[95] Perugini, *Concordata Vigentia,* pp. 34-35, n. 5. Ottaviani argues that the juridic primacy of the Catholic Church which is mentioned in the Constitution of 1921 is more than a mere primacy of honor.—*Institutiones Iuris Publici Ecclesiastici,* II, 402-403, n. 423.

[96] The years of 1933 and 1934 were marked by political crisis in Austria. Ehler and Morall briefly describe these conditions: "In 1933 he [Chancellor Dollfuss (+ 1934)] suspended the hardly workable Austrian parliament, dissolved the armed formations of the Socialist Party and proscribed the Nazi Party entirely, following a series of bomb outrages staged by its members. In February 1934, the Socialist Party was violently suppressed and on May 1, 1934, the Government of Chancellor Dollfuss, now authoritarian and supported by all Catholic political forces (who remained the only legal organizations in the country), enacted a new Constitution transforming Austria into a Corporative."—*Church and State,* p. 497. An English translation of the Articles of the Constitution of 1934 is contained in *Church and State,* pp. 501-509. For a discussion of the post-war problems surrounding this concordat of 1934 consult: Willibald M. Plöchl, "Church and State in Austria," *The Jurist,* XII (1952), 400-416. The concordat text is found in *AAS,* XXVI (1934), 249-283, and in Perugini, *Concordata Vigentia,* pp. 263-307.

ing, for ninety-four percent of the population were at least nominally Catholic.[97]

Chapter two of the Constitution (Articles 27-31) was concerned with the general rights of citizens. Article 27 guaranteed everyone in Austria freedom of worship and conscience, provided that his activity did not oppose public order and good morals. This article removed all religious tests for public office.[98]

Article 28 specified the right of assembly for worship:

> The adherents of a sect, if it is not legally recognized in Austria as a religious body, can associate with a view to regular worship, or with a view to any other manifestation of religious belief. Such a group has not the character of a religious community, unless the sect in question is permitted by the State. When it is the religious community assumes a juridic personality and has a right to claim the State's protection in the exercise of its religion; but it is subject to State supervision.[99]

Article 29 recognized the right of legally established Church bodies to regulate their own internal affairs and to own and administer property within the framework of the law. Article 30 indicated the special position enjoyed by the Catholic Church:

> The affairs of Churches and religious bodies recognized by law, in which the interest of the State are also involved, are regulated by special legal provisions.
>
> In this connection other rights than those mentioned in Art. 29 may be recognized to each Church or religious body, according to their nature and general importance in the State.
>
> As regards the Catholic Church such regulation took place, in principle, in the agreement reached between the Federation and the Holy See.
>
> Articles 1 and 2; Art. 5. par. I, sects. 1-3; Art. 6, sects 1-2; Art. 10, par. I, sec. 1; Art. 13, pars. 1-4; Art.

---

[97] Cf. *Church and State,* p. 498. Ottaviani, *op. cit.,* II, p. 357, note 13.— In 1934 Austrian citizens numbered 6.76 millions, of whom 93.7% were Catholic, 3.1% Protestant, and 2.9% Jews.

[98] *Church and State,* p. 501.

[99] *Ibid.,* p. 502.

> 14, 1st sentence and par. I of annexed protocol; Art. 15, par. I; and Art. 16, par. I of the Concordat concluded on June 5, 1933, between the Holy See and the Austrian Republic shall have the force of Constitutional law from the moment of their publication.
>
> As regards the other Churches and sects recognized by law, such regulation shall take place by means of a law after an agreement has been reached with them.[100]

Finally, Article 31, among other items, said that "any Church or religious community recognized by law has the right to give religious instructions to its members in schools and to exercise direct control over such instructions.[101]

The Austrian Concordat must be understood within the framework of the foregoing constitutional articles, because the concordat was promulgated about the same time as the constitution. The position of the Church in Austria was cast in general terms in the concordat's first article:

> The Republic of Austria assures and guarantees to the Holy Roman Catholic Church in its various rites the free exercise of its spiritual power and the free and public exercise of worship.[102]

No concordat defining the juridic position or status of Church and State exists between the Holy See and Ireland, but it would be a gross understatement to say that a merely cordial relationship flourishes between these two societies. Although the Holy See does not consider the Constitution adopted by Eire on December 29, 1937, as ideal in every detail in matters pertaining

[100] *Ibid.*, pp. 502-503. Ehler and Morrall make the following comment on Article 30: ". . . the Catholic Church was given a special position through the inclusion of some of the important provisions of the Concordat in the Constitution (Art. 30, pars. 3 and 4). These concerned chiefly the juridical position of the Church in Austrian public law, school affairs, and guarantees for the material conditions of the Church in Austria; the ecclesiastical estates and property, as well as State salaries for holders of poor benefices (the so called "congrua") were safeguarded."—*Ibid.*, p. 498.

[101] *Ibid.*, p. 503. Ottaviani, *op. cit.*, II, pp. 357-358, n. 406. He discusses the legal status of the Concordat from its promulgation until after World War II.

[102] Perugini, *Concordata Vigentia*, p. 264, Art. 1 (trans. by writer).

to religion, no doubt these matters have the sanction of the Holy See. The Irish Constitution does have a peculiar significance for the concepts under consideration in this thesis, because it represents a concrete solution, arrived at by a Catholic nation, of the current problem of a religiously pluralistic society.

The Constitution gives a place to religion in public affairs: "The State acknowledges that the homage of public worship is due to God Almighty. It shall hold His name in reverence, and shall respect and honor religion."[103] Ireland grants the Church a preferred status in these words: "The State recognizes the special position of the Holy Catholic Apostolic and Roman Church as the guardian of the faith professed by the great majority of the citizens."[104]

The Catholic Church is not *de facto* the sole religion practiced by all the citizens of Ireland, so Ireland finds it impossible to extend establishment to the Church. It also considers that it is politically expedient to give legal recognition to several other religious denominations. Eire's Constitution states that "the State also recognizes the Church of Ireland, the Presbyterian Church in Ireland, the Religious Society of Friends in Ireland, as well as the Jewish Congregations and other religious denominations existing in Ireland at the date of the coming into operation of this Constitution."[105]

---

[103] *Church and State,* p. 598, Art. 44, I (1).

[104] *Ibid.,* p. 599, Art. 44, I (ii).

[105] *Ibid.,* p. 599, Art. 44, I (iii). Ehler and Morrall make some pertinent remarks on this entitre article which are worth quoting in full: Article 44 (on religion) is a consistent Catholic-liberal synthesis, in which section 1 (i) rejects the idea of the "lay" State acknowledging no religious influence, while 1 (ii) makes special mention of the Catholic Church; it is, however, noteworthy that the recognition of the Church's privileged status is based on the fact that it is "the guardian of the Faith professed by the majority of its citizens," a formula derived ultimately, not from Catholic theory, but from the wording of Napoleon's Concordat with the papacy in 1801 (see Chap. VII, doc. no. 2) / *ibid.,* pp. 249 ff. /—a word accepted only with reluctance by Pope Pius VII. The recognition of non-Catholic bodies, 1 (iii), of freedom of conscience and profession of religion (2, i), the ban on State endowments (2, ii) and the implicit disavowal of State preference for the Catholic religion in civil life and education (2, iii and iv),

Haiti and the Holy See in 1940 negotiated a convention to regulate all matters of Church property.[106] In conformity with Article I of the Concordat of 1860, the State of Haiti recognized "the juridic personality of the Roman Catholic Apostolic Church and its particular institutions, determined by the Code of Canon Law, such as dioceses, seminaries, parishes, and religious congregations."[107] The Concordat of 1860 granted the Church a preferred position among the religions practiced in Haiti (Art. 1) and assured the ordinaries of freedom in the government of the Church in order to exercise everything connected with the pastoral ministry according to the tenor of canon law.[108] For the government of Haiti to conform to the Concordat of 1860, it must continue to extend to the Church the preferred position which it guaranteed a hundred years ago. The Convention of 1940 contains no statement rejecting this preferred status of the Church, and so it is logical to conclude that Haiti still honors this pledge of 1860.

### 3. Equal Status in Law

Eight States, or about half of the Conventions considered under the juridic status of the Church, guarantee the Catholic Church

---

laying down the principle of State aid to all religious denominations, while not being in accord with Ultramontane conceptions of a Catholic State, may be reconciled with Pope Leo XIII's moderately qualifying statements in the Encyclical *Immortale Dei.—Ibid.*, p. 595. (The second part of Article 44, sections of which are alluded to in the preceding quotation, are considered later in this section of the thesis.)

For the French Concordat of 1801 consult: *Raccolta di Concordati*, I, pp. 562 ff., and *Church and State*, pp. 252-254. For a brief treatment of Church-State relations between the Holy See and Napoleon at the time of the signing of the Concordat of 1801, cf. Raymond Corrigan, *The Church and the Nineteenth Century* (Milwaukee: Bruce Publishing Co., 1948), pp. 95-107; Ross W. Collins, *Catholicism and the Second French Republic, 1848-1852* (New York: Columbia University Press, 1923), pp. 14 ff.; Hales, *The Catholic Church in the Modern World*, pp. 52-74; Leo Gershoy, *The French Revolution and Napoleon* (New York, 1933), pp. 348-370, especially pp. 366-370.

[106] "Convenzione con la Repubblica di Haiti sui Beni Ecclesiastici e sulle Fabbricerie," *Raccolta di Concordati*, II, 224-231.

[107] *Ibid.*, p. 224, Chap. I, Art. 1 (trans. by writer).

[108] Cf. "Concordato fra Pio IX e la Repubblica di Haiti," *Raccolta di Concordati*, I, 929 and 932-933.

equal treatment with the various recognized religious sects in their respective territories. This undoubtedly reflects the adaptation of the Church to the exigencies of the modern system of government. Everyone of these States is on the Continent of Europe: Latvia (1922), Bavaria (1925), Lithuania (1927), Prussia (1929), Baden (1933), Germany (1933), Portugal (1940), and Yugoslavia (1935).

Latvia was among the new republics which arose after the First World War. Following treaties with Germany on July 15, 1920, and with Russia on August 11, 1920, Latvia emerged a free and independent nation. In 1921 it was *de iure* enrolled among the League of Nations. The Holy See extended a factual recognition of its independence at the time of the birth of the Republic, and worked also to establish diplomatic relations. The first Apostolic Delegate for Lithuania, Latvia and Estonia was designated on October 25, 1922.[109]

The Republic of Latvia was the first nation in the post-war period to negotiate a concordat with the Holy See. This agreement was signed on May 30, 1922, and became effective on November 3, 1922.[110] By means of this instrument Latvia solemnly pledged that the Catholic religion would enjoy a free and public exercise of worship and recognized the juridic personality of the Catholic Church. This juridic personality would be accorded all the rights which the Civil Code of Latvia recognized in other legal personalities.[111]

---

[109] Perugini, *Concordata Vigentia,* p. 1. Malbone W. Graham, *The League of Nations and Recognition of States: The Diplomatic Recognition of Border States—Part III, Latvia,* The University of California, Social Science Studies, vol. III (Berkeley: Univ. of California Press), pp. 441-452, especially pp. 443-444, 447.

[110] "Concordat entre le Saint-Siège et le Gouvernement de Lettonie," Perugini, *Concordata Vigentia,* pp. 3-8; *AAS,* XIV (1922), 577-581; *Raccolta di Concordati,* II, 6 ff.

[111] Perugini, *Concordata Vigentia,* p. 3, Art. 1. Perugini notes that Latvia is divided into three parts: Livonia, so named specifically, and Courland (Curlandia), which are predominantly Protestant, and Latgale (Polish Livonia), which is inhabited by Catholics.—*Ibid.,* p. 1. The concordat assured this Catholic segment of the population equal protection and recognition at law. Graham, *op. cit.,* pp. 391-408.

Concordat negotiations between the Holy See and Bavaria were initiated in 1920. These negotiations were protracted for four years. Both parties signed the document in 1924, and the concordat became effective on January 24, 1925.[112] The German Concordat of 1933 expressly mentioned that the Bavarian Concordat was not abrogated in consequence of the negotiations of 1933.[113]

The first article of the Bavarian Concordat stated that the government of Bavaria guaranteed "the free and public exercise of the Catholic religion." The German or Weimar Constitution of 1919 in Article 137, § 1, decreed that "no State religion exists, nor is any religion dominant or in any way privileged," and section 3 of the same article guaranteed every religious denomination independent administration of its property and ruled out State and local interference in the filling of religious offices.[114]

From the wording of the German Federal Constitution it is clear that the Bavarian Concordat could not grant an established position or a preferred position to the Catholic Church. On the other hand, the guarantees of free exercise of religion in the Bavarian Concordat and in the Weimar Constitution, which are cited in the preceding paragraph, and other articles of a similar nature which are discussed later in this article of the dissertation, are ample proof that the State of Bavaria extended more than a guarantee of toleration to the Catholic Church. Accordingly, the Bavarian government granted the Catholic Church a status in law that was no less than that granted to other religions in Bavaria. In a word, Bavaria extended to the Catholic Church a juridic position which may be termed "equal status in law."

---

[112] "Konkordat zwischen Seiner Heiligkeit Papst Pius XI und dem Staate Bayern," Perugini, *Concordata Vigentia,* pp. 10 ff.; *AAS,* XVII (1925), 41-56.

[113] *AAS,* XXV (1933), 390-391, Art. 2; Perugini, *Concordata Vigentia,* p. 232, Art. 2; *Church and State,* p. 487, Art. 2.—"The Concordats concluded with Bavaria (1924), Prussia (1929), and Baden (1932), and the rights and privileges of the Catholic recognized therein remain unchanged within the territory of the States ('Laender') concerned. . . ."

[114] Perugini, *Concordata Vigentia,* p. 11, Art. 1, § 1, and on page 9 Perugini reproduces the relevant sections of the German Constitution (trans. by writer); cf. also Ottaviani, *op. cit.,* II, pp. 371, 373, n. 414, parts one and two.

Lithuania was the next nation to bestow this legal status upon the Church in a concordat concluded with the Holy See on September 27, 1927. During World War I this country gained independence *de facto,* and it was recognized *de iure* by the Holy See on November 10, 1922.[115]

The Lithuanian Constitution of August 1, 1922, granted full religious freedom to all religious denominations.[116] The Constitution guaranteed freedom of conscience and declared that no special rights or privileges were to be given because of creed. This document established no State religion.[117]

The Holy See sought to strengthen its ties with the new republic and to specify this guarantee of religious freedom and equality before law more clearly in a solemn international agreement.[118]

---

[115] Joseph Prunskis, *Comparative Law, Ecclesiastical and Civil, in Lithuanian Concordat,* The Catholic University of America, Canon Law Studies, No. 222 (Washington, D. C.: The Catholic University of America Press, 1945), pp. 17-40.

[116] Section 83. The State recognizes the equal right of all religious organizations existing in Lithuania to administer their affairs in accordance with the requirements of their canons or statutes, to freely publish their religious doctrines and to practice their cult ceremonies, to establish and manage their cult buildings, schools, educational and charitable institutions, to establish convents, religious congregations and fraternities, to impose upon their members dues for the needs of religious organizations, and to acquire and manage personal and real property.

Religious organizations shall possess the rights of legal entities in the State.—This article is from the official English text reproduced in M. W. Graham, *New Governments of Eastern Europe* (New York, 1927), pp. 720-735. Cf. also Prunskis, *op. cit.,* p. 6; Perugini, *Concordata Vigentia,* pp. 57-58.

[117] Section 10. All citizens of Lithuania, men and women, are equal before the law. No special privileges can be given to, nor shall rights of citizens be restricted because of race, creed, or nationality.

Section 13. Citizens shall have the right of freedom of religious belief and conscience.

The belonging to any religion or the profession of one's convictions shall not form the basis for justification of an offense or for refusing to perform public duties.—Graham, *New Governments of Eastern Europe, loc. cit.;* Prunskis, *op. cit.,* p. 7. Ottaviani, *op. cit.,* II, p. 393, note 420.—Ottaviani also notes that the Constitution did not establish a State religion.

[118] The text of the concordat may be found in *AAS,* XIX (1927), 425 ff., and Perugini, *Concordata Vigentia,* pp. 59-70. The population of Lithuania was predominantly Catholic: Roman Catholic, 80.33%; Lutheran (Evangel-

The concordat, which was finally brought into being in 1927, contained many articles specifying this liberty and equality.[119] The first article promised freedom to the Catholic Church in terms almost identical to the Polish Concordat:

> Article 1. The Catholic Church, without distinction of Rite, shall enjoy in the Republic of Lithuania all the liberties requisite for the exercise of her spiritual power and jurisdiction, and for the proper conduct and administration of her affairs and property, conformably with the Divine Law and the Sacred Canons.[120]

Conditions were so altered both politically and religiously in Prussia after the First World War, that its leaders, in imitation of Bavaria, felt compelled to negotiate a new concordat with the Holy See. The Prussian Concordat was signed on June 4, 1929, and became effective on August 13, 1929.[121] Catholics were in the

ical), 9.56%; Russian Orthodox, 2.62%; all other forms of Christianity, 0.08%; Hebrew, 7.30%; all other non-Christian bodies, 0.07%.—Prunskis, *op. cit.*, p. 21.

[119] One of the reasons for the delay was the land dispute between Poland and Lithuania. In March 15, 1923, the Conferences of Ambassadors assigned the disputed Vilnius region to Poland. The Vatican accepted the decision of the Conference and assigned the Vilnius region to the Polish hierarchy, i.e., Vilnius was included in the Polish ecclesiastical province under the Polish Concordat of 1925 (*AAS,* XVII (1925), 273-287). The Holy See had to get in touch with the Polish president before a bishop was appointed to the See of Vilnius (Art. XI), and the bishop of Vilnius had to take an oath of fidelity to the Polish president (Art. XII). The Lithuanian populace reacted vehemently, and diplomatic relations between its government and the Vatican were temporarily disrupted.—Cf. Prunskis, *op. cit.*, pp. 32-36.

[120] Translation from: Amleto Giovanni Cicognani, *Canon Law,* authorized English version by J. M. O'Hara and F. Brennan (2nd rev. ed., Philadelphia: The Dolphin Press, 1925), p. 472. For the French edition, cf. *AAS,* XIX (1927), 425-433, and Perugini, *Concordata Vigentia,* pp. 59-70. Prunskis, *op. cit.*, pp. 10-16.—Here he discusses whether the Concordat is still in force.

[121] The text may be found in *AAS,* XXI (1929), 521-543; Perugini, *Concordata Vigentia,* pp. 174-202. Prussia was one of the States of the German Federal Republic, so what is stated above regarding Bavaria and the Weimar Constitution is applicable to Prussia. There could be no State religion, nor any dominant or privileged religion, and all religious sects were granted equal freedom and equal protection at law. Cf. also Ottaviani, *op. cit.*, pp. 373-374, n. 414, part two.

minority in Prussia, and so the Holy See was gratified to have an added solemn guarantee of equality with various religious sects and of the free profession and exercise of the Catholic religion.[122]

Baden, another German State, signed with the Holy See a concordat which endorsed a similar pledge of equality at law and of the free exercise of worship for the Catholic Church. The State of Baden promised in applying the Constitution of the German Reich and the Constitution of the Republic of Baden to safeguard the legal protection afforded to the freedom of the profession and the exercise of the Catholic religion.[123]

Although the Holy See had concluded separate conventions with three German States to protect the rights of the Catholic Church, these rights were placed in danger because of the political conditions existing in the central government.[124] In an effort to safeguard these rights the Holy See negotiated a concordat with the Hitler government, as it had done with the government of Mussolini four years earlier. This international agreement encom-

[122] Cf. *AAS*, XXI (1929), p. 522, Art. 1; Perugini, *Concordata Vigentia*, p. 175, Art. 1.

[123] *AAS*, XXV (1933), p. 177, Art. 1; Perugini, *Concordata Vigentia*, p. 207, Art. 1.

[124] During the nineteen-twenties the Catholic Center Party was very influential and supplied the German Republic with most of its Reich chancellors. In January of 1933, Hitler managed by constitutional means to ascend the ladder of power. A general election was held in March, 1933, and "the number of votes of the Centre Party shrank considerably under the Nazi pressure against its adherents, and at the beginning of July the Party had to decide—like all other non-Nazi parties—on its own dissolution."—*Church and State*, p. 484.

At this time Hitler was chancellor, and Franz von Papen, a Catholic politician and a former chancellor, was kept on as vice-chancellor. The vice-chancellor represented the Hitler government in negotiations with the Holy See for a concordat which was designed to settle the position of the Catholic Church in the whole of Germany. "The negotiations took the shape of a compromise with Catholicism in which the 'Fuehrer' was prepared to concede generous conditions to the Church in matters important to her . . . ; in return he demanded the Vatican's acquiescence in the disappearance of the Centre Party and the prohibition of any participation of the German clergy in politics. On these lines the Concordat was signed on July 20, 1933."—*Ibid.*, p. 485. Cf. also Hales, *The Catholic Church in the Modern World*, pp. 292-294.

passed the entire Reich and left the conventions with the individual German States unimpaired.[125]

The concordat did not secure any privileged position for the Catholic Church, but it did in fact enable the Church to force the Hitler government to respect its rights more than the Protestant denominations were able to do in the absence of such an international convention. As Ehler and Morrall phrase it, "the Concordat does not appear unsatisfactory for the Church and the Papacy, particularly if compared with the treatment which the German Protestant Churches had to undergo simultaneously on the part of the Nazis."[126] This national concordat promised freedom to the Catholic Church:

> The German Reich guarantees freedom of profession and public practices of the Catholic religion. It recognizes the right of the Catholic Church to regulate and manage its own internal affairs independently within the limits of the law applicable to all and to issue—within the framework of its own competency—laws and ordinances binding on its own members.[127]

Although things looked grim for the Catholic Church in the late nineteen-thirties in certain parts of Europe, the anti-clerical spirit which had been so violent earlier in the century in Portugal gradually subsided, and conditions reached such a favorable state that

---

[125] "Concordat between Pope Pius XI and the Hitler Government of Germany, July 20, 1933," Church and State, p. 487, Art. 2: The Concordats concluded with Bavaria (1924), Prussia (1929), and Baden (1932), and all the rights and privileges recognized therein remain unchanged within the territory of the States ("Laender") concerned . . .; cf. *AAS,* XXV (1933), pp. 390-391, Art. 2, and Perugini, *Concordata Vigentia,* p. 232, Art. 2. An English translation of the text may also be found in *The Persecution of the Catholic Church in the Third Reich,* Appendix I, pp. 516 ff.

[126] *Church and State,* p. 486.

[127] *Ibid.,* p. 487, Art. 1; *AAS,* XXV (1933), p. 390, Art. 1; Perugini, *Concordata Vigentia,* p. 231, Art. 1. For a brief discussion of the circumstances surrounding and preceding the negotiation of this concordat cf. Hales, *The Catholic Church in the Modern World,* pp. 291-298. Cf. also Ottaviani, *op. cit.,* II, pp. 374-376, n. 414, part two (C) for a brief commentary on this concordat.

it was possible to negotiate a concordat in 1940.[128] This new spirit was evident in the very first article in which "the Portuguese Republic recognizes the juridic personality of the Catholic Church," and by which "friendly relations with the Holy See shall be assured by the traditional form in which they were formerly expressed. . . ."[129]

Some years prior to this concordat arrangement the new Portuguese Constitution guaranteed the free exercise of religion, and the government renewed this guarantee with respect to the Catholic Church in the concordat.[130] This Portuguese Constitution retained the separation of Church and State:

> Without prejudice to the provisions of concordats in the matter of the *Padroado,* the State shall maintain the regime of separation of the Catholic Church and any other religion or cult within the Portuguese territory, and the

[128] "Concordat between the Holy See and the Republic of Portugal," *The Canon Law Digest* (ed. T. L. Bouscaren and J. J. O'Connor, 4 vols., Milwaukee: Bruce Publishing Co., 1934-1958), II, 11-19 (hereafter cited *Digest*); *AAS*, XXXII (1940), 217 ff. For a summary of the Holy See—Portuguese relations between 1910 and 1940, consult Ottaviani, *op. cit.*, II, pp. 395-396, n. 421.

[129] *Digest,* II, pp. 11-12, Art. 1; *AAS,* XXXII (1940), 218. By traditional form is meant the exchange of ambassadors. Relations with the Holy See had been disrupted early in the century. King Carlos I of Portugal (1889-1908) and Crown Prince Louis Philip (1887-1908) were boldly assassinated in the streets of Lisbon on February 1, 1908. This assassination was attributed to the anti-clerical element in Portugal. The anti-clerical party fomented a revolution on October 3, 1910. Theophilus Braga (1843-1924) became president of the provisional government which expelled religious congregations and seized their property. This anti-clerical policy finally culminated in the Law of Separation of Church and State on April 20, 1911. Pope Pius X condemned these anti-Catholic actions in the Encyclical *Iamdudum,* May 24, 1911. For the text consult *AAS,* III (1911), 218-223. Cf. *All Things in Christ, Encyclicals and Selected Documents of St. Pius X* (ed. Vincent A. Yzermans, Westminster, Md.: The Newman Press, 1954), pp. 176-181; Edward Prestage, "Portugal," *The Catholic Encyclopedia* (ed. Charles G. Herberman, Edward A. Pace, *et alii,* 15 vols., Index and Supplement, New York: 1907-1921), XII, 305.

[130] Cf. "Portuguese Constitution of April 11, 1933, as amended on August 1, 1935," *Church and State,* p. 514, Sec. X, Art. 45. For the concordat pledge consult *AAS,* XXXII (1940), p. 225, Art. 16, and *Digest,* II, p. 23, Art. 16.

> diplomatic relations between the Holy See and Portugal, with reciprocity of representation.[131]

Even though the Concordat of 1940 was favorable in many respects to the Catholic Church and agreed to respect canon law in several areas, it did not depart from the basic principle of non-establishment contained in the Portuguese Constitution.[132] Nor did the Concordat grant the Catholic Church a privileged position. The logical conclusion must be that the equality extended to all religions by the Constitution remained unaltered.[133]

Another nation extended an equal status in law position to the Catholic Church—Yugoslavia. The political and religious structure of Yugoslavia was a complex one, and the religious distribution did not coincide with nationalities.[134] The Eastern Orthodox

---

[131] *Church and State,* pp. 514-515, Art. 46. Cf. also Ottaviani, *op. cit., loc. cit.,* for a brief discussion of the articles of the Constitution relating to religion.

[132] Examples of favorable matters are found in Articles 3, 7, 8, 11, 12, 13, 20, 21, 22, 24, 25, 27, 28.

[133] Ottaviani, *op. cit.,* II, p. 396, n. 421.—Ottaviani states that the Concordat does not contain anything about the principle of separation stated in the Constitution, but, in practice, it does show some preference for the Catholic Church, e.g., it recognizes the juridic personality of the Church and accepts the teaching of Catholic doctrine in schools, etc.

Section X, Art. 45, of the Constitution:

> The public and private practice of any religion shall be free. Religious bodies may organize themselves freely, in accordance with the rules of their hierarchy and discipline, in such manner as to form associations and organizations whose civil existence and juridic personality shall be recognized by the State. This shall not apply to the practices of any religious body which are incompatible with life and physical integrity of the human individual and with good morals.—*Church and State,* p. 514.

[134] Joseph S. Roucek, *Balkan Politics: International Relations in No Man's Land* (Stanford, California: Stanford University Press, 1948), p. 84 (hereafter cited Roucek. *Balkan Politics*). Roucek gives the following statistics:

| *Nationalities* | *Percent* | *Churches* | *Percent* |
|---|---|---|---|
| Yugloslavs (Serbs, Croats, Slovenes) | 82.87 | Greek Orthodox | 48.70 |
| Other Slavs | 1.46 | Roman Catholic | 37.45 |
| Germans | 4.22 | Greek Catholic | 0.32 |
| Hungarians | 3.90 | Old Catholic | 0.05 |
| Albanians | 3.67 | Protestant (Lutheran) | 1.26 |
| Rumanians | 1.93 | Protestant (Calvinist) | 0.40 |
| Turks | 1.26 | Other Christian | 0.12 |
| Italians | 0.11 | Moslem | 11.20 |
| Others | 0.58 | Jewish | 0.49 |
| | | Others | 0.01 |

faith was professed mainly by the Serbs, the Rumanians, and the Albanians, and its strength was south of the Sava and the Danube. The Serbian migrations had further expanded it in the East. The Croats, the Slovenes, and the greater number of the German and Hungarian minorities professed the Catholic faith. Roucek remarks that "the Catholic Church possessed considerable property and, like the Orthodox Church, received a state subsidy; it appointed its clergy in agreement with Belgrade."[135]

The Kingdom of Yugoslavia was established on December 1, 1918. The Croats and Slovenes under Dr. Koroshetz, a Catholic priest, convened a National Council in Ljubljana, which was attended by representatives of Bosnia-Herzegovina. This Council soon assumed the character of an unofficial government. In November, 1918, the premier of Serbia, Pashitch, met with Yugoslav leaders and members of the National Council in Geneva. They agreed to establish a joint Serbo-Yugoslav government, and the Council sent a deputation to Prince Alexander of Serbia (1888-1934) with a request that he serve as Regent. In the meantime, Montenegro's National Assembly deposed King Nicholas I (1878-1921) and united with Serbia. A short time later Alexander proclaimed the unification of the Serbs, Croats, and Slovenes into one kingdom.[136]

In 1921 Alexander was crowned King of Yugoslavia. Parliamentary government proved unable to cope with the problems of national unity. During the ten years of its existence, it averaged three cabinets a year. On the tenth anniversary of the founding of the State, the Croats remained at home. As Roucek observes, "The only way out of this political impasse seemed the one pursued by the King—dictatorship."[137]

On January 6, 1929, King Alexander dissolved the parliament and abolished the Constitution of the Kingdom of 1921. The old

---

There are about eight million Serbs, three and a half million Croats, and one and a half million Slovenes, according to Roucek's statistics. (These statistics were published in 1935.—*Ibid.*, p. 85, note 9.) Cf. Ottaviani, *op. cit.*, II, pp. 392-393, note 101.

[135] *Balkan Politics*, p. 85.

[136] Roucek, *Balkan Politics*, pp. 80-81.

[137] *Ibid.*, p. 98.

official title of the Kingdom of the Serbs, Croats and Slovenes was replaced on October 3, 1929, by the Kingdom of Yugoslavia. All confessional schools were integrated with a strict nationalistic system of education.[138]

On September 3, 1931, King Alexander I proclaimed a new constitution, and "elections" were held on September 12, 1931. The party of Zhivkovitch won the election.[139] On April 4, 1932, Zhivkovitch resigned, and the nation witnessed a succession of premiers. Popular unrest increased. King Alexander I was assassinated by an extremist on October 9, 1934, in Marseilles.[140]

Alexander's son, Peter II, a child of eleven, became the new sovereign. A regency headed by Prince Paul Karageorgevitch was established, and Prince Paul was able to improve relations between the Serbs and the Croats. In December, 1936, the Prince received Dr. Matchek, the leader of the Croat opposition. The following January a meeting took place between Premier Stoiadinovitch and Matchek. A few months later Stoiadinovitch presented to parliament a concordat granting the Roman Catholic Church a status equal to that of the Serbian Orthodox Church. This was a conciliatory gesture toward the Catholic Croats and Slovenes. The concordat had been signed with the Holy See in July, 1935, but had not been submitted for parliamentary approval. This approval was not gained, because the sharp objectives raised by the Orthodox Church forced the government to withdraw the concordat. Although the Holy See was willing to accept this equal status in law with the Orthodox Church as agreed upon in the concordat, the concordat had to be abandoned, because of Serbian Orthodox opposition.[141]

---

[138] *Ibid.*, pp. 90-100.

[139] Roucek describes in some detail the measures taken to assure this party victory. The party dutifully ratified all the government measures in January of 1932.—*Balkan Politics*, pp. 100-101.

[140] Roucek enumerates all those who were connected with the assassination plot.—*Ibid.*, 101.

[141] *Ibid.*, pp. 102-104, 85. Roucek has a brief, but excellent, discussion of the religious and cultural differences between the Croats and Serbs. These differences account in no small way for the Orthodox reaction to any measure which strengthens the ties of the government to Rome.—*Ibid.*, pp.

Eight States, some in more explicit terms than others, extended a pledge of equal status in the public law of their respective territories. In some of these States the Catholic population was at least nominally in the majority, while in others the Catholics definitely constituted a minority. Yet, in each case the Holy See conformed to the will of the rulers and accepted a position at least theoretically less favorable than it had obtained from some European governments. This indicates two things. The Holy See is willing to adjust its position and yield in its demand that it be the only recognized religion in a given nation, when the greater good of souls is involved. Furthermore, the Holy See is content, although not fully satisfied, if it receives adequate guarantees of freedom and equal treatment.

### 4. Inferior Status in Law

Rumania guaranteed the Catholic religion a free exercise of worship, but extended to the Church a legal status which in public law was even less favorable than that of equality among all the legally recognized denominations. The Catholic Church was inferior in law to the preferred Orthodox belief. The Holy See felt that the religiously and politically prudent course of action was to accept this status, even in a most solemn international agreement like a concordat. This marked the first post-war convention with a schismatic nation.[142]

87-91. For the concordat text consult: "Concordato Firmato con la Jugo-Slavia," *Raccolta di Concordati,* II, pp. 202 ff. Willibald Plöchl, "Reflections on the Nature and Status of Concordats," *The Jurist,* VII (1947), 16. The author notes that ratification of the Yugoslavian Concordat was abandoned by both parties, when it became clear that its conclusion would not bring about its ultimate purpose. Both Montenegro and Serbia had negotiated concordats with the Holy See before the First World War. Both of these States, which were predominantly non-Catholic, guaranteed the Catholic Church free and public exercise of its religion in these solemn conventions. Pope Leo XIII concluded a concordat with Nicholas I of Montenegro on August 18, 1886.—*Raccolta di Concordati,* I, pp. 1048 ff. Pope Pius X signed a concordat with Peter I of Serbia (1903-1921) in 1914.—*Raccolta di Concordati,* I, pp. 1102 ff.

[142] Cf. Roucek, *Balkan Politics,* pp. 209-250, for a history of Rumania, especially after World War I.

After the First World War the substantial territorial increment of Rumania brought thousands of additional uniate Catholics under the jurisdiction of this government. The Catholics in union with Rome accounted for approximately one-sixth of Rumania's population.[143] The Rumania Constitution of 1923 made provision to protect these Catholics and other minority groups, especially by guaranteeing them freedom of conscience and a free exercise of religion.[144] However, the Orthodox religion was given a preferred status in law over all other religious denominations in Rumania.[145]

Article 22 of the Constitution envisioned one law for regulating the Orthodox religion, and another for specifying the relations between the State and the other religious denominations. The law for the Orthodox Church was passed on May 6, 1925. The first article of this law declared that the Orthodox Church was the dominant Church (*Ecclesia dominans*) in the State of Rumania, and reaffirmed its autonomy in the sense that it was subject to no external, i.e., supra-national hierarchy. The law regulating other denominations was passed on April 22, 1928. It contained

[143] Perugini, *Concordata Vigentia,* p. 142; Roucek, *op. cit.,* p. 214; Ottaviani, *op. cit.,* II, p. 403, n. 424, note 132. Ottaviani notes that in the 1930 census, there were eighteen million citizens in Rumania, and about one-sixth of these were uniate Catholics.

[144] Article 22 of the Constitution states that the State grants equal liberty and protections to all religions, in so far as their exercise does not interfere with the maintenance of public order, or good morals, or the State laws of organization. Cf. Perugini, *Concordata Vigentia*, p. 142, note 2, and Ottaviani, *op. cit.,* II, p. 404, n. 424.

[145] Article 22 of the Constitution also states that the Orthodox Christian Church and the Greek Catholic are the Rumania Churches. The Orthodox Church being the religion of the majority of the Rumanians is the dominant and privileged Church, and the Greek-Catholic Church is given priority over the remaining religions. This article also mentions that relations between Church and State are to be regulated by one law. Cf. Perugini, *Concordata Vigentia,* pp. 142-143, especially note 3. Albert Galter states that, "the greater number of Rumanian Catholics belong to the Church of the Oriental Rite, called 'The Uniate Church' or 'The Greek-Catholic Church.' In the Constitution of 1923 it was referred to as the Rumanian Catholic Church, and as such enjoyed a certain position of dignity after the 'dominant Church,' namely the National Orthodox Church."—*The Red Book of the Persecuted Church* (trans. from the French, Westminster, Md.: The Newman Press, 1957), p. 295 (hereafter cited Galter, *The Red Book*).

three main divisions: 1) general dispositions (Arts. 1-20); 2) relations between the State and religious sects (Arts. 21-40); 3) mutual relations between the sects (Arts. 41-50), to which were added some final short dispositions.[146]

In the first article of the 1928 law the State sanctioned the same freedom and protection for all sects, provided that their exercise did not disturb the public order, good morals, and the laws of the State. The State also recognized individual liberty of conscience and profession of religion (Arts 3-4), but forbade denominational political associations and also moral and material dependence of any denomination on extra-national authorities, except for the Catholic Church, whose relations with the State were regulated by a special convention.[147]

This special convention or concordat was signed on May 10, 1927, almost a year before the promulgation of the 1928 law regarding religious denominations, and took force on July 7, 1929.[148] For the Holy See to conclude a concordat with a nation whose public law granted the Catholic Church an inferior juridic position indeed appears to be a great concession. One might expect to find a *Modus Vivendi,* such as the Church negotiated with Czechoslovakia in 1928, but to solemnize this inferior status and give it permanent stature in an international agreement, such as a concordat, is a departure from the ordinary manner of acting on the part of the Holy See.[149]

The Holy See had a serious reason for the course of action which it followed. In the absence of the concordat Roman Catholics

[146] Ottaviani, *op. cit.,* II, p. 405, n. 424, and Perugini, *Concordata Vigentia, loc. cit.*

[147] Ottaviani, *op. cit.,* II, pp. 405-406, n. 424.

[148] Perugini, *Concordata Vigentia,* pp. 143-144, and Ottaviani, *op. cit.,* p. 406, n. 424. The text of the concordat may be found in *AAS,* XXI (1929), 441-456, and Perugini, *Concordata Vigentia,* pp. 145-161. After the concordat in 1929 the Latin Rite organization in Rumania consisted of one archiepiscopal see at Bucharest with four suffragan dioceses: Alba Julia, Satu Mare, Timisoara and Iasi.—Galter, *The Red Book,* p. 297. The ecclesiastical organization for the Greek Rite and the Armenian Rite was also settled by the concordat.—*AAS,* XXI (1929), 441-443.

[149] "Modus Vivendi inter Sanctam Sedem et Rempublicam Cecoslovham," Perugini, *Concordata Vigentia,* pp. 73-75, and also *AAS,* XIX (1929), 65-66.

would have been subject to an intolerable prohibition, namely, the clause of the 1928 law, which forbade any moral or material dependence upon external authorities. The concordat prevented the Catholic Church in Rumania from being reduced, at least in law, to a National Church.

Undoubtedly, this convention strengthened the supra-national character of the Rumanian Catholic Church, but it did not alter the basic juridic standing which the Church was given in the Constitution. The initial article of the concordat contained a guarantee of religious freedom: "The Catholic Apostolic Roman religion of every Rite shall be practiced and exercised freely and publicly in the entire Kingdom of Rumania."[150] The rights of the Catholic Church and its members were further safeguarded by article ten of the concordat, which pledged that the Catholics who were Rumanian citizens would receive a treatment from the State which could not be inferior to that which would be accorded to other denominations according to the Constitution.[151]

The significant phrase in article ten is "according to the constitution." If this phrase were not present, the presumption would be that the Rumanian Catholics enjoyed an equal status in law with all the other religions in Rumania. Read in the light of the Constitution this article means that the Catholic Church enjoys the same status as all the other religions, except the Orthodox religion, which is accorded a preferred position, as described above.[152]

In solemn agreements with Italy, Spain, and the Dominican Republic the Holy See stabilizes the maximum degree of legal recognition for the Catholic Church—Establishment. The concordats with Poland, Haiti, and Austria guarantee the Church a preferred position, which is not the ideal status for the Church,

---

[150] *AAS,* XXI (1929), 441, and Perugini, *Concordata Vigentia,* p. 145 (trans. by writer).

[151] *AAS,* XXI (1929), p. 445, Art. 10, and Perugini, *Concordata Vigentia,* p. 150, Art. 10.

[152] Perugini gives the reader an idea of the pluralistic society in Rumania. In addition to the Orthodox and the Catholics, there are Calvinists, Evangelical-Lutherans, Unitarians, Greek-Armenians, Jews, and Moslems.—*Ibid.,* p. 143.

but is nevertheless a coveted position in the modern religiously pluralistic society. The pledge of equal protection and right before the law, which the conventions with Latvia, Lithuania, Germany, Yugoslavia, Bavaria, Prussia, and Portugal contain, is the increasingly more common legal position extended to the Church. It is not the most desired status, and the pontiffs frankly state this, but it assures the freedom necessary for the fulfillment of the mission of the Church and it fortifies the friendly relations of the Holy See with the contracting nation. Finally, the Church recognizes a fourth condition as acceptable, i.e., more than merely tolerable, and this is an inferior position in law. The Rumanian Concordat secures for the Church a direct recognition at law, rather than an indirect recognition through the Orthodox Patriarch, a condition prevalent in dissent nations when they were under Arab and Turkish domination. From these concordat considerations it can be argued that the Church has not abandoned its traditional claim to the right of establishment, but it has adapted itself to the exigencies of the modern world and its religious pluralism and has, above all, striven to maintain the freedom of action and legal recognition of the juridic independence of the Church and its supra-national character. This freedom and legal recognition enable the Church to carry out its preaching and teaching mission with a minimum of civil interference.[153]

### *Section 2. Free Exercise of Religion and the Ministry*

The Church was not satisfied with a general statement of principle that recognized its right to unfettered existence as expressed in an establishment or an equal protection clause. Whenever possible, it negotiated for specific guarantees of the free exercise of religion and of the ministry.

[153] Willibald M. Plöchl, "Reflections on the Nature and Status of Concordats," *The Jurist,* VII (1947), 16. Plöchl sums up this idea:

> The ultimate aim of the concordat, therefore, is to realize and fulfill freedom of religion and of religious worship and conviction. For the Church, this means that the Catholic is at liberty to live according to his religion and the norms of ecclesiastical law, that the Church authorities can exercise their functions accordingly, and that both clergy and the faithful are protected against violation of their legitimate rights.

The principle of non-interference by the civil government in the ecclesiastical rule of the diocese was specified by particular guarantees, such as the right of the bishop of the diocese to promulgate pastoral letters, bulletins, laws, ordinances, and other decrees relative to the spiritual governing of the clergy and the faithful.[154] Another common manifestation of this non-interference policy was the promise of free communication between the Holy See and the local ordinaries.

The freedom of action necessary for a minister of the Gospel was recognized by many States by means of his exemption from military service and other civil duties incompatible with a priestly vocation, and also by the recognition of rights and privileges proper to clerics.[155] Several States, such as Bavaria, Italy and Germany, guaranteed a special State protection to the clergy when they were fulfilling their ecclesiastical duties. Yugoslavia, Poland, and the Dominican Republic extended to clerics engaged in the activities of the ministry the same degree of protection as they did to their civil employees.

To insure the free exercise of religion, worship and the ministry, several nations respected and explicitly upheld the inviolability of Catholic churches, chapels, and cemeteries.[156] A detailed exposition of the above stated guarantees and of the additional pledges made by the States which signed concordats with the Holy See follows in the succeeding paragraphs in chronological sequence.

The Latvian Concordat set the pattern for the guarantees of free exercise which appear in most of the post-war concordats. This government acknowledged its incompetence for regulating the

---

[154] E.g., the Yugoslavian Concordat of 1935, Art. 6, and the German Concordat of 1933, Art. 4.

[155] E.g., in the following concordats: Latvian, Arts. 10, 17, 19; Bavarian, Art. 1, sec. 3; Polish, Arts. 4, 5, 23; Lithuanian, Arts. 4, 5, 20; Italian, Arts. 3, 4; German, Arts. 5, 6, 7, 8; Austrian, Art. 1, sec. 3; Spanish (1953), Art. 14; and Dominican (1954), Art. 11, sec. 3.

[156] E.g., the Latvian Concordat, Arts. 14, 15, 16; the Italian Concordat, Arts. 9, 10; the Polish Concordat, Arts. 7, 15; the Lithuanian Concordat, Arts. 6, 16.

affairs of the Church, and agreed that "for all ecclesiastical matters the Archbishop of Riga shall be subject directly to the Holy See.[157] A practical expression of this policy of non-interference was contained in Article VIII of the concordat, which stated that members of the cathedral chapter, pastors, and in general all ecclesiasticals are to be nominated by the Archbishop according to the norms of canon law.[158] The government also granted exemption from military service and other civil duties, such as being a juror or tribunal member, which were incompatible with a priestly vocation.[159]

There was not a sufficient number of clergy of Latvian nationality when the concordat was concluded, so the government granted the Archbishop the right during this period of transition to enlist the aid of a foreign clergy. These clergymen were to express freely the duties assigned to them by the Archbishop. The Archbishop in turn was obliged to submit the names of these foreign priests to the government, which was then to determine whether it objected to them on political grounds.[160]

Catholic churches, chapels, and cemeteries were considered to be the property of the Catholic Church in Latvia.[161] These properties were to be administered by ecclesiastical authority and they could not be destroyed or confiscated, nor could they be destined for the use of another against the wishes of the ecclesiastical au-

---

[157] Perugini, *Concordata Vigentia,* p. 3, Art. 3 (trans. by writer). Cf. also *CIC,* canon 329, § 1. The concordat only mentioned Riga, but Galter gives the following as the status of the Church in Latvia: "Before 1918 there were only two dioceses of Mohilev and Kaunas, but after the establishment of Latvian independence the former diocese of Riga was reconstituted and in 1920 a Lett bishop was consecrated to that see, which was subsequently raised to the dignity of an archdiocese (1923). In 1927 a new bishopric was erected at Liepaja (Lietan), and at the same time the Archbishop of Riga received the title of Metropolitan."—*The Red Book,* p. 56.

[158] Perugini, *Concordata Vigentia,* p. 5, Art. 8; cf. also *CIC,* canon 403 and canon 1432 for the conferral of benefices; canon 455 for the naming of pastors; and canon 152 for the appointing to ecclesiastical offices.

[159] Perugini, *Concordata Vigentia,* p. 5, Art. 9; cf. also *CIC,* canon 121, regarding military exemption, and canon 139, regarding incompatible offices.

[160] Perugini, *Concordata Vigentia,* p. 6, Art. 11. This right of political objection is discussed in detail in a later part of this chapter.

[161] When the concordat was concluded there was only one archdiocese in Latvia, as noted above.

thorities.[162] Furthermore, the immunity of these Catholic churches, chapels, and cemeteries was to be in keeping with the norms of canon law.[163]

Bavaria recognized the autonomy of the Church in fulfilling its mission. The government acknowledged the right of the Church to promulgate, within the area of its competency, laws and decrees binding its members, and promised, moreover, neither to impede nor to make difficult the exercise of this right.[164] The independence of the Church was further assured by the admission of the Church's right to remain undisturbed in the exercise of worship. This assurance was implemented by a pledge of state protection when the members of the Church were carrying out their ecclesiastical duties.[165]

Religious orders and congregations could freely establish foundations according to the norms of canon law, and they were not subject to state limitations regarding residence, number, or quality of membership, except for Art. 13, § 2.[166]

The Polish Concordat contained all the guarantees mentioned in the discussion of the Latvian and Bavarian Concordats with some variations. In Article one of the Polish Concordat the Church was guaranteed freedom in the exercise of its ecclesiastical jurisdiction and spiritual power, and the same liberty in the administration and management of its affairs and property in conformity

---

[162] Perugini, *Concordata Vigentia*, p. 18, Art. 14. Perugini notes that this article is in conformity with Article I, which recognizes the Catholic Church as a juridic person with all the rights which the Civil Code of Latvia accords to civil persons, and these rights include the right to possess and administer property.—*Ibid.*, p. 6, note 8. Cf. also *CIC*, canon 1495.

[163] Cf. Perugini, *Concordata Vigentia*, p. 6, Art. 15, and also *CIC*, canons 1160 and 1178, regarding the exemption of sacred places from the civil authority, and canon 1179, for the right of asylum.

[164] Perugini, *Concordata Vigentia*, p. 11, Art. 1, sec. 2.

[165] Perugini, *Concordata Vigentia*, pp. 11-12, Art. 1, sec. 3; cf. Ottaviani, *op. cit.*, II, p. 373, n. 414, part two.

[166] Perugini, *Concordata Vigentia*, p. 12, Art. 2. Article 13, § 2, is discussed later in the dissertation. It demands that all superiors be German citizens and reside in Bavaria.

with the divine law and the canon law.[167] The Polish bishops and clergy were promised free and direct communication with the Holy See, and in the exercise of their duties the bishops enjoyed the same free communication with their clergy and flock. This freedom was further specified by a pledge of freedom to publish their instructions, directives and pastoral letters.[168] The Polish government agreed to more than a mere non-interference policy towards the Church. This was manifested in several ways. In the exercise of their ministry the clergy were given a special juridic protection.[169] Clerics, seminarians, religious and novices enjoyed a broad military service exemption; in fact, it was more extensive than the military exemption given by Latvia. Clerical exemption from civil duties incompatible with the ministry and state in life was the same as in the Latvian Concordat.[170]

The Polish government promised to respect the immunity of Catholic chapels, churches, and cemeteries, provided that the public security in no way suffered.[171] Latvia honored this immunity according to the norms of canon law, but it did not add the restric-

---

[167] Perugini, *Concordata Vigentia,* p. 33, Art. 1. Lithuania gave the same guarantees.—*Ibid.,* p. 59, Art. 1. For the disregard of the Polish Concordat by the Polish Communist regime consult: Ottaviani, *op. cit.,* II, p. 403, n. 423.

[168] Perugini, *Concordata Vigentia,* p. 34, Art. 2. Lithuania gave the same guarantees in its concordat.—*Ibid.,* p. 60, Art. 2. Similar pledges of free communication were incorporated into a number of the nineteenth and early twentieth-century concordats. E.g., The Bavarian Concordat (1817)—*Raccolta di Concordati,* I, p. 568, Art. 3; The Concordat of Ecuador (1862)—*Raccolta di Concordati.* I, pp. 986, Art. 6; The Concordat with Montenegro (1886)—*Raccolta di Concordati,* I, p. 1049, Art. 5; The Serbian Concordat (1914)—*Raccolta di Concordati,* I, p. 1049, Art. 5.

[169] Perugini, *Concordata Vigentia,* p. 35, Art. 5.

[170] Perugini, *Concordata Vigentia,* p. 35, Art. 5; cf. also *CIC,* canons 121, 139. The Lithuanian Concordat promised the same juridic protection as the Polish Concordat, and also the same exemption from military service and civil duties. It did further specify the exemption from civil duties, for it said that ecclesiastics shall be free from civil functions incompatible with the priestly vocation, as specified in the canon law.—Perugini, *Concordata Vigentia,* pp. 60-61, Art. 5. Cf. also *CIC,* canons 138, 139, 141, and 142.

[171] Perugini, *Concordata Vigentia,* p. 35, Art. 6.

tive clause "provided that public security does not suffer from this immunity."[172]

Italy gave many of these same guarantees of free exercise of the ministry. The Catholic Church could freely exercise its spiritual power and jurisdiction, and its ministers were promised protection from the State in the exercise of their spiritual ministry.[173] The usual guarantees of free communication between the Holy See and the bishops, and also of the bishops with their clergy and flock were stated in the Italian Concordat.[174] Freedom to publish pastoral letters and other directives was defined in rather specific terms.[175]

---

[172] Perugini, *Concordata Vigentia,* p. 6, Art. 15. Lithuania extended the same guarantee of immunity in its concordat as Poland, including the restrictive clause: Art. VI: Immunity is guaranteed to Churches, chapels and cemeteries, so far as is consistent with public safety.—Cicognani, *Canon Law,* p. 473. Cf. also *CIC,* canons 1179, 1160 and 1206.

[173] In the sense of Article I of the treaty, Italy assures the Catholic Church the free exercise of spiritual power, the free and public exercise of worship, and of jurisdiction in ecclesiastical matters in accordance with the provisions of the present concordat, and, if necessary, shall grant to ecclesiastics protection through its authorities, with regard to acts of the spiritual ministry. —*Church and State,* p. 394, Art. 1; *AAS,* XXI (1929), p. 276, Art. 1; Perugini, *Concordata Vigentia,* p. 113, Art. 1. Perugini enumerates things which would interfere with the sacred character of the Eternal City, which the second paragraph of the first article of the concordat pledges to preserve; e.g., productions in theaters and movie houses which offend religion and good morals; billboards, posters, speeches, and the like, which praise apostates, heretics, atheists, wicked men, etc.—*Concordata Vigentia,* p. 113, note 46.

[174] The Holy See shall communicate and correspond freely with bishops, with the clergy and with the whole Catholic world, without any interference on the part of the Italian government. Similarly, the bishops shall communicate with their clergy and with all the faithful in matters concerning their pastoral ministry.—*Church and State,* p. 394, Art. 2; AAS, XXI (1929), p. 276, Art. 2; Perugini, *Concordata Vigentia,* pp. 113-114, Art. 2. It is interesting to note that the concordat makes use of the phrase "without any interference on the part of the Italian government," and this phrase is understood as part also of the next sentence which speaks about the exercise of the pastoral ministry.

[175] Both the Holy See and the bishops can freely publish and also affix inside the buildings used for public worship or for the offices of their ministry—or on the outer doors thereof—all the instructions, orders, pastoral letters, diocesan bulletins and other documents concerning the spiritual gov-

The Italian Concordat granted no absolute immunity to places of worship. In general, they were exempt from occupation, but when necessity required it, they could be occupied. The ordinary was to be consulted before the requisition of the building, or, if this was impossible, as soon after the occupation as possible.[176]

The public places of worship were exempt from the jurisdiction of law-enforcing agencies, for "except in cases of urgent necessity, the public force (i.e., the police force) must not enter the buildings open for worship for the purpose of carrying out their duties, without first advising the ecclesiastical authorities thereof."[177] Furthermore, no building open for public worship could be demolished without the approval of the competent ecclesiastical authority.[178] Public worship in churches was given another safeguard against lay interference. The council for the maintenance of the church (*consilium fabricae*) was not allowed to interfere with services of public worship, even if it was composed entirely or predominantly of laymen.[179]

---

ernment of the faithful which they see fit to issue within the scope of their jurisdiction.—*Church and State,* p. 394, Art. 2, *AAS, loc. cit.,* Perugini, *Concordata Vigentia, loc. cit.*

[176] As a rule, buildings open for public worship shall be exempt from requisition and occupation.

In case a grave necessity should make it necessary to occupy a building open for public worship, the authority which proceeds to the occupation must previously make arrangements with the ordinary, unless reasons of absolute urgency oppose it. In such an event, the authority proceeding to the occupation has to inform the ordinary immediately.—*Church and State,* p. 395, Art. 9; *AAS,* XXI (1929), p. 279, Art. 9; Perugini, *Concordata Vigentia,* p. 118, Art. 9; also *CIC,* canon 1178.

[177] *Church and State,* p. 395, Art. 9; *AAS, loc. cit.;* Perugini, *Concordata Vigentia, loc. cit.* Canon 1179 is the ecclesiastical law underlying this paragraph. It states that a church enjoys the right of asylum. Any fugitive from justice who seeks refuge in a church may not be forced to leave, except in a case of grave necessity, and then only with the consent of the ordinary, or at least the consent of the pastor of the church.

[178] *AAS,* XXI (1929), p. 279, Art. 10; Perugini, *Concordata Vigentia,* p. 118, Art. 10; *Church and State,* pp. 395-396, Art. 10.

[179] *Church and State,* p. 400, Art. 29; *AAS,* XXI (1929), p. 286, Art. 29; Perugini, *Concordata Vigentia,* p. 129, Art. 29. For the administration of church property cf. *CIC,* canons 1182-1187 and 1518-1528. Canon 1184 specifically states that the council of the church maintenance (*consilium*

The great detail of the Italian Concordat concerning matters of Church immunity from lay and from civil interference reflects the deep concern of the Holy See over the infringement of rights to carry out its preaching, teaching and governing mission in spiritual matters. In Italy the State had a monopoly on education, except for brief periods of religious instruction. In 1927 the pope was compelled to dissolve the Catholic boy scouts, and in 1931 Mussolini forced Pius XI to curtail to a large degree the scope of Catholic Action activities in Italy. In the midst of such conditions the Catholic Church considered that the prudent course of action was to negotiate a concordat and a treaty with the Italian totalitarian regime. Both Mussolini and Pius XI realized that peace between the Church and the State would enable Italy to take a more effective stand against Communism. These leaders knew that the sixty-year-old quarrel had weakened the position of the Church and of the State. After two years of secret negotiation, Mussolini's government and the Holy See reached a satisfactory solution to the "Roman Question." The Vatican regained its territorial sovereignty, but not the return of the Papal States, and Catholicism was again recognized as the official State religion. Pius XI knew that he was negotiating with a government which might attempt to violate the rights of the Church under some pretext such as the preservation of public order. He tried to prevent this by means of detailed guarantees in the concordat and in the treaty. However, the rights of the Church continued to be violated, and two issues remained the source of much conflict—Catholic Action and Catholic education.[180]

The Church temporarily does yield the exercise of her preaching and teaching rights when public security or public order are at stake, but it insists that the competent ecclesiastical authorities be consulted before the State undertakes such a trespass. This is the

---

*fabricae*) may in no way interfere in those matters that pertain to the spiritual office of the pastor. Canons 1522 and 1523 outline the duties of such administrative personnel.

[180] Cf. Hales, *The Catholic Church in the Modern World*, pp. 288-289; *Church and State*, pp. 383-385. Mussolini's "observance" of the concordat is discussed under the previous section with Pius XI and his encyclical letter *Non abbiamo bisogno* (June, 1931).

Holy See's way of insisting upon its own competence to judge whether circumstances are so extreme that its rights ought to be suspended for the sake of the public order. Nevertheless, the Church is realistic and knows that there will be emergencies which will prompt State authorities to act, because the delay required to consult with the ecclesiastical authorities might work grave injury to citizens or to the State. The Holy See sanctions this course of action, provided that Church authorities are given an accounting as soon as possible. From the content of the Italian concordat and other concordats here under discussion, it seems legitimate to form the opinion that the right of the Church to fulfill its mission, which includes the right to preach freely, is conditioned by the public order of the State. However, it is the prerogative of the Church to judge when its right of free exercise ought to yield temporarily to the right of the State to maintain public order and security.[181]

Even though the Catholic Church enjoyed an inferior position in the law of Rumania, the Rumanian government made a number of pledges in the concordat which guaranteed the Catholic Church a wide degree of free exercise in the ministry. Rumania extended the usual guarantee of free communication in spiritual matters and Church affairs between the ordinaries and the Holy See, and between the bishop and his clergy and flock.[182]

The government agreed that "the ordinaries will have complete freedom in the exercise of their ecclesiastical functions and in the government of their own dioceses."[183] The right of these same ordinaries to preach and to teach was assured in these words:

[181] The meaning of public order in canonical literature is the subject of a recent dissertation: John Henry Hackett, *The Concept of Public Order* (Washington, D. C.: The Catholic University Press, 1959), The Catholic University of America Canon Law Studies, No. 399. In his conclusions on page ninety-one Hackett states that "public order may be defined as a pattern of conduct in conformity with a law which is essential to the security of society in that it is indispensable to the protection of a necessary public good."

[182] *AAS,* XXI (1929), p. 443, Art. 4; Perugini, *Concordata Vigentia,* pp. 147-148. For a summary of this concordat consult Ottaviani, *op. cit.,* pp. 406-407, n. 424.

[183] *AAS,* XXI (1929), p. 444, Art. 8; Perugini, *Concordata Vigentia,* p. 149, Art. 8 (trans. by writer).

"They will be able to exercise all the rights and prerogatives belonging to the pastoral ministry in conformity with the discipline approved by the Catholic Church, and will be free to give religious, moral, and ecclesiastical instructions as their sacred ministry demands."[184] The Rumanian rulers further pledged their non-interference in ecclesiastical affairs when they accepted the statement that "the other members of the Catholic clergy will depend exclusively upon them (the ordinaries) in all that concerns their nomination and the exercise of the sacred ministry."[185] However, this free exercise of the ministry must be understood within the framework of Article 22 of the Constitution which guarantees equal liberty and protection to all religions, in so far as their exercise does not interfere with the maintenance of public order, good morals, and the State laws of organization.[186]

The State recognized the juridic personality of the Catholic Church as represented by its legitimate ecclesiastical authorities according to the common law of the country. Parishes, monasteries, abbies, chapters, and other legally erected canonical organizations were considered juridic personalities, and the complete possession of their property was guaranteed by the State according to the Rumanian Constitution.[187]

The Catholic Church and her members, Rumanian citizens, were promised the same treatment from the State as was accorded to other religious bodies in Rumania according to the Rumanian Constitution.[188] The 1928 Law of Cults and Article XXII of the Constitution granted every religion equal freedom and protection, provided that the exercise of this liberty did not disturb the public

---

[184] *AAS, loc. cit.;* Perugini, *Concordata Vigentia, loc. cit.* The only condition annexed to this liberty was that, if these instructions were published, the Minister of Religion would be apprised of this fact.

[185] *AAS, loc. cit.* (trans. by writer); Perugini, *Concordata Vigentia, loc. cit.* These nominations were to be called to the attention of the Minister of Religion.

[186] Cf. Perugini, *Concordata Vigentia,* p. 142, note 2, and Ottaviani, *op. cit.,* p. 404, n. 424.

[187] *AAS,* XXI (1929), p. 445, Art. 9; Perugini, *Concordata Vigentia,* pp. 149-150, Art. 9.

[188] *AAS,* XXI (1929), p. 445, Art. 10; Perugini, *Concordata Vigentia,* p. 150, Art. 10.

order, good morals and the law of organization of the State.[189] When this Article is harmonized with the Articles discussed above, it appears that the free exercise of the ministry as granted to bishops and their clergy is subject to three limitations: considerations of the public order, of good morals, and of the law of organization of the State. However, Articles VI to IX of the Law of Cults of 1928, which forbids any Church to be dependent upon an outside authority, makes an exception for the Catholic Church, whose relations with the State are regulated by a special convention. If this exceptive clause could be extended to Article I of the 1928 law, then the restriction of this law on the free exercise does not bind the Church. However, the same three restrictions are contained in the Rumanian Constitution, and thus it seems that the Catholic Church is still restricted by these three limitations in its preaching mission.

The Concordat with the German Reich contained the guarantees of free exercise, free communication, and special protection. In a general statement of principle in the initial Article the government recognized "the right of the Catholic Church to regulate and manage its own affairs independently within the limits of the laws applicable to all, and to issue—within the framework of its competence—laws and ordinances binding on its members."[190] In this same article the "German Reich guarantees freedom of profession and public practice of the Catholic religion."[191] The Reich honored the freedom of contact between the Holy See and the Catholic clergy and faithful in Germany. This same freedom of communication was applied "to the bishops and other diocesan authorities in their contact with the faithful in all matters of their pastoral ministry."[192] This free communication with the faithful was made

---

[189] Cf. Perugini, *Concordata Vigentia,* p. 142, note 2, and Ottaviani, *op. cit.,* II, p. 405, n. 424.

[190] *Church and State,* p. 487; *AAS,* XXV (1933), 390; Perugini, *Concordata Vigentia,* p. 231. Cf. Ottaviani, *op. cit.,* II, pp. 374-376, n. 414, for a summary and brief commentary on this concordat.

[191] *Church and State, loc. cit.*

[192] *Church and State,* p. 488, Art. 4; *AAS,* XXV (1933), p. 391, Art. 4; Perugini, *Concordata Vigentia,* pp. 233-234, Art. 4.

more specific, and it included the issuance of pastoral letters, newspapers, instructions, and similar matters.[193]

The State accorded the clergy protection during the performance of their duties:

> The clergy enjoy in the discharge of their spiritual activities the same protection of the State as State officials. The State will proceed according to the general provisions of its law in case of any outrage directed against the clergy personally, or against their ecclesiastical character, or in case of any interference with the duties of their office and, if necessary, will provide official protection.[194]

This protection was very extensive inasmuch as it embraced the entire priestly or spiritual activity of the cleric, which of course included State protection while he performed his duties of preaching.

The German Reich also recognized the juridic personality of Church institutions.[195] In general, the Church had the right to

---

[193] Instructions, ordinances, pastoral letters, official diocesan gazettes, and other enactments concerning the spiritual guidance of the faithful, issued by the ecclesiastical authorities within the framework of their competence (see Art. 1, § 2) may be published without hindrance and made known to the faithful in the ways hitherto usual.—*Church and State,* p. 488, Art. 4; *AAS, loc. cit.,* Perugini, *Concordata Vigentia,* p. 234, Art. 4, and also note 11.

[194] *Church and State,* p. 488, Art. 5; *AAS,* XXV (1933), p. 392, Art. 5; Perugini, *Concordata Vigentia,* pp. 234-235, Art. 5. Perugini cites two penal laws in protection of State officials which would be applicable to clerics under this concordatory provision.—*Ibid.,* pp. 234-235, note 12. Cf. also *CIC,* canon 119, which deals with the right of the cleric to reverence and respect (*ius ad reverentiam*), and canon 2343, which inflicts penalties upon those who lay violent hands upon clerics and religious.

[195] Catholic parishes, parish and diocesan associations, episcopal sees, bishoprics and chapters, religious orders and congregations, as well as institutions, foundations and property of the Catholic Church administered by ecclesiastical authority, shall retain or acquire respectively juridic personality, recognized by the State according to the general provisions of the Civil Law. They shall remain publicly recognized corporations as far as they have been hitherto; the same rights may be granted to others in accordance with the general law applicable to all.—*Church and State,* p. 489, Art. 13; *AAS,* XXV (1933), p. 395, Art. 13; Perugini, *Concordata Vigentia,* p. 240, Art. 13.

confer all ecclesiastical offices and benefices independently of State interference.[196]

Although the Reich did not guarantee any freedoms not already found in concordats previously considered, the Holy See did obtain a more extensive guarantee of freedoms, especially in the free exercise of ministerial activities, and a more specific pledge of protection for its clerics in the exercise of this ministry than it had

[196] Article 14. As a rule, the Church has the right to appoint freely to all Church dignities and benefices without any co-operation on the part of the State or of civil corporations, unless any other arrangement has been made in previous Concordats mentioned in Article 2. As far as the appointment to episcopal sees is concerned, the arrangement reached with regard to the Metropolitan See of Freiburg, in the diocese of the upper Rhine, shall be applicable to the two suffragan bishoprics of Rottenburg and Mainz, as well as the bishopric of Meissen. The same applies in the said two suffragan bishoprics as regards the appointments to the Cathedral Chapters and the settlement of the rights of patronage.—*Church and State,* p. 489;

*AAS,* XXV (1933), p. 396, Art. 14; Perugini, *Concordata Vigentia,* pp. 240-241. The German Concordat also contains articles relative to schools, but this matter is not the object of discussion in this work. Articles pertinent to the school question may be found in the following concordats: Bavarian, 4, 5, 7, 8, 9, 11; Polish, 13; Lithuanian, 13; Italian, 35, 36, 37, 38; Rumanian, 18, 19, 20; Baden, 11; German, 21, 22, 23, 24, 25, 28, 31; Austrian, 6, 16; Latvian, 10. This list is simply an illustrative one. Cf. also John J. Doyle, *Education in Recent Constitutions and Concordats* (Washington, D. C.: The Catholic University of America Press, 1933). The nineteenth-century concordats also contain articles on education: All these references are to *Raccolta di Concordati,* I—"Concordato fra Pio VII e Ferdinando Re delle Due Silicie," p. 621, Art. 2; "Concordato fra Pio IX e la Repubblica di Costa Rica," pp. 800-801, Art. 2; "Concordato fra Pio IX ed Isabella II Regina di Spagna," p. 771, Art. 2; "Concordato fra Pio IX e la Repubblica Guatemala," pp. 810-811, Art. 2; "Concordato fra Pio IX e Francesco Giuseppe I Imperatore d'Austria," p. 882, Art. 5; "Concordato fra Pio IX e Federico Granduca di Baden," p. 885, Art. 7. This article was elaborated upon by Cardinal Antonelli in a letter dated September 30, 1859—*ibid.,* p. 913, sec. 16; "Concordato fra Pio IX e la Repubblica di Honduras," p. 937, Art. 2; "Concordato fra Pio IX e la Repubblica di Venezuela," pp. 971-972, Art. 2; "Convenzione fra Leo XIII e Niccolo I Principe di Montenegro," p. 1049, Art. 8 and p. 1054, Art. 12; "Concordato fra Pio X e Pietro I Re di Serbia," p. 1001, Art. 10; "Concordato fra Pio IX e Guglielmo I Re del Wurttemburg," p. 858, Art. 7; cf. also the Concordat with Ecuador, *Church and State,* p. 275, Arts. 3, 4, which concordat is also found in *Raccolta di Concordati,* pp. 984-985, Arts. 3, 4.

received in other concordats. This concordat demonstrates the desire of the Church to obtain the widest breadth of freedom to carry out its mission and, at the same time, the most extensive legal protection to enable its ministers to perform the charge of preaching and teaching all men.

The Concordat with Yugoslavia followed the pattern established by earlier concordats concluded after World War I. It contained guarantees of a free communication with the Holy See, and a free communication between the bishops and the faithful, and of the free exercise of ecclesiastical jurisdiction, and of protection for the ministers of the Gospel.

Yugoslavia acknowledged the direct and exclusive dependence of diocesan ordinaries upon the Holy See and guaranteed a free communication between the Holy See and the clergy.[197] Ordinaries were promised a free communication with the clergy and with the faithful, and the freedom to publish acts dealing with the pastoral government of the diocese, and the right to call synods to consider the problems relating to the sacred ministry.[198]

The ordinaries were also given full liberty in the exercise of their ecclesiastical jurisdiction and in the use of all rights and prerogatives proper to their office. The Catholic clergy were considered by Yugoslavia to be subordinate to their proper ordinary in conformity with the laws of the Church.[199]

The clergy were extended the same degree of police protection in the exercise of their ministry as was given to State employees. The government promised to prevent, in conformity with the common law, offenses against the dignity and person of clerics, in the same fashion as it safeguarded the free exercise of their ministry. The article covering protection was probably modeled after the one in the German Concordat, because its pledges of protection are similar.[200]

---

[197] "Concordato Firmato con la Jugoslavia" (1935), *Raccolta di Concordati,* II, p. 205, Art. 6. For a discussion of the present status of religious liberty in Yugoslavia cf. Ottaviani, *op. cit.,* II, pp. 392-393, n. 420.

[198] *Raccolta di Concordati, loc. cit.*

[199] *Raccolta di Concordati,* II, p. 205, Art. 7.

[200] *Raccolta di Concordati, loc. cit.* For the German Concordat Article cf. *AAS,* XXV (1933), p. 392, Art. 5.

The Haiti Convention, which was concerned with ecclesiastical property, stated that the pastor of a parish church would be free to exercise his pastoral ministry, and that he would be held accountable in this matter to his ecclesiastical superiors.[201]

Portugal formulated a new Constitution in 1933. It contained an article which guaranteed the free exercise of religion:

> Art. 45. The public and private practice of any religion shall be free. Religious bodies may organize themselves freely, in accordance with the rules of their hierarchy and discipline, in such a manner as to form associations or organizations whose civil existence and juridical personality shall be recognized by the State.
>
> This shall not apply to the practices of any religious body which are incompatible with the life and physical integrity of the human individual and with good morals.[202]

The guarantee of religious freedom and the meaning of the restrictive clause of Article 45 of the Constitution with respect to Catholics was stated in the Concordat of 1940: "The Catholic Church is guaranteed the free exercise of all of its acts of worship, private and public, without prejudice to the exigencies of police and traffic control."[203] The significant phrase in this Article is "without prejudice to the exigencies of police and traffic control." The Holy See in a solemn agreement has conceded to have the exercise of worship restrained by police and traffic control. This limitation is more specific than the general restraint of a free exercise by the demands of public order and tranquility. Processions, outdoor masses, and religious rallies may more easily interfere with traffic regulations than they will with the public order of a State.

Although Portugal required the Church to adjust its activities to conform to police and traffic regulations, as a matter of general

---

[201] "Convenzione con la Repubblica di Haiti sui Beni Ecclesiastici e sulle Fabbricerie" (1940), *Raccolta di Concordati,* II, p. 226, Chap. 1, Art. 32.

[202] "The Portuguese Constitution of April 11, 1933, as amended on August 1, 1935," *Church and State,* p. 514, Sec. X, Art. 45.

[203] *Digest,* II, p. 15, Art. 16; *AAS,* XXXII (1940), p. 225, Art. 16. For a discussion of the Constitution and the Concordat consult Ottaviani, *op. cit.,* II, pp. 395-397, n. 421.

principle the State recognized the exclusive right of the Church to govern its own internal life.[204] This right was further determined by the pledge of the government not to exercise prior restraint upon communications of the Holy See relative to Church government and the pastoral ministry, and not to censor correspondence between the same Holy See and the clergy and the faithful of Portugal.[205] The policy of non-interference was also implicit in the guarantee that "the Catholic Church in Portugal can freely organize in accordance with the rules of canon law, and thus establish associations and organizations whose juridic personality is recognized by the State."[206]

With the exception of "urgent public necessity, such as war, flood, or fire," the State could not demolish or expropriate places or objects of public worship without the permission of the competent ecclesiastical authority. When such expropriation did take place the proper ecclesiastical authority would be consulted regarding the amount of the indemnity.[207] The Holy See again permitted its rights to be curtailed by State action, but in this case the area of independent State action was much more restricted. Only acts of God, i.e., fire, flood or some other natural disaster, or an act of an enemy of the State in the form of war, constituted legitimate grounds for such civil action, and the Church was eventually to be indemnified.

The Portuguese government extended more than negative pledges of non-interference in ecclesiastical activities. The State guaranteed that "in the exercise of their ministry, ecclesiastics enjoy the protection of the State in the same way as do the public authorities," and these same "ecclesiastics are exempt from the

---

[204] The Catholic Church is guaranteed the free exercise of its authority: within the proper sphere of its competency, the Church has the freedom to exercise acts of its powers of jurisdiction and of orders without interference. —*Digest*, II, p. 12, Art. 2; *AAS*, XXXII (1940), p. 219, Art. 2; *Raccolta di Concordati*, II, p. 233, Art. 2.

[205] *Digest*, II, *loc. cit.; AAS*, XXXII (1940), *loc. cit.; Raccolta ci Concordati*, II, *loc. cit.*

[206] *Digest*, II, p. 12, Art. 3; *AAS*, XXXII (1940), p. 219, Art. 3; *Raccolta di Concordati*, II, pp. 233-234, Art. 3.

[207] *Digest*, II, pp. 13-14, Art. 7; *Raccolta di Concordati*, II, p. 236, Art. 7.

duty of acting as jurors, members of tax tribunals or commissions, and other charges of the same nature, which are considered by canon law as incompatible with the ecclesiastical state."[208] These legal assurances of protection and exemption together with the promise of non-interference in religious matters and the guarantee of a free exercise of worship, both public and private, form a solid juridic basis for the unfettered exercise of the Church's preaching mission in Portugal.

Spain eventually followed its neighbor's example and concluded the long projected concordat with the Holy See on August 23, 1953. The government recognized "in the Catholic Church the character of a perfect society," and it guaranteed to this Church "the free and full exercise of its spiritual power and jurisdiction, such as the free and public exercise of cult."[209] The choice of the words "perfect society" is a felicitous one and has far reaching implications.[210] In recognizing the Church as a perfect society Spain acknowledges the autonomy of the Church in regulating its own affairs and the juridic right of the Church to use all the means necessary or useful for the accomplishing of its supernatural end or mission, the salvation of souls. One of the chief means to obtain this end is preaching the Gospel. The government safeguards this important means by the guarantee of a full and free exercise of the Church's spiritual power and jurisdiction in such matters as the free and public exercise of worship. This freedom of spiritual power and jurisdiction is further specified by the promise of free communication between the Holy See and the members of the Church.[211] As in other countries which grant this

---

[208] *Digest,* II, pp. 14-15, Arts. 11-13; *AAS,* XXXII (1940), p. 224, Arts. 11, 13; *Raccolta di Concordati,* II, p. 237, Arts. 11, 13.

[209] *AAS,* XXXXV (1953), p. 626, Art. 2, i (trans. by writer). The Dominican Republic in its 1954 Concordat made the same act of recognition and guarantee.—*AAS,* XXXXVI (1954), p. 435, Art. 3, i.

[210] For a discussion of the Church as a perfect society cf. Ottaviani, *op. cit.,* I, pp. 53 ff.

[211] In particular, the Holy See will be able to freely promulgate and publish in Spain whatever measure relates to the government of the Church, and to communicate without impediment with the prelates, the clergy and the faithful of the country, in the same way that these (above-mentioned) will be able to do with the Holy See.—*AAS,* XXXXV (1953), p. 626, Art. 2, n. 2

free communication, the same freedom is extended to ordinaries and other ecclesiastical authorities in all that refers to the local clergy and the faithful.[212]

In both Spain and the Dominican Republic "clerics and religious will not be obliged to assume public posts or offices which, according to the norms of Canon Law, may be incompatible with their state."[213] In addition to the guarantees of the Dominican Concordat as cited above in connection with the Spanish Concordat, the Dominican government promised that "the clerics will enjoy in the exercise of their ministry the special protection of the State."[214] The Catholic religion continued to be the State religion, so such protection for the Established Church was to be expected. This form of Church-State relationship (one which the Catholic religion was recognized to be the true religion, and its rights according to divine and canon law were honored in public law, and its activities were favored and protected) was the ideal public law recognition envisioned by Leo XIII in his encyclicals *Libertas* and *Immortale Dei.*

When the Church was commissioned to preach to all nations, the means of communication were primitive according to modern standards. With the invention of the printing press the media for reaching the masses were greatly improved. The Church immediately used this method to convey its pastoral messages to the world. Concordat after concordat acknowledged this right of the Church to communicate freely with the faithful in this manner. In the twentieth century another revolution occurred in the field of communication, first the radio and more recently the television. The Church adopted these new advances in the science of com-

---

(trans. by writer). The Dominican Concordat contains the same pledge.—*AAS,* XXXXVI (1954), p. 435, Art. 3, n. 2.

[212] *AAS,* XXXXV (1953), *loc. cit.; AAS,* XXXXVI (1954), *loc. cit.*

[213] *AAS,* XXXXV (1953), p. 632, Art. 14; *AAS,* XXXXVI (1954), p. 440, Art. 11, n. 3. Both nations added the provision that such persons "to occupy public offices or posts . . . will need the *nihil obstat* of their proper ordinary and of the ordinary of the place in which they are to discharge their activity. When the *nihil obstat* has been revoked, they will no longer continue exercising their activities." (Both translations are by the writer.)

[214] *AAS,* XXXXVI (1954), p. 440, Art. 11, n. 1 (trans. by writer).

munication in order to fulfill more effectively its preaching mission. The recognition of the right of the Church to use these media of communication not only independently of State regulation, but even with State patronage, was expression in the Spanish Concordat.[215] This Article of the Spanish Concordat will find expression in concordats which will be negotiated in future years, for it is simply an application of the claim of the Church to preach freely to all nations.

An examination of the free exercise articles contained in the twentieth-century concordats shows that the Church negotiates not only for vague guarantees and pledges of freedom in the ministry, but also for specific promises of the free exercise of religion, of Church administration, of communication, and of government. The Holy See seeks to preserve these rights more securely by obtaining special guarantees of State protection for the ministers of religion, and specific assurances that the inviolability of its places of worship will be respected.

The Church is willing to have the exercise of these rights limited by the demands of the public order and tranquility, and conditioned by the demands which follow disasters, such as flood, fire, and war. In some instances the Church is even willing to sanction the limitations imposed upon the free exercise of its mission by police and traffic regulations.

### *Section 3. Church Concessions Made to the Various States With Respect to Ministers of Religion*

The Church as a perfect society endowed with a supernatural mission to save souls has a right superior to that of any natural society to use the means necessary or useful for the accomplishment of this mission. The appointment of personnel, the formulation of their qualifications, and the control of their activities are by right the sole concern of the Church. The mission of the Church

[215] The State will be careful that in the institutions and methods of forming public opinion, in particular on radio and television programs, a fitting post for exposition and defense of the true religion be given to priests and religious in agreement with their respective ordinaries.—*AAS,* XXXXV (1953), p. 647, Art. 29 (trans. by writer).

constitutes it as a supra-national body, and its objectives are not contrary to, but beyond, the interests of any one nation. Therefore, by right neither national boundaries nor local regulations may hinder the essential activities of the Church. When there is an area of seeming conflict, it is the right of the superior society, the Church, to resolve the issues and settle the differences of opinion.

However, churchmen are realists and they know that at times they must be content to negotiate for less than their full rights, in order that the Church may enjoy the peace and freedom necessary for the carrying out of its mission of preaching, of teaching, and of saving souls. For this reason the Holy See made several concessions to civil governments in concordats which it concluded since the First World War. Among these concessions were: the requirement that clerics take a special oath of fidelity to the State, the right of the State to object to the nomination of candidates for bishoprics on the grounds of political unacceptability, and the requirement that archbishops, bishops, chancery officials, and religious superiors be citizens of the respective State in which they hold office.

### 1. Oath of Fidelity

Several concordats contain the stipulation that a bishop must take the oath of fidelity to the State before he assumes office.[216]

### 2. Political Objection to Ministers of Religion

The government of Latvia was granted the privilege of raising objections from a political point of view to the candidate chosen by the Holy See for the Archbishopric of Riga.[217] This *jus praenotificationis officiosae* is a *jus objiciendi,* but it is not a *nihil*

---

[216] E.g., Concordat of Latvia, Art. 5; Lithuania, Art. 12; Poland, Art. 12; Czechoslovakia, Art. 5; Italy, Art. 20; Rumania, Art. 6; Germany, Art. 12. The Czechoslovakian oath is significant for its conciseness: *Juro et promitto, sicuti decet Episcoporum, fidelitatem Reipublicae Cecoslovachae necnon nihil me facturum quos sit contra salutem, securitatem, integritatem Reipublicae.*—Perugini, *Concordata Vigentia,* p. 75, Art. 5.

[217] Perugini, *Concordata Vigentia,* p. 3, Art. 4.

*obstat,* or a *jus exclusivae* or a veto power.[218] It is a privilege conceded to a State by force of which, before any person is appointed to a public ecclesiastical office, his name is secretly and confidentially given to the civil government some time prior to his official appointment, so that the government may have an opportunity to raise objections of a political nature, if there are any, against this person, and explain these objections to the competent ecclesiastical superior.

In the present context the *jus praenotificationis officiosae* does not extend to all offices, but primarily to the office of the archbishop, the bishop, and the coadjutor with a right of succession. The weight of this clause differs with the various governments, and each concordat which contains such a clause must be investigated to determine the precise weight for the said country. The purpose in this present paragraph is not to determine the exact meaning of each *jus praenotificationis officiosae,* but only to indicate that such a privilege exists in concordat practice, whereas it is not demanded by American constitutional law.

As Prunskis observes, the Lithuanian Concordat does not define the meaning of the phrase "political objections," but the *Modus Vivendi* of Czechoslovakia enables the reader to arrive at a general understanding of the phrase.[219] The Czechoslovakian governmen could raise political objections against a candidate based on natural security, such as, the candidate chosen by the Holy See was guilty of irredentist or separatist political activity directed against the constitution, or against the public order of the country.[220] In the Concordat with Baden the political objection

[218] Cf. Ottaviani, *op. cit.,* I, pp. 434-451, n. 234-n. 242 for a complete discussion of these notions. The German Concordat explicitly states that this privilege is not a right to vote.—Perugini, *Concordata Vigentia,* p. 242, Art. 14 and the additional protocol on this article.—*Ibid.,* p. 257; *Church and State,* pp. 490, 495.

[219] *Comparative Law, Ecclesiastical and Civil, in the Lithuanian Concordat,* p. 72.

[220] *AAS,* XX (1928), p. 66, Art. 4; Perugini, *Concordata Vigentia,* pp. 74-75, Art 4. Perugini states that this is the meaning of the phrase "objections of a political nature against a nominee" found in several of the concordats.—*Ibid.,* p. 75, note 9.

could not be based solely on membership in a political party.[221]

The president of Poland was granted the same privilege as Latvia with respect to all archbishops, bishops, and coadjutors with the right of succession.[222] The concordat between the Holy See and Italy contained a similar concession:

> Before proceeding to the nomination of an archbishop, a diocesan bishop or a coadjutor *cum iure successione,* the Holy See shall communicate the name of the person chosen to the Italian government in order to make sure that the government has no objections of a political nature to the nomination.[223]

The Prussian government was given permission to pass judgment on the political acceptability of archbishops, bishops, coadjutors with the right of succession, and prelates *nullius.*[224] Rumania and Austria could also raise objections on political grounds to the nominees for bishoprics.[225] Baden was permitted to raise objections based on grounds of a general political nature to the nominee for the archbishopric.[226] The Portuguese government enjoyed a similar privilege of objection on general political grounds:

> The Holy See, before proceeding to the appointment of a resident Archbishop, bishop, or a coadjutor with the right of succession, without prejudice to the provisions made in regard to patronage and semi-patronage, shall communicate the name of the person chosen to the Portuguese government, to ascertain whether there are any objections

---

[221] Perugini, *Concordata Vigentia,* p. 210, Art. 2.

[222] Perugini, *Concordata Vigentia,* p. 39, Art. 11. The Lithuanian Concordat contains an identical article.—*Ibid.,* p. 63, Art. 12.

[223] *Church and State,* p. 389, Art. 19; *AAS,* XXI (1929), p. 282, Art. 19; Perugini, *Concordata Vigentia,* p. 123, Art. 19.

[224] Perugini, *Concordata Vigentia,* p. 182, Art. 6, § 1, and p. 184, Art. 7.

[225] *AAS,* XXI (1929), p. 443, Art. 5, and Perugini, *Concordata Vigentia,* p. 148, Art. 5; for Austria, cf. Perugini, *Concordata Vigentia,* p. 269, Art. 4, n. 2.

[226] Perugini, *Concordata Vigentia,* p. 210, Art. 2. Germany enjoyed a similar privilege.—*Church and State,* p. 490, Art. 14, n. 2, and the additional protocol on this Article.—*Ibid.,* p. 495. Perugini, *Concordata Vigentia,* p. 242, Art. 14, n. 2, and the additional protocol.—*Ibid.,* p. 257.

> of a general political character against the candidate. The silence of the government, after thirty days from the aforesaid communication, shall be interpreted in the sense that there are no objections. All proceedings contemplated in this article shall remain secret.[227]

Although the privilege of the political objection to candidates for Church offices was not *de iure* a veto power, it did constitute a restriction upon the right of the Church in selecting the candidates whom the Church considered best qualified to fill the offices which direct the preaching and teaching of the Gospel in the respective countries.

### 3. Citizenship Requirements

The purpose of this paragraph is not to determine the specific nature of every citizenship requirement in each nation, but to cite examples of its existence in concordats and to compare this condition with the state of affairs in the United States.

The Latvian Concordat required that "the archbishop and bishops shall be of Latvian nationality."[228] It also contained a citizenship requirement for the members of the cathedral chapter, the deans (*les doyens*), and the pastors (*les cures titulaires*).[229]

The citizenship requirement was more flexible in Bavaria. A cleric could not be assigned to the direction and administration of a diocese, or to some pastoral or educational activity, unless he was a citizen of Bavaria or one of the other German States. In a word, any German citizen was eligible for the said offices.[230] Superiors of religious orders or congregations who held legal residence in Bavaria were also obliged to be citizens of Bavaria or one of the other German States. If the superior had his per-

---

[227] *Digest,* II, p. 14, Art. X; *Raccolta di Concordati,* II, pp. 236-237, Art. X.

[228] Perugini, *Concordata Vigentia,* p. 3, Art. 2 (trans. by writer).

[229] *Ibid.,* p. 6, Art. 12.

[230] Perugini, *Concordata Vigentia,* pp. 25-26, Art. 13, § 1. The German concordat contains a similar Article.—*Church and State,* p. 490, Art. 14, § 2, n. 1, and Perugini, *Concordata Vigentia,* p. 241, Art. 14. The Austrian Concordat has a similar citizenship clause.—Perugini, *Concordata Vigentia,* p. 283, Art. 11, § 2.

manent residence outside of Bavaria and was a citizen of another country, he could make his visitation of the houses of his group in Bavaria either himself or through his delegate.[231]

The *Modus Vivendi* with Czechoslovakia required that provincial superiors and the superiors of the houses directly dependent upon the generalate (*la maison generalice*) be Czech citizens.[232] Archbishops, bishops of dioceses, coadjutors with the right of succession, and the ordinary for the armed forces had to be Czechoslovakian subjects.[233]

In Rumania all the canons of the cathedral chapter were obliged to be citizens, unless the Holy See and the royal government reached a special agreement in a particular case.[234] Pastors had to be Rumanian citizens who were free from any definitive sentence against them for crimes committed against the State. The consent of the government had to be obtained when the ordinary nominated a foreigner for the post of pastor. Even this pastor had to become a Rumanian citizen in the course of time.[235] Perugini gives an insight into the reason for this legal requirement in Rumania. Rumanian pastors also enjoyed the office of a civil official, e.g., in celebrating marriage, so it was repugnant for a non-Rumanian to hold a civil post.[236] In the case of religious orders and congregations in Rumania, their provincials and members, Rumanian citizens, had to have permanent residence within the country.[237]

Austria required that the provincials have legal residence in

---

[231] Perugini, *Concordata Vigentia,* p. 26, Art. 13, § 2. The German concordat contains a similar statement.—*Church and State,* p. 490, Art. 15, and Perugini, *Concordata Vigentia,* pp. 242-243, Art. 15.

[232] *Ibid.,* p. 74, Art. 4.

[233] *Loc. cit.*

[234] *AAS,* XXI (1929), p. 445, Art. 11, § 2; Perugini, *Concordata Vigentia,* p. 151, Art. 11, § 2.

[235] *AAS,* XXI (1929), p. 446, Art. 12, § 2; Perugini, *Concordata Vigentia,* p. 151, Art. 12, § 2.

[236] *Ibid.,* p. 151, note 26. Italy established a prohibition against non-Italians holding benefices in Italy.—*AAS,* XXI (1929), p. 284, Art. 22, and *Church and State,* p. 399, Art. 22.

[237] *AAS,* XXI (1929), p. 448, Art. 17, and Perugini, *Concordata Vigentia,* p. 154, Art. 17.

Austria, and that they be Austrian citizens. The superior of an order or of a province who lived outside of Austria and was of another nationality could make a visitation of the houses of the congregation or order in Austria either personally or through a delegate.[238]

The concordat between the Holy See and the Dominican Republic presents a sharp contrast to the aforementioned concordats with their many clauses hindering the unqualified selection of ministers of religion by the Church. The good of souls is the primary factor affecting the choice of a candidate, and not his nationality, nor his political affiliation:

> The ecclesiastical authorities will be able to use the services and the co-operation of the foreign clergy, secular or religious, and confer upon the foreign priests dignities, offices and ecclesiastical benefices, when they judge it fitting for the welfare of the country, diocese or prelature.[239]

Instead of placing impediments in the way of a foreign clergy, the Dominican Republic agrees that "the foreign priests and both men and women religious whom the ecclesiastical authority invites to the country, in order to exercise the ministry and to carry out the activities of the Apostolate, will be exempt from any immigration measure or import duty."[240]

This sound attitude of the Dominican Republic is more in keeping with the general principle enunciated in the Code of Canon Law, viz., that the Church has the right to preach the Gospel everywhere independently of civil regulation, than the policy of restriction practiced by a number of the nations which concluded concordats with the Holy See since World War I.[241]

---

[238] *Ibid.*, pp. 281-282, Art. X, § 3.

[239] *AAS*, XXXXVI (1954), p. 439, Art. 10, § 2 (trans. by writer).

[240] *AAS*, XXXXVI (1954), p. 439, Art. 10, § 2 (trans. by writer).

[241] Cf. *CIC*, canon 1322, § 2. For a statement of the present condition of the Catholic Church in Latvia, Lithuania, Poland, Rumania, Yugoslavia, Czechoslovakia, and other nations under Communist domination consult Galter, *The Red Book*.

ARTICLE III. A COMPARATIVE STUDY: FIRST AMENDMENT FREEDOMS, PAPAL PRONOUNCEMENTS AND CONCORDAT PRACTICE

### *Section 1. No Establishment Clause . . . "separation and co-operation"*

The juridic status of the Roman Catholic Church, as well as every other religious sect, in the United States today is "equality at public law." In the light of the Supreme Court decisions of the past fifteen years it is evident that the "no establishment clause" of the First Amendment has been interpreted to mean that Congress may not establish a religion, nor enforce the legal observance of religion by law, nor compel American citizens to worship God in a way contrary to their consciences. However, the Court has not yet resolved what constitutes an establishment. Apparently, the use of a public school classroom as a place in which to administer religious instruction is a form of establishment. Co-operation of the public school authorities in "release time" programs in which instruction classes are conducted off public school property is not an establishment.

In the McCollum case the majority interpreted separation of Church and State to mean "absolute separation" connoted by the metaphor "wall of separation." The McCollum doctrine of "absolute separation" has been modified by the Zorach formula, which Konvitz correctly describes as "separation and co-operation." Douglas, delivering the majority opinion, said: "The First Amendment, however, does not say that in every and all respects there shall be a separation of Church and State. Rather, it studiously defines the manner, the specific ways, in which there shall be no concert or union or dependency one on the other."

The immediate problem confronting the Court is the determination of the meaning of the word "co-operation." The content of this term will probably be clarified piecemeal by future Supreme Court decisions. Zorach's majority looked to traditional practice for a descriptive definition of the term co-operation. Co-operation, at the least, includes in this definition a public recognition of God by invocations in courtrooms and legislative assemblies; references to the Almighty in laws, public rituals, and other official ceremonies; police and fire protection for religious institutions; official co-operation to enable students and other citizens to attend the form of worship dictated by conscience; the use of public parks for religious services and rallies; and the appointment of military chaplains.

The spirit of this co-operation is embodied in the following words:

> We are a religious people whose institutions presuppose a Supreme Being. We guarantee the freedom to worship as one chooses. We make room for as wide a variety of beliefs and creeds as the spiritual needs of man deem necessary. We sponsor an attitude on the part of the government that shows no partiality to any group and lets each flourish according to the zeal of its adherents and the appeal of its dogma. When the state encourages religious instruction or co-operates with religious authorities by adjusting the schedule of public events to sectarian needs, it follows the best of our traditions. For it then respects the religious nature of our people and accommodates the public service to their spiritual needs. To hold that it may not would be to find in the Constitution a requirement that the government show a callous indifference to religious groups. That would be preferring those who believe in no religion over those who do believe.[242]

---

[242] 343 U.S. 306, 313, 314 (1952). The question of state aid for Churches, parochial schools, hospitals, etc., is not discussed in this work for reasons already outlined. In general, the principle is that no Church or religious sect may receive direct government subsidy. Individual citizens may receive certain emoluments, which may indirectly aid a religious sect, but this is *per accidens*. The title for such assistance is not religious affiliation, but the safeguarding of the health and welfare of American citizens. This right is considered judicially more fundamental than a title of religious affiliation. For a consideration of this question of state aid consult: Francis J. Powers, C.S.V., "The Supreme Court and the Constitutional Prohibition Against 'An Establishment of Religion,'" *The Jurist,* XII, 282-314 (July, 1952); E. R. Barry, "Public Benefit and School Bus Transportation," *The Jurist,* VI, 425-431 (July, 1946); Kenneth R. O'Brien and Daniel E. O'Brien, "Separation of Church and State in Restatement of Inter-Church and State Common Law," *The Jurist,* VII, 259-279 (July, 1947).

The present condition of Church-State relations existing under the American Constitutional System can be adequately termed "separation and co-operation." Precisely because the American system of public law jurisprudence is a dynamic one, it is difficult to predict with accuracy what the juridic content of these terms will be a quarter of a century from today. To the writer, however, the guess appears reasonable, that the present juridic meaning of "separation" will remain fairly constant, but the juridic content of "co-operation" will continue to move steadily away from the McCollum attitude and expand in a direction more favorable to Church bodies. It is the writer's conviction that religion and government will profit by this increased spirit of co-operation.

How does the juridic status of religion in the United States, expressed in the phrase "equal at law," compare with Roman Catholic concordat practice and the pronouncements of modern popes? The juridic position of the Catholic Church in the United States compares favorably with the legal status of the Church as guaranteed in concordats since World War I. Only three Latin nations, Italy, Spain, and the Dominican Republic, have granted the Roman Catholic Church an "established position" in their concordat agreements. Three nations, Austria, Haiti, and Poland, pledged a "preferred position" for the Church in their solemn conventions. Eight European States or nations, Latvia, Lithuania, Germany, Yugoslavia, Baden, Portugal, Prussia, and Bavaria wrote an "equal status of religion" clause into their formal documents. It is significant that the Holy See has accepted the condition of equality at law as a permanent status for the Church in international agreements solemnly binding both parties for an indefinite period. In the absence of any such agreement, the Catholic Church enjoys the same legal status in the United States.

There is an important consideration which should not be passed over lightly. Ordinarily, treaty agreements are more subject to serious violation and repudiation than rights secured in the common law and tradition of a country. This is particularly true of a nation steeped in Anglo-American legal heritage. It is the considered opinion of the writer that the equal status at law position of the Church in America enjoys greater solidarity than it would possess, if it were solely the product of an international convention.[243]

In the Rumanian Concordat the Holy See agreed to accept a "less than equal status at law" position for the Catholic Church. There is no need to labor the obvious; the legal position of the Catholic Church in the United States is superior.

The juridic content of the "equal status at law" concept is the same under the First Amendment and in the concordat practice—no State religion and no dominant religion.[244]

The present formula for Church and State relations in the United States is "separation and co-operation." How does this compare with the traditional formula of the Catholic Church as expressed in the phrase "distinction and co-operation?"[245] Pope Pius XII said in 1955 that these two powers must not "ignore one another, still less be in conflict with one another."[246] The majority of the Court in the Zorach case said the equivalent. The First Amendment, they said, does not mean that the State and religion should be alien to each other—hostile, suspicious, and even unfriendly, nor that government should be indifferent toward religion.[247]

The Court and the modern popes agree on the negative definition of "separation and co-operation" and "distinction and co-operation." They both mean that there should be no domination of one society over the other, and no hostility between them. There is a difference in the positive definition. The popes maintain that the

---

[243] Cf. Rommen, *The State in Catholic Thought*, p. 591. He makes similar observations.

[244] The reader must avoid the error of equating the "equal status" concept with the "free exercise" concept. The notion of free exercise is discussed in some of the succeeding paragraphs.

[245] The history of this concept, which originated with Saint Pope Gelasius (d. 496), was forceably recalled to our minds by Pope Leo XIII, and is found in several pronouncements of Pope Pius XII. Cf. Wilfred Parsons, S.J., *The First Freedom, Considerations on Church and State* (New York: Declan X. McMullen Co., Inc., 1948), pp. 80-94.

[246] *The Pope Speaks,* II, 210; *AAS,* XLVII (1955), 678. Rommen, *op. cit.,* pp. 600-603. Rommen accurately describes this hostile form of separation, and notes that the United States does not fall within this category.

[247] 342 U.S. 306, 312, 313, 314.

ideal is the establishment of the Catholic Church with a full recognition of its Canon Law. During the nineteenth century most of its concordat arrangements realized this ideal in the practical order, but in this century only three concordat negotiations have accomplished this goal.

Does this mean that the "separation and co-operation" formula of American Church and State relations is rejected by the popes? No, the modern popes have explicitly commended the juridic conditions existing in the United States, but they do not hold them aloft as ideal. However, in the particular circumstances of time and place, the American solution may properly be regarded as good for the United States.

Pope Leo XIII, in his encyclical *Immortale Dei,* 1885, clearly enunciated the teaching of the Church:

> The Church, indeed, deems it unlawful to place the various forms of divine worship on the same footing as the true religion, but does not, on that account, condemn those rulers who, for the sake of securing some greater good or hindering some great evil, allow patiently custom or usage to be a kind of sanction for each kind of religion having its place in the State. And, in fact the Church is wont to take earnest heed that no one shall be forced to embrace the Catholic faith against his will. . . .[248]

In his encyclical on *The Catholicity in the United States, Longinqua Oceani,* January 6, 1895, he applied this teaching specifically to the American situation:

> But, moreover (a fact which it gives pleasure to acknowledge), thanks are due to the equity of the laws which obtain in America and to the customs of that well-ordered Republic. For the Church amongst you, unopposed by the

---

[248] *The Church Speaks to the Modern World,* p. 178, No. 36; *ASS,* XVIII (1885), 174-175. For an excellent treatment of this text consult: Giacomo Cardinal Lercaro (Archbishop of Bologna), "Religious Tolerance in Catholic Tradition," *Catholic Mind,* LVIII, 19-20 (January-February, 1960). This is translated by *Catholic Mind* from the French version of J. Thomas-d'Hoste, which appeared in *Documentation Catholique,* Maison de la Bonne Presse, 5, rue Bayard, Paris (VIII), France, March 15, 1959.

> Constitution and the government of your nation, fettered by no hostile legislation, protected against violence by the common laws and the impartiality of the tribunals, is free to live and act without hindrance. Yet, though all this is true, it would be very erroneous to draw the conclusion that in America is to be sought the type of the most desirable status of the Church, or that it would be universally lawful and expedient for State and Church to be, as in America, dissevered and divorced. The fact that Christianity with you is in good condition, nay, is even enjoying a prosperous growth, is by all means to be attributed to the fecundity with which God has endowed his Church, in virtue of which, unless men or circumstances interfere, she spontaneously expands and propagates herself; but she would bring forth more abundant fruit if, in addition to liberty, she enjoyed the favor of the laws and the patronage of public authority.[249]

Co-operation, as interpreted in the Zorach case, appealed to the American tradition of recognizing God in the courtroom, in the legislative hall, in the fundamental law of the land, and in congressional enactments. Leo XIII in the Encyclical *Libertas* declared that the State is bound to recognize God and his laws, and to consider the good of souls by making legislative enactments in conformity with the laws of God. He condemned those who denied that God and his authority should be given recognition in both public and private affairs, or only in public affairs, for such a denial leads to godlessness and absolute separation of Church and State. The pope unhesitatingly condemned the notion of absolute separation, but he sanctioned the position of those who, although not favoring a separation of Church and State, believe that the Church must adapt itself to the times and conform to what is required by the modern system of government, provided it is based upon some equitable adjustment consistent with truth and justice. American "separation and co-operation" falls within this second category.

The most authoritative interpretation of the Catholic Church's

---

[249] *The Great Encyclical Letters of Leo XIII*, pp. 323-324. Cf. Rommen, *op. cit.*, pp. 603-605. He considers the United States to be the best example of this milder separation.

position on matters of Church and State on the domestic scene may be gleaned from the pronouncements of the American bishops. The Catholic bishops have expressed their opinion on this matter at various times, but the most explicit statement was made in 1948, shortly after the Supreme Court handed down the McCollum decision.[250] The bishops found the acceptance of the "absolute separation" doctrine expounded in the Everson and McCollum cases very distasteful, and also detrimental to both Church and State.[251]

The American bishops were not unaware of the tremendous problems which exist in the religiously pluralistic society of America. They firmly believed that a solution could be found to the question of Church and State relations which would be acceptable to all, and yet not detrimental to Catholic principles:

> That concrete problem, delicate as it is, can, without sacrifice of principle, be solved in a practical way when good will and a spirit of fairness prevail. Authoritative Catholic teaching on the relations between Church and State, as set forth in papal encyclicals and in treaties of recognized writers on ecclesiastical law, not only states clearly what these relations should normally be under ideal conditions, but also indicates to what extent the Catholic Church can adapt herself to the particular conditions that may obtain in different countries.[252]

Then a particular application of these principles was made to the United States:

> Examining, in the full perspective of that teaching, the position which those who founded our nation and framed

---

[250] "The Christian in Action," November 21, 1948, *Our Bishops Speak*, pp. 145 ff.

[251] *Ibid.*, p. 151.—If this practical policy be described by the loose metaphor "a wall of separation between Church and State, that term must be understood in a definite and typically American sense. It would be an utter distortion of American history and law to make that practical policy involve the indifference to religion and the exclusion of co-operation between religion and government implied in the term separation of Church and State as it has become the shibboleth of doctrinaire secularism."

[252] *Ibid.*, p. 150.

> its basic law took on the problem of Church-State relations in our own country, we find that the First Amendment to our Constitution solved the problem in a way that is typically American in its practical recognition of existing conditions and its evident desire to be fair to all citizens of whatever religious faith.[253]

The American hierarchy summed up its position in these words:

> We feel with deep conviction that for the sake of both good citizenship and religion there should be a reaffirmation of our original American tradition of free co-operation between government and religious bodies—co-operation involving no special privilege to any group and no restriction on the religious liberty of any citizen. We solemnly disclaim any intent or desire to alter this prudent and fair American policy of government in dealing with the delicate problems that have their source in the divided religious allegiance of our citizens.[254]

The Zorach formula of separation and co-operation is undoubtedly in agreement with what the American bishops sincerely believe to be the best arrangement for the United States. The writer is of the opinion that the bishops would prefer that a more substantial content be given to "co-operation," yet the present interpretation of the Court and the practice of the American government is definitely in conformity with, or at least in the direction of, the position adopted by the American hierarchy.

Religion in the United States enjoys a solid juridic basis in public law. This statement is substantiated by the freedom granted to the exercise of religion in the United States. On a television program during the month of February, 1960, Senator Wayne Morse said in substance, "I always told my students that the substantive rights guaranteed by a nation are only as good as the procedural rights which protect them. Don't look to what a country says it grants on paper, look rather to its procedures. These will tell you what rights a State really honors." The same

---

[253] *Loc. cit.*

[254] *Ibid.*, p. 153. Cf. also Francis J. Connell, "The Relationship Between Church and State," *The Jurist*, XIII (1953), 411-414, II.

observation may be made in connection with the juridic position of the Church. A nation may grant establishment and all kinds of preferential rights to the Church in a solemn document, but its governmental machinery may deprive the Church of any real semblances of rights and freedom. The writer can demonstrate that the juridic position of the Church in the United States is both solid and genuine by appealing to his investigation of the Court's interpretation and defense of the First Amendment freedoms.

The juridic position of the Catholic Church in the United States is less than ideal, but still practically and morally acceptable, even as a permanent condition, in the light of concordat practice, papal pronouncements, and episcopal statements. What is the position of the right of the Catholic Church to preach, when judged within this same framework? In general, the exercise of this right is in agreement with papal pronouncements and episcopal statements, and in several instances it is superior to the degree of free exercise accorded in concordats.

Both the Supreme Court and the modern popes are in perfect agreement on at least one point—no one can be forced to embrace a religious belief contrary to the dictates of his conscience. When subjective beliefs are at variance with objective truth, may this error ever be permitted to be propagated? Yes, both the Court and modern popes agree that the guiding norm must not be "suppression of error whenever and wherever possible." Such intolerance may produce a greater evil. The guiding norm implicitly established by the Court is the common good of the nation. Pius XII explicitly declared that the final norm of judgment is the international common good. Viewed within the area of each one's respective competence and the practical circumstances with which the Court and the Holy See are faced, these norms are not at variance with each other.[255]

Securing an important phase of the common good, such as the public order, in a religiously pluralistic society is not as simple a task as it is in a country whose population is traditionally and almost one hundred per cent Catholic in culture and belief. Leo

---

[255] Cf. also Lercaro, "Religious Tolerance in Catholic Tradition," *Catholic Mind*, LVIII, 19-20 (Jan.-Feb., 1960).

XIII and Pius XII were aware of this difference, and both looked benignly and with no small satisfaction upon the solution existing in the United States. It would be a misstatement to assert that these pontiffs considered the American solution as ideal in every respect. But it is true to state that Pius XII had America in mind when he said that "there is a political tolerance, a civil tolerance, a social tolerance, in regard to adherents of other religious beliefs which, in circumstances such as these [a religiously pluralistic society] is a moral duty for Catholics."[256]

### *Section 2. Preaching and Public Order*

The past thirty-five years of Supreme Court activity demonstrates clearly the difficult task involved in finding a norm adequate enough to balance the claims of the right of free speech and the demands for civil peace and public order. The present standard is "clear and probable danger," the Dennis test, applied with juridic "reasonableness." Religious speech or preaching is given an even more favorable position than secular speech, in the balancing of these equities. A supplementary norm sometimes applied by the Court is the doctrine of "avoidability of a clash." Therefore, preaching enjoys a privileged position in the United States.

The balance between the factors of the relative value of speech, on the one hand, and of the public safety and order, on the other, will shift with times and circumstances. In periods when the security of the nation is gravely threatened, the liberty accorded free speech will be less than the freedom granted to speech in times of reduced national peril. Preaching is an integral part of free speech, and so the relative degree of freedom which it possesses will fluctuate in the same manner.

Concordats both of the past and of the present century acknowledge the importance of state maintenance of public peace and security, so the Holy See has agreed to place the right of preaching below that of the public order. For example, by the Concordat

---

[256] Powers, *Papal Pronouncements on the Political Order,* p. 122, n. 181; *AAS,* XXXVIII (1946), 393; cf. also Lercaro, "Religious Toleration in Catholic Tradition," *Catholic Mind,* LVIII, 21-24 (Jan.-Feb., 1960).

with France (1801), Pius VII permitted the public exercise of the Catholic religion to be governed by "police regulations which the government shall deem necessary for public tranquility." A similar article was embodied in the Concordat with Portugal in 1940: "The Catholic Church is guaranteed the free exercise of all acts of worship, public and private, without prejudice to the exigencies of police and traffic control." However, this comparison cannot be made in every detail, for two reasons: 1. the French concordat is more inclusive, since it embraced the entire public order; 2. the political situation in each country was vastly different, the one in Portugal was more favorable to the Church.[257]

It is difficult to deduce a principle in this matter from concordatory practice, since the act of acknowledging the maintenance of public peace and security may have a different weight in various countries. The precise meaning depends on constitutional and political circumstances which cannot be covered by one juridical formula. In a police state or a totalitarian country the concessions made by the Holy See in this respect can lead, and have led, as experience demonstrates, to severe, though legalized, restrictions on the right of preaching.

---

[257] For the French Concordat of 1801, cf. *Church and State,* p. 252, Art. 1, and *Raccolta di Concordati,* I, p. 562, Art. 1; for the Portuguese Concordat of 1940, cf. *Digest,* II, p. 15, Art. 16, and *AAS,* XXXII (1940), p. 225, Art. 16. Leo Gershoy shows that Napoleon abused the concordat phrase:

> . . . Bonaparte made effective the police regulations given him by article one of the concordat; namely, that the worship of the Catholic religion should be "in conformity with the police regulations which the government shall deem necessary for public tranquillity." These "regulations," which not only filled in the omissions of the Concordat, but also provided for the state regulation of Protestantism, were known as the Organic Articles. The Concordat and the Organic Articles were combined into one text, so as to give the impression that the "regulations" were an integral part of the arrangement that had been made with the papacy, and issued as a single law on April 8, 1802. The pope, however, knew nothing of the Organic Articles until they were passed, and he never accepted them as provisions of the Concordat.—*The French Revolution and Napoleon* (New York, 1933).

Bonaparte's action violated the spirit of the concordat and, as Gershoy observes, "the Organic Articles were an error and Bonaparte lived to regret them."—*Loc. cit.* For a discussion of the Organic Articles, cf. Graham, *Vatican Diplomacy,* pp. 267-274.

### *Section 3. Preaching and Prior Restraint*

These considerations logically lead to a discussion of the Supreme Court doctrine of prior restraint of freedom of expression. The majority of the cases reviewed by the Court during the past twenty years have involved Jehovah's Witnesses, and so, beyond a doubt, the doctrine applies to the exercise of preaching. The formula of the Court has been fairly consistent, and at present prior restraint is still suspect, but no longer unconstitutional on its face. The restriction placed upon prior restraint is not absolute, but, on the other hand, the Court will not uphold any form of blanket prohibition.

When traffic on the street or highway is involved, the Court is prone to look more benignly upon state control. The requirement in a clearly drawn and non-discriminatory statute that a permit first be obtained to parade in the streets, even for religious purposes, is considered a legitimate exercise of police power.

The Supreme Court norms of prior restraint are definitely in conformity with papal pronouncements and concordat practice. The right to preach, as such, is never directly denied. Some extrinsic circumstance is always involved. Only when it can be foreseen according to definite norms of law that preaching will interfere with the public order may a public official refuse to grant permission to preach. The state does not regulate the content of the preaching, but it maintains the public order according to a set of definite standards fixed by law. In fact, the American law of prior restraint is superior to concordat practice in a number of ways. It requires no loyalty oath from bishops, the official preachers of the various dioceses, as do at least six twentieth-century concordats. American law does not demand the privilege to object on political grounds to the appointment of bishops and other ministers of religion, as in greater number the twentieth-century concordats. Finally, American law does not contain a citizenship requirement for bishops, pastors, religious superiors, and religious permanently residing in the country, as do several twentieth-century concordats. These concordat concessions are at least indirect acts of prior restraint upon the right of preachers of the Catholic religion, since Catholic preachers not fulfilling the above stated requirements could not exercise their office of preaching in the absence of a special arrangement.

### *Section 4. Preaching and Subsequent Punishment*

The doctrine of the Supreme Court on free speech and public order is reflected more precisely in cases involving subsequent punishment. In Cantwell *v.* Connecticut the Court declared that the free exercise of religion is not an absolute: "Conduct remains subject to regulation for the protection of society." However, a preacher must go to extremes before the Supreme Court will hold that he has violated public order. The Terminiello case, 1949, definitely placed the right of free speech above public order, because the Court underwrote a near riot. The Feiner case, 1952, restored speech to a position below public order. It is important to keep in mind that Terminiello spoke indoors, and his right to free speech was upheld, even though the mob disrupted civil peace out-of-doors. Feiner spoke on a busy street corner, and was more directly responsible for creating hazardous traffic conditions.

The Court has consistently maintained that libel, profanity, obscenity, threats, fighting words apt to instigate a riot, and other words of personal abuse are outside the scope of constitutional protection. Any preacher who engages in such verbal expressions from the pulpit, park or street corner, will not be given the protection of the law under the guise of preaching. It is almost unnecessary to say that such a position as this adopted by the Court is in conformity with Catholic legal principles.

Justice Douglas made it clear in the Fowler case, 1953, that a public official is not competent to judge when an address by one preacher is a sermon, and a talk by another is not. This is both preferring one religion over another and unduly regulating free speech. Douglas regarded sermons as much a part of religious services as prayers, and he stated that no public official may assume to "approve, disapprove, classify, regulate or control in any manner sermons delivered at religious meetings."[258] The opinion of the Court, as reflected in the majority opinion delivered by

[258] 345 U.S. 67, 70 (1953).

Douglas, is quite explicit and needs no further clarification. It is certainly in keeping with the teaching of the modern popes and in accord with the best portion of concordat practice.

### *Section 5. Conflict of Competence*

In the opinion of the writer the Supreme Court doctrine of subsequent punishment of preachers is at variance with the ideal standards propounded in papal pronouncements and realized in some concordats. The Church has no direct review of the norms for determining when such violations of the public order occur. However, in the practical order, the Holy See realizes the difficulty with which a government is faced in a religiously pluralistic society. In such circumstances the Holy See not only permits its Catholic citizens to conform to this arrangement, but declares that it is their moral duty to do so. There have also been instances in concordat practice where the Holy See has agreed to submit its preaching right to police regulations without any right of Church review. Finally, the Church through its members has an indirect right of review. Catholic citizens are able to form pressure groups, as do many other religious bodies and business associations, to assure the passage of just and equitable police regulations.

The writer has not singled out ways in which the American constitutional guarantee of the right to preach is below the norms established in papal pronouncements and in some concordats. This inferiority can be stated in one sentence: In areas where Church competence and State competence overlap and there is involved a question of the public order, the Church asserts its claim for competence in the judgment to be passed; the American Supreme Court claims the same competent authority for the State. In some conventions the Church has deemed it prudent to yield this right to the civil authority, e.g., Article 16 of the Portuguese Concordat.

In the final analysis, the condition which prevails in American jurisprudence works no harm to Church or State. The exercise of the right to preach is ordinarily more than sufficiently guaranteed for the Catholic Church with a view to its duty of preaching to all nations. Only the extreme or peripheral religious and political elements find the liberty of speech guaranteed by the

Constitution of the United States too narrow. The Court cases reveal these two groups to be the Communists in the area of political expression, and the Jehovah Witnesses in the realm of religious expression.[259]

---

[259] In practice, religious leaders, such as bishops, are frequently consulted before local police officials take action against a minister of religion. This procedure is beyond the law, and, therefore, no adequate records are available to substantiate this statement. However, this method of procedure is a matter of fairly common knowledge.

On March 18, 1960, in Chicago, the Apostolic Delegate to the United States, Archbishop Egidio Vagnozzi, addressed a Loyola University symposium on the writings and influence of Pope Leo XIII. Excerpts of his address were published in the April 2, 1960, issue of *America.* The writer penned the present section prior to this address, and so it is comforting to the writer to learn that his thoughts are in accord with those of the Archbishop. Two paragraphs are especially significant:

> In the practical field of relations with civil powers, the Catholic Church shows, with reciprocal international agreements called concordats, a considerable variety of provisions in particular questions, depending on local traditions, customs and practices. In fact, it is extremely difficult to define the neat line of demarcation between the domain of the Church and that of the State. Actually, even in some traditionally and predominantly Catholic lands, no preferential juridic recognition is granted to the Catholic Church.
>
> As far as the United States is concerned, I feel that it is a true interpretation of the feelings of the hierarchy and of American Catholics in general to say that they are well satisfied with their Constitution and pleased with the fundamental freedom which their Church enjoys; in fact, they believe that this freedom is to a large extent responsible for the expansion and consolation of the Church in this great country. Whether they remain a minority or become a majority, I am sure American Catholics will not jeopardize their cherished religious freedom in exchange for a privileged position.—*America,* CIII (1960), 6.

For a recent appraisal of the current role of religion in the United States consult: "Religion in American Society," *The Annals,* 332 (November, 1960), 1-155.

## CONCLUSIONS

1. Neither New York nor New Jersey had *de iure* an establishment of the Church of England during colonial times. New York had *de facto* an establishment of the Anglican Church, and New Jersey probably had a similar establishment. (Colonial Sections.)
2. The Toleration Act of William and Mary was responsible for as much intolerance in the colonies as tolerance. In the Puritan Establishments and in Virginia it secured a greater degree of freedom for a number of Protestant dissenters, but in several of the other colonies it either provoked or stabilized an intolerance towards Roman Catholics and other dissenters. (Colonial Sections.)
3. During the last quarter of the eighteenth century the majority of the colonies favored legal disestablishment. However, there is ample legal evidence to show that most of the colonies did not equate disestablishment with absolute separation of Church and State, but rather favored some form of union or co-operation less than establishment. (Statehood Sections.)
4. Over half of the twentieth-century concordats extended an "equal status in law" position for the Church. A partial explanation for this fact may be found in the social and religious composition of the negotiating States. Many of the twentieth-century concordats were made with nations in which the society was religiously pluralistic. (Part III, Article II.)
5. The Church is willing to negotiate for less than an unrestricted right to exercise its preaching duties and other ministerial activities. Oaths of fidelity to the State by the Church's clerics, citizenship requirements, and the priority of the public order and tranquility over the preaching and teaching right of the Church and over the inviolability of its places of worship are the usual concessions. (Part III, Articles I and II.)
6. It is evident from concordat practice and papal pronouncements that the Catholic Church believes that the *ideal* position for the Church in the public law of each State is establishment. It is equally clear that the Church cannot in principle approve *com-*

*plete* separation of Church and State. However, not all degrees of separation fall under this condemnation. The governments of modern religiously pluralistic societies may seek some adjustments consistent with truth and justice, in the hope that a greater good will be secured. (Part III, Article I.)

7. The position of the Catholic Church in the United States—equality at law—compares favorably with concordat practice in the twentieth century. It is less than the ideal of establishment as expressed in some concordats of this century and in the writings of modern popes. However, this form of legal status of the Church in the United States meets with the approval of the modern popes and the American hierarchy. (Part III.)

8. The dynamic formula for relations between Church and State in papal writings is distinction and co-operation. The present Supreme Court formula for relations between Church and State is separation and co-operation. The "separation," as defined by the Court, is acceptable in the light both of the papal pronouncements and of the statement of the American hierarchy made in 1948. The term "co-operation," as described by the Court, is not ideal in every respect in the light of concordat practice, of the papal pronouncements, and of the statement of the American bishops. However, it is in conformity with, or at least in the direction of, the position adopted by the American hierarchy, by Leo XIII, and by Pius XII. (Part III.)

9. The right to preach, as interpreted by the Supreme Court of the United States, is a value placed at present below that of the public order. This judgment is not at variance with a segment of concordat practice during the twentieth century or with papal principles. (Pp. 152, 153, 162; Part III.)

10. The American law on prior restraint of preaching is superior to a number of aspects in the concordat practice of the twentieth century. Part II, Article III; Part III, Article II.)

11. Libel, profanity, obscenity, threats, "fighting words" apt to stir up a riot, and other words of personal abuse are outside the sphere of American constitution protection. A preacher who would engage in the use of such forms of speech within a church, on a street corner, or in a public park would not be defended by the

constitutional protection guaranteed to preachers. This position is in conformity with Catholic legal principles. (Pp. 150, 158, 159, 162.)

12. Subsequent punishment of preachers is at variance with the *ideal* standards propounded in papal pronouncements and realized in some concordats. The problem is ultimately reduced to the apparent conflict between the right of the State to regulate the activities of its citizens and the right of the Church to fulfill its divinely given mission to preach to all men. In a word, there exists a conflict of competency. The Catholic Church and the United States government claim an equal competence in all the areas of conflict. (Part II, Article IV; Part III, Article III.)

13. In the practical order there is no real difficulty. The right to preach is given an even broader scope of constitutional protection than secular speech. The content of a sermon may only rarely be regulated in any manner by the State prior to delivery. Only if there is a clear and probable danger that the sermon will incite to riot, and when there is no other way to resolve the conflict, may a preacher be ordered to desist from his preaching. The preachers of the Catholic Church in their normal manner of delivering sermons in churches or in other public places will experience no serious difficulty under the present American system of law. (Pp. 137, 157, 162, 163; Part III, Article III.)

## BIBLIOGRAPHY

### Sources


*Acta Apostolicae Sedis*, Romae, 1909-

*Acta Sanctae Sedis*, 41 vols., Romae, 1865-1908.

*Acts of the Assembly Passed in the Province of Maryland from 1692-1715*, London, 1723.

*Acts and Laws of His Majesties Colony of Connecticut in New England*, London, 1715-1730, 1750.

*Acts and Resolves of the Province of Massachusetts Bay, I-V, 1692-1780*, Boston, 1869-1886.

*Acts of the General Assembly of the Provinces of New Jersey, 1702-1776*, ed. Samuel A. Allison, Burlington, N. J., 1776.

*Archives of Maryland*, 61 vols., Maryland Historical Society, Baltimore, 1883-1944.

*Canon Law Digest, The*, vols. I-IV, 1917-1957, eds. T. L. Bouscaren-James J. O'Connor, Milwaukee: Bruce Publishing Co., 1934-1958.

Clark, Walter (ed.), *The State Records of North Carolina*, 25 vols., Goldsboro, N. C., 1904-1908.

*Codex Iuris Canonici*, Pii X Pontificis Maximi iussu digestus, Benedicti Papae XV auctoritate promulgatus, actus a Petro Card. Gasparri, Romae, 1918.

*Coloniall Laws of Massachusetts, The*, reprinted from the edition of 1672 with supplements through 1686, prepared under the supervision of William H. Whitman, Boston, 1887.

*Colonial Laws of New York from the Year 1664 to the Revolution, The*, 5 vols., Albany, 1894.

*Colonial Records of Pennsylvania*, 16 vols., Philadelphia, 1852; Harrisburg, 1851-1853.

*Connecticut Acts and Laws*, an unbound copy in the Anglo-American section of the Library of Congress, Washington, D. C., May Session, 1791 (Second Thursday), 403-404.

*Connecticut Acts and Laws*, a bound photo-static copy in the Anglo-American section of the Library of Congress, Washington, D. C., October Session, 1792.

Cooper, Thomas (ed.), *Statutes at Large of South Carolina*, I-IV, Columbia, S. C., 1836-1839.

*Ecclesiastical Records of the State of New York*, 7 vols., published under the direction of Hugh Hastings, Albany, 1901.

*Grants, Concessions and Original Constitutions of the Province of New Jersey, The Acts between 1664-1702, The*, eds. Aaron Leaming and Jacob Spicer, Philadelphia, 1758.

Hening, William Waller (ed.), *Statutes at Large Being a Collection of All the Laws of Virginia from the First Session of the Legislature,* I-XIII, old series, New York, Philadelphia, Richmond, 1820-1823.

Kilty, William (ed.), *The Laws of Maryland,* 2 vols., Annapolis, 1779-1780.

*Laws and Liberties of Massachusetts, The,* reprinted from the 1648 edition in the Henry E. Huntington Library, with an introduction by Max Farrand, Cambridge: Harvard University Press, 1929.

*Public Statutes of the State of Connecticut, The,* Book I, Hartford, 1808.

*Raccolta di Concordati su Materie Ecclésiastiche tra la Sancta Sede e le Autorità Civili,* a cura Angelo Mercati, nuova edizione anatatica con supplemento, 2 vols., Romae: Tipografia Vaticana Poliglotta, 1954.

*Records of the Colony of Rhode Island and Providence Plantation in New England, 1636-1792,* ed. J. R. Bartlett, 10 vols., Providence, R. I., 1856-1858.

*Statutes at Large of Pennsylvania from 1682-1801, The,* 13 vols., Philadelphia: C. M. Busch, 1896.

Thorpe, Francis N. (ed.), *Federal and State Constitutions, Colonial Charters, and Other Organic Laws of the States, Territories, and Colonies, now or hitherto forming the United States of America,* 7 vols., Washington, D. C., 1909.

### Reference Works

*All Things in Christ, Encyclicals and Selected Documents of St. Pius X,* ed. Vincent A. Yzermans, Westminster, Md.: The Newman Press, 1954.

Aspects of Liberty, Essays Presented to Robert Cushman, eds. Milton R. Konvitz and Clinton Rossiter, Ithaca, N. Y.: Cornell University Press, 1958.

Bancroft, George, *History of the United States,* 2 vols., New York, 1888.

Brierly, J. L., *The Law of Nations: An Introduction to the International Law of Peace,* 4 ed., London: Oxford University Press, 1949.

*Catholic Encyclopedia, The,* 15 vols., ed. Charles Herberman, Edward Pace et alii, New York, 1907-1914.

*Church and State Through the Centuries,* trans. and ed. Sidney Z. Ehler and John Morrall, London: Burns and Oates, 1954.

*Church Speaks to the Modern World, The Social Teachings of Leo XIII, The,* ed. Etienne Gilson, Garden City, New York: Image Books, 1954.

Cicognani, Amleto G., *Canon Law,* trans. Joseph M. O'Hara and Francis Brennan, 2 rev. ed., Philadelphia: The Dolphin Press, 1935.

Cobb, Sanford H., *The Rise of Religious Liberty in America,* New York, 1902.

*Collections of the Massachusetts Historical Society,* vol. X, *Ecclesiastical History of Massachusetts,* Boston, 1809.

*Collections of New Hampshire Historical Society,* 11 vols., Concord, 1824-1915.

Collins, Ross W., *Catholicism and the Second French Republic,* 1848-1852, New York: Columbia University Press, 1923.

*Constitution of the United States of America, Analysis and Interpretation,* ed. Edward S. Corwin, Washington, D. C.: The United States Government Printing Office, 1953.

Corrigan, Raymond, *The Church and the Nineteenth Century,* Milwaukee: Bruce Publishing Co., 1948.

Corwin, Edward S., *The Constitution and What It Means Today,* 11 ed. rev., Princeton, N. J.: Princeton University Press, 1954.

Coulter, E. Merton, *Georgia, A Short History,* Chapel Hill: The University of North Carolina Press, 1947.

Cushman, Robert F. and Robert E., *Cases in Constitutional Law,* New York: Appleton-Century-Crofts, Inc., 1958.

Doyle, John J., *Education in Recent Constitutions and Concordats,* Washington, D. C., The Catholic University of America Press, 1933.

Elson, Henry W., *History of the United States,* New York, 1926.

Gershoy, Leo, *The French Revolution and Napoleon,* New York, 1933.

Graham, Malbone W., *New Governments of Eastern Europe,* New York, 1927.

———, *The League of Nations and Recognition of States: The Diplomatic Recognition of Border States*—Part III, *Latvia,* The University of California Social Science Studies, Vol. III, Berkeley: The University of California Press, 1942.

Graham, Robert A., *Vatican Diplomacy: A Study of Church and State on the International Plane,* Princeton, N. J.: Princeton University Press, 1959.

*Great Encyclical Letters of Leo XIII, The,* ed. John J. Wynne, New York, 1903.

*Encyclical Letter on the Mystical Body,* trans. of *Mystici Corporis Christi* of Pius XII, with discussion club outline, by Gerald C. Treacy, New York: The Paulist Press [no date].

Galter, Albert, *The Red Book of the Persecuted Church,* trans. from the French, Westminster, Md.: The Newman Press, 1957.

Hackett, John Henry, *The Concept of Public Order,* Canon Law Studies No. 399, Washington, D. C.: The Catholic University of America Press, 1959.

Hales, Edward, *The Catholic Church in the Modern World,* London: Eyre and Spottiswoode, 1958.

Hanley, Thomas O'Brien, *Their Liberties and Rights,* Westminster, Md.: The Newman Press, 1959.

Harte, Thomas J., *Papal Social Principles,* Milwaukee: Bruce Publishing Co., 1956.

Hazen, Charles D., *Fifty Years of Europe,* New York, 1919.

*History of Nations, The,* vol. IV, Italy, ed. J. Higginson Cabot, New York, 1928.

Howe, Mark De, Wolfe, *Cases on Church and State in the United States,* Cambridge, Mass.: Harvard University Press, 1952.

Husslein, Joseph, *Social Wellsprings,* 2 vols., Milwaukee: Bruce Publishing Co., 1940-1942.

Hutchinson, Thomas, *The History of the Colony of Massachusetts-Bay,* 3 vols., ed. Lawrence S. Mayo, Cambridge, Mass.: Harvard University Press, 1936.

Hyman, Harold M., *To Try Men's Souls: Loyalty Tests in American History,* Berkeley, California: The University of California Press, 1959.

Jensen, Merril, *The New Nation: A History of the United States During the Confederation, 1781-1789,* New York: Knopf, 1950.

Johnson, Alvin W. and Yost, Frank H., *Separation of Church and State in the United States,* Minneapolis: University of Minnesota Press, 1948.

Kelly, Francis C., *Blood-Drenched Altars,* 2 ed. rev., Milwaukee: Bruce Publishing Co., 1935.

Konvitz, Milton R., *Fundamental Liberties of a Free People: Religion, Speech, Press, Assembly,* New York: Cornell University Press, 1957.

Morison, Samuel E. and Commager, Henry S., *The Growth of the American Republic,* 4 ed. rev., 2 vols., New York: Oxford University Press, 1955.

Myers, Gustavus, *History of Bigotry in the United States,* New York: Random House, 1943.

O'Brien, F. William, *Justice Reed and the First Amendment, The Religion Clause,* Washington, D. C.: Georgetown University Press, 1958.

O'Callaghan, E. B., *The Documentary History of the State of New York,* 4 vols., arranged under the Secretary of State, Albany, 1849-1851.

———, *History of New Netherlands,* 2 vols., New York, 1855.

Ottaviani, Alaphridus, *Institutiones Iuris Publici Ecclesiastici,* 2 vols., *Ius Publicum Internum et Jus Publicum Externum,* 3 ed., Romae: Typis Polyglottis Vaticanis, 1947.

*Our Bishops Speak, 1919-1951,* ed. Raphael M. Huber, Milwaukee: Bruce Publishing Co., 1952.

Padover, Saul K., *The Complete Jefferson,* New York: Tudor: 1943.

*Papal Encyclicals in Their Historical Context, The,* ed. Anne Fremantle, New York: G. P. Putnam's Sons, 1956.

Parsons, Wilfred, *The First Freedom, Considerations on Church and State,* New York: Declan X. McMullen Co., Inc., 1948.

*Persecution of the Catholic Church in the Third Reich,* facts and documents translated from German, London: Burns and Oates, 1940.

Perugini, Angelus, *Concordata Vigentia,* Romae, 1934.

Powers, Francis, *Papal Pronouncements on the Public Order,* Westminster, Md.: The Newman Press, 1952.

———, *Religious Liberty and the Police Power of the State,* Washington, D. C.: The Catholic University Press, 1948.

Pritchett, C. Herman, *Civil Liberties and the Vinson Court,* Chicago: The University of Chicago Press, 1954.

Prunskis, Joseph, *Comparative Law, Ecclesiastical and Civil, in Lithuanian Concordat,* Canon Law Studies No. 222, Washington, D. C.: The Catholic University of America Press, 1945.

Rommen, Heinrich, *The State in Catholic Thought,* St. Louis: Herder Book Co., 1950.

Roucek, Joseph S., *Balkan Politics: International Relations in No Man's Land,* Stanford, California: The Stanford University Press, 1949.

Ryan, John A. and Boland, Francis J., *Catholic Social Principles,* rev. ed. of *The State and the Catholic Church,* New York: The Macmillan Co., 1940.

Sotillo, Laurentius R., *Compendium Iuris Publici Ecclesiastici,* 2 ed. rev., Santander: Editorial Sal Terrae, 1951.

Stokes, Anson Phelps, *Church and State in the United States,* 3 vols., New York: Harper, 1950.

Taylor, A. J. P., *The Struggle for the Mastery of Europe,* London: The Oxford University Press, 1954.

Torpey, William George, *Judicial Doctrines of Religious Rights in America,* Chapel Hill: The University of North Carolina Press, 1948.

*Transactions and Collections of the American Antiquarian Society,* Cambridge, 1857.

Van Doren, Carl, *The Great Rehearsal: the Story of the Making and Ratifying of the Constitution of the United States,* New York: Viking Press, 1948.

Werline, Albert W., *Problems of Church and State in Maryland During the Seventeenth and Eighteenth Centuries,* South Lancaster, Mass., 1948.

Zollman, Carl, *American Church Law,* St. Paul: West Publishing Co., 1934.

Zwierlein, Frederick J., *Religion in New Netherlands,* Rochester, N. Y., 1910.

## Articles

Anderson, William, "The Bill of Rights, the Fourteenth Amendment, and the Liberty of Conscience," *Aspects of Liberty, Essays Presented to Robert Cushman,* Ithaca, N. Y.: Cornell University Press, 1958, pp. 287-307.

Barry, E. R., "Public Benefit and School Bus Transportation," *The Jurist,* VI (July, 1946), 425-431.

"Christian in Action, The," *Our Bishops Speak,* ed. Raphael M. Huber, Milwaukee: Bruce Publishing Co., 1952, pp. 149-153.

Connell, F. J., "The Relation between Church and State," *The Jurist,* XIII (1953), 398-414.

Green, John Raeburn, "The Bill of Rights, the Fourteenth Amendment and the Supreme Court," *Michigan Law Review,* XLVI (1948), 868.

Lecaro, Card. Giacomo, "Religious Toleration in Catholic Tradition," *Catholic Mind,* LVIII (Jan.-Feb., 1960), 12-14.

Murray, John C., "Freedom, Responsibility and Law," *The Catholic Lawyer,* II (1956), 214-223.

———, "Law or Prepossessions," *Essays in Constitutional Law,* ed. with an introduction by Robert McCloskey, New York: Alfred A. Knopf, 1957, pp. 316-347.

O'Brien, Kenneth R. and Daniel E., "Separation of Church and State in Restatement of Inter-Church and State Common Law," *The Jurist,* VII (July, 1947), 259-279.

Parsons, Wilfred, "There Is a Persecution in Mexico," *America,* XLVIII (Oct. 15, 1932), 34-36.

Plöchl, Willibald M., "Church and State in Austria," *The Jurist,* XII (1952), 400-416.

———, "Reflections on the Nature and Status of Concordats," *The Jurist,* VII (1947), 10-44.

Powers, Francis J., "The Supreme Court and the Constitutional Prohibition against 'an Establishment of Religion,'" *The Jurist,* XII (July, 1952), 282-314.

Prestage, Edward, "Portugal," *The Catholic Encyclopedia,* ed. Charles G. Herberman, Edward A. Pace *et alii,* XII, New York, 1911-1914, 297-307.

Sorauf, Frank J., "Zorach *v.* Clauson: The Impact of a Supreme Court Decision," *The American Political Science Review,* LIII (September, 1959), 777-791.

Summers, C. W., "The Sources and Limits of Religious Freedom," *Illinois Law Review,* XLI (1946), 53.

Vagnozzi, Egidio, "Address to a Loyola University Symposium, March 18, 1960," *America,* CIII (1960), 6.

Warren, Charles, "The New Liberty Under the Fourteenth Amendment," *Harvard Law Review,* XXXIX (1926), 431-465.

White, Robert J., "The Legal Status of the Church," *The Jurist,* I (1941), 20-49.

## Papal Pronouncements

*Acerba animi, AAS,* XXIV (1932), 409-419.

*Au milieu, ASS,* XXIV (1891-1892), 519-529.

*Ci riesce, AAS,* XLV (1953), 794-802.

*Ci torna, AAS,* XXXIX (1947), 493-498.

*Dacchè piacque, AAS,* XXXVII (1945), 256-262.

*Diuturnum illud, ASS,* XIV (1881), 3-14.

*Divini Redemptoris, AAS,* XXIX (1937), 65-106.

*Ecco che già, AAS,* XXXVIII (1946), 391-397.

*Firmissimam constantiam, AAS,* XXIX (1937), 189-199.

*Gravissimum apostolici muneris*, *AAS*, XXXIX (1906), 30-33.
*Iamdudum*, *AAS*, III (1911), 217-224.
*Immortale Dei*, *ASS*, XVIII (1885), 161-180.
*In hac quidem*, *AAS*, XIII (1921), 521-524.
*Libertas*, *ASS*, XX (1887), 593-613.
*Longinqua oceani*, *ASS*, XXVIII (1895), 387-399.
*Mit brennender Sorge*, *AAS*, XXIX (1937), 145-167.
*Mystici Corporis*, *AAS*, XXXV (1943), 193-248.
*Non abbiamo bisogno*, *AAS*, XXIII (1931), 285-312.
*Paterna sane*, *AAS*, XVIII (1926), 175-179.
*Sapientiae Christianae*, *ASS*, XXII (1890), 385-404.
*Vehementer nos*, *ASS*, XXXIX (1906-1907), 2-16.
*Vous avez voulu*, *AAS*, XLVII (1955), 672-682.

## Cases Cited

Abrams *v.* United States, 250 U.S. 616 (1919).
West Virginia State Board of Education *v.* Barnette, 319 U.S. 624 (1943).
Breard *v.* Alexandria, 341 U.S. 622 (1951).
Barr *v.* Matteo, 360 U.S. 564 (1959).
Beauharnais *v.* Illinois, 343 U.S. 250 (1952).
Bridges *v.* California, 314 U.S. 252 (1941).
Butler *v.* Michigan, 352 U.S. 380 (1956).
Cantwell *v.* Connecticut, 310 U.S. 296 (1940).
Chaplinsky *v.* New Hampshire, 315 U.S. 568 (1942).
Cox *v.* New Hampshire, 312 U.S. 569 (1941).
De Jonge *v.* Ore. 299 U.S. 353 (1937).
Debs *v.* United States, 249 U.S. 211 (1919).
Dennis et al. *v.* United States, 341 U.S. 494 (1951).
Douglas *v.* Jeannette, 319 U.S. 157 (1943).
Everson *v.* Board of Education, 330 U.S. 1 (1947).
Feiner *v.* New York, 340 U.S. 315 (1951).
Fiske *v.* Kansas, 274 U.S. 380 (1927).
Follett *v.* Town of McCormick, 321 U.S. 573 (1944).
Fowler *v.* Rhode Island, 345 U.S. 67 (1953).
Gitlow *v.* New York, 268 U.S. 652 (1925).
Hague *v.* C.I.O., 307 U.S. 496 (1939).
Herndon *v.* Lowry, 301 U.S. 242 (1937).
Howard *v.* Lyons, 360 U.S. 593 (1959).
Jamison *v.* Texas, 318 U.S. 413 (1943).
Jones *v.* Opelika, 316 U.S. 584 (1942).
Kingsley Books *v.* Brown, 354 U.S. 436 (1957).
Kingsley Pictures Corp. *v.* Regents of New York University, 360 U.S. 684 (1958).
Kovacs *v.* Cooper, 336 U.S. 77 (1949).

Kunz *v.* New York, 340 U.S. 290 (1951).
Lovell *v.* Griffin, 303 U.S. 444 (1938).
NAACP *v.* Alabama, 357 U.S. 449 (1958).
Niemotko *v.* Maryland, 340 U.S. 268 (1951).
Marsh *v.* Alabama, 326 U.S. 501 (1946).
Martin *v.* Struthers, 319 U.S. 141 (1943).
McCollum *v.* Board of Education, 333 U.S. 203 (1948).
Murdock *v.* Pennsylvania, 319 U.S. 105 (1943).
Near *v.* Minnesota, 283 U.S. 697 (1931).
Panhandle Oil Co. *v.* Knox, 277 U.S. 218 (1928).
Poulos *v.* New Hampshire, 345 U.S. 395 (1953).
Prince *v.* Massachusetts, 321 U.S. 158 (1944).
Public Utilities Commission *v.* Pollak, 343 U.S. 451 (1952).
Roth *v.* United States, 354 U.S. 467 (1957).
Reynolds *v.* United States, 98 U.S. 145 (1879).
Saia *v.* New York, 334 U.S. 558 (1948).
Schenck *v.* United States, 249 U.S. 47 (1919).
Schneider *v.* Town of Irvington (State), 308 U.S. 147 (1939).
Staub *v.* Baxley, 355 U.S. 313 (1957).
Terminiello *v.* Chicago, 337 U.S. 1 (1949).
Thomas *v.* Collins, 323 U.S. 516 (1945).
Thornhill *v.* Alabama, 310 U.S. 88 (1940).
Tucker *v.* Texas, 326 U.S. 517 (1946).
Whitney *v.* California, 274 U.S. 357 (1927).
Youngdahl *v.* Rainfall, Inc., 355 U.S. 131 (1957).
Zorach *v.* Clauson, 343 U.S. 306 (1952).

## PERIODICALS

*Annals, The,* Philadelphia, 1890-
*America,* New York, 1909-
*American Political Science Review, The,* Baltimore, 1907-
*Catholic Lawyer, The,* Brooklyn, New York, 1955-
*Catholic Mind,* New York, 1903-
*Clergy Review, The,* London, 1931-
*Harvard Law Review,* Cambridge, Mass., 1887-
*Illinois Law Review,* Chicago, 1906-
*Jurist, The,* Washington, D. C., 1941-
*Michigan Law Review,* Ann Arbor, 1902-
*Pope Speaks, The,* Washington, D. C., 1954-

## ABBREVIATIONS

*ASS—Acta Sanctae Sedis*
*AAS—Acta Apostolicae Sedis*
*CIC—Codex Iuris Canonici*

## BIOGRAPHICAL NOTE

William Nessel was born on February 2, 1929, in Philadelphia. He received his elementary education in the school of Our Lady Help of Christians, and his secondary education at the Northeast Catholic high school in Philadelphia. In 1946 he entered the novitiate of the Oblates of Saint Francis de Sales in Childs, Maryland.

After profession he attended the Catholic University of America, where he received an A.B. in Philosophy and an M.A. in Politics. He pursued his theological studies at the De Sales Hall School of Theology in Hyattsville, Maryland, and was ordained to the priesthood on June 9, 1956.

In the fall of 1957 the writer returned to the Catholic University of America and enrolled in the School of Canon Law. He received the degree of the Baccalaureate in Canon Law in June, 1958, and the degree of Licentiate in Canon Law in June, 1959.

INDEX

www.ingramcontent.com/pod-product-compliance
Lightning Source LLC
LaVergne TN
LVHW050254080826
844660LV00012B/637

* 9 7 8 0 8 1 3 2 2 5 7 0 8 *